TROUP-HARRIS-COWETA REGIONAL LIBRARY
LA GRANGE MEMORIAL LIBRARY

3 6379 1010 1158 9

Public Library Service
State Dept. of Education
156 Trinity Avenue, S. W.
Atlanta, Georgia 30303

CL1 10/94

823
.0872     Panek, LeRoy.
PAN          An introduction to
           the detective story

MAY 04 1988

TROUP - HARRIS - COWETA
REGIONAL LIBRARY
LaGrange, Georgia   30240

__ LaGrange Memorial Library
__ Bookmobile
__ Ethel W. Kight Library
__ Grantville Public Library
__ Harris County Public Library
__ Hogansville Public Library
__ Newnan-Coweta Public Library
__ Senoia Public Library

GAYLORD

D0938896

# *An Introduction to the Detective Story*

# An Introduction
# to the
# Detective Story

## LeRoy Lad Panek

Public Library Service
State Dept. of Education
156 Trinity Avenue, S. W.
Atlanta, Georgia 30303

Bowling Green State University Popular Press
Bowling Green, Ohio 43403

Copyright © 1987 Bowling Green State University Popular Press

Library of Congress Catalogue Card No.: 87-70502

ISBN: 0-87972-377-7  Clothbound
      0-87972-378-5  Paperback

**Cover design by Gary Dumm and Greg Budgett**

# Contents

*To Claire*

# Preface

Books about detective stories tend to start with apologies, suggesting there is something vaguely wrong with adults who spend their time reading detective stories and something definately akilter in those who spend their energy analyzing and interpreting them. The following book, however, is not an apology or a defense or a "personal" look at detective fiction. It treats and analyzes the detective story as literature. To this end, I have traced the origins of the form, presented the literary and cultural forces that have influenced it, followed its development, and discussed some of the major authors who have contributed to its evolution and popularity. Throughout, I have supplied readers with essential basic information about the writers and movements that I examine; it is not, however, merely a collection of received opinions. I have tried to ask myself new questions about the detective story and its development, and I hope that my answers provide readers with some new insights about the form. I have, of course, omitted mention of a number of important writers and even a greater number of significant books. One cannot cover everything in a field as vast as that of detective fiction. Readers interested in detailed analyses of specific writers can find them by working through the specialized bibliographies listed at the end of the book.

Criticism of the detective story is at a transitional point. Much earlier criticism is either solely directed at fans or at academics. That is, either criticism rests on the obvious and superficial or on highly complex and abstract intellectual structures. Some articles and books, however, take a middle road, hoping to make observations and provide analyses which will appeal to both the lay and the academic reader. I hope that this book falls in with the latter category.

Because this book is intended for a wide variety of readers, I have dispensed with the machinery and some of the stodginess of the typical academic book. Readers will, therefore, find no footnotes, but for those who wish to consult my sources or to find more detailed information, I have appended a section of Further Readings. The dignity of the subject and the demands of the reader have controlled much of what follows, but I also wrote this book to inform and amuse myself. This I do not view as self-indulgence, but as an essential ingredient in any book worth writing or reading.

Finally, I wish to extend my thanks to the library staff at Western Maryland College and to my colleagues for assisting in my research and for listening to my enthusiasms. My thanks, too, go to Betsy, Larry, and Paul of Basically Computers for the patience and assistance they offered to a novice word processor. For corrections and suggestions, I owe the mysterious F.M.N. at least a drink, if not a dinner.

# Chapter 1
# Beginnings

James Burke, in his television series *Connections*, demonstrated an engaging and athletic capacity for tying together apparently separate facts in the history of human technology. He connected things like the founding of marine insurance companies with the invention of plastic, events divided by continents and hundreds of years, to say nothing of their apparent dissimilarity. From one point of view, Burke was absolutely right in defining technology as a web of historical connections: human life and human experience form an insoluble whole as well as a host of compartmented instances. Each of our biological processes stretches back to carbon atoms flirting in the primordial goo, and human technology traces to a Lucy-like creature bashing some sort of antediluvian rodent with a rock. Our literature, too, echoes back over the "once upon a times" of countless generations.

P.G. Wodehouse, for instance, connects back to drunken Greeks celebrating their god. To apply this approach to the subject of the detective story means looking back in literary history, back before Sherlock Holmes and back before Dupin. Given the requisite, slightly tipsy mood, one can argue that God was the first detective, discerning man's felonious intent and punishing it, or that Cronos was the first bungling detective, gobbling down a stone and letting the real criminal go free to do him dirty. Even though Father Rivas, in Greene's *Honorary Consul*, argues along these lines, it seems absurd to chase the roots of a distinctly modern literary form back to first causes as big as the First Cause. Cases have, nevertheless, been made for tracing the character types as well as the conventional mental processes found in the detective story back to the antique world. If one wishes to string out a lengthy series of connections for the detective story, there is certainly no lack of terminals in the history of human culture. But will the resultant machine work?

Going as far back as possible, some people hold up two episodes from the Apocryphal books of the Old Testament as the earliest examples of the detective story; they are, if you will, proto-crypto detective tales. In the first of these, Daniel saves the virtuous Susanna from the false accusations of

1

two lecherous elders who have not had the sense to collude on the details of their charges concerning Susanna cavorting with a lover in the garden. All Daniel does is take their testimony separately, and the inconsistencies in their stories vindicate Susanna's innocence. The second of these scriptural tales recounts Daniel's unmasking the scam run by the priests of Bel. Daniel knows that the priests have been profiting from all of the offerings to their idol, and so he scatters ashes on the floor of the temple and bids the Babylonian king to lock and seal it. The next day all of the offerings have vanished, but the priests' footprints, left when they made off with the swag, remain on the ash-covered floor. In both of these narratives, we witness God making manifest His justice and His presence; in both instances, nevertheless, justice and truth depend on the use of human reason and insight by Divinely-inspired agents. Some people would go as far as suggesting these stories give us an early example of analyzing testimony and observing material evidence. The Bel story we can see, again granted the slightly tipsy mood, as the progenitor of Poe's "Maelzel's Chess-Player" or John Dickson Carr's *The Crooked Hinge.*

The classical world, too, has given ingenious historians of the detective story several instances which they hold up as progenitors of the form. First, there is Herodotus' recounting of "The Story of Rhampsinitus' Treasure House." Here, by means of a secret passage, two brothers dip into the treasury of the King of Egypt. When a mantrap springs on one of them, his brother decapitates him and carries off the head along with his ration of the king's gold. Understandably irked, the king displays the corpse left in the treasure house, hoping to pounce upon the grieving family. But his guards succumb to the occupational disease of accepting drink from strangers, and brother number two carries off the body. Driven to what can only be called extremes, the king puts his daughter into a brothel, instructing her to charge not drachma or shekels for her favors, but to demand from each of her swains a story of his cleverest exploit. The thief enters and pays up by boasting about his robberies and the princess grabs his arm; the thief, however, has brought along an extra arm which he leaves in her grip. At this point, the king throws up his hands and offers his daughter in marriage to the man, thief, fratricide, and lecher that he is, who has been so deucedly clever. Now it does seem to pull credulity out of joint to see this tale as a precursor of detective fiction. Surely some Egyptian jokester was putting Herodotus on, or Herodotus, in the fashion of later travellers, is putting us on, or both. Nevertheless, reasonably reputable writers include this fish story in their histories of detective fiction—one telling us that it illustrates the psychological method of detection. Piffle. We can, if we want to, see Herodotus' fiction as an example of the hoax or joke, both of which are germane to Poe, but this washes tipsiness over into the hallucinations of drunkenness.

The other source of connections to the detective story in the ancient world cannot be ridiculed quite so easily. If the detective story depends upon the scientific method (which it does for a brief spell in the twentieth century), we need to wire back through Francis Bacon to Archimedes. Archimedes' discovery of specific gravity while sloshing about in his bath can be forced into some of the patterns of the detective story: the important client (King Hiero of Syracuse, or Doyle's King of Bohemia), the dramatic discovery based on relating separate things (bath water equals specific gravity, or Sayers' air-locked motorcycle equals a bubble in the blood), and even the inclusion of zany humor (Archimedes bounding about in the buff, or Anthony Berkeley's Roger Sheringham detecting a bull).

If one is diligent, and detective story fans are nothing if they are not diligent, one can unearth examples of rigorous thinking, the use of evidence, and the hero as the unraveller of the antagonist's artifice in virtually every epoch or clime. They pop up in Homer and Virgil and Aesop. Persian examples exist, as well as examples from China. The history of human endeavor and literature illustrating it could hardly exist without rigorous thinking, the use of evidence, and heroes unravelling villains' jiggery-pokery. To return, however, to the historical frame, examples of proto-crypto detective tales continue in the middle ages. There are the clever ruses of the beast fable and the *Fabliau*, the Robin Hood tales, and murder-will-out stories like Chaucer's "The Prioress' Tale." The king's spy flours the floor around Iseult's bed in an attempt to keep an eye on her nocturnal activity. Not many historians get tremendously exercised by these—even if they can be made as relevant as some of the material I have cited earlier. The avoidance of medieval material rests on the partly valid assumption that the detective tale cannot exist when the rule of law does not exist and the techniques of evidence-gathering include the rack, the rubber hose, or electric shock to the genitals. If we do accept this, however, we ought also to recognize that Herodotus' Egyptian king had a pretty cavalier attitude, at best, toward the law. But this is quibbling.

When we arrive at the Renaissance, the emphasis shifts in the search for the repeated elements which constitute the detective story network. By the Elizabethan era, there are so many people exhibiting reason and cleverness, in prose and verse, that no one even tries to follow this side of the argument anymore. Look, there were Francis Bacon and Thomas Browne promoting inductive reasoning; there was Hieronimo looking for clues to his son's murder in *The Spanish Tragedy*; there was Surly, in *The Alchemist*, sniffing out the con game run by Subtle and Face; there was the reader as detective peering into Spenser's dark conceits in *The Faerie Queen*. But these are not the areas of the intellectual life of the Renaissance where browsers in the field of detective history have fed. Not that there is not plenty of suggestive material to be found in Renaissance literature. A pretty good case can be made for seeing the Elizabethan revenge play as a source for detective fiction and plenty of twentieth century novels in particular. Revenge plays from *The Spanish Tragedy* through *Hamlet* develop specific attitudes toward crime, criminals, and the legitimate use of evidence. They look both into the psyche of the criminal and the detective. Indeed, Shakespeare gives us the standard narrative patterns of the crime before the opening of the story (*Hamlet*), the crime in the middle (*Macbeth*), and the crime at the end (*Othello*). Lots of recent detective writers do, in fact, respond to Elizabethan drama: Blake's' *Thou Shell of Death* starts from Tourneur's *Revenger's Tragedy*, and Christie's *The Mousetrap* is only one of a whole flock of works which play off of Shakespeare. We could make a reasonably good case for dating the detective tale from the renaissance, but it would be a deductive one: because later writers use renaissance writers as inspiration, the detective tale must have begun in the sixteenth century. It would also be misleading in that detective fiction did not grow out of the masterworks of Elizabeth's reign.

Rather than begetting a tradition of crime literature compounded of sublime verse, powerful psychological insight, and absorbing action, Elizabethan drama popped and fizzled into the middle-class absurdities of Dryden, Tate, and Lillo. Where the renaissance did contribute something which led, with jumps and shifts, to the detective story was in the creation of the rogue hero and in the invention of popular literature about crime. As Professor Chandler points out in *The Literature of Roguery*, the printers of the sixteenth and seventeenth centuries produced an almost inexhaustible supply of books and pamphlets about crime and criminals. As well as following the picaresque novel, Chandler discusses Beggar-Books, Cony-Catching Pamphlets, Prison Tracts and Repentances, Canting Lexicons, and Scoundrel Verse. Now, none of these kinds of books is about detectives. They warn readers about the sorrows of a life of crime as well as about the ways in which criminals ply their trades. In his cony-catching tracts, for instance, Robert Greene, says he has palled around with crooks and sharpers "as a spy to have an insight into their knaveries," and he details how cut-purses and allied trades work their crafts, topping this off with illustrative examples of purse-cutting drawn mostly from the tradition of the jest book. With these renaissance stories about crime (so the argument goes), the culture got away from its total absorption in the moral condemnation of crime inculcated by the heavily didactic "Murder-will-out" stories of the middle ages and moved toward an interest in the cunning and craft of the malefactor as well as towards accepting crime as a fit subject for entertaining fiction. All we need, then, for the detective story is a slight moral realignment, which establishes the detective as a worthy character with his own intricate skills and craft.

The eighteenth century witnessed such an immense growth of popular literature about criminals it would have probably produced some kind of crime novel without the interventions of Godwin, Lytton, Dickens, Collins, and Poe. Replacing narratives about the careers and practices of cheats, gamesters, and pirates which dominate most sixteenth—and early seventeenth-century crime journalism, we find a great deal of literature about a new sort of criminal, the highwayman (the term itself first appearing in 1649). These new criminals of the eighteenth century, like Dick Turpin, Spring-Heeled Jack Shepherd, and Jonathan Wild, achieved lasting fame because of the tracts, pamphlets, and biographies written about them. The highwayman even occasionally rose into the world of regular literature, as in Gay's *Beggar's Opera* (1728) and Fielding's *The History of the Life of the Late Mr. Jonathan Wild* (1743). Daniel Defoe, in fact, contributed to the flood of popular tracts about crime and criminals with his life of John Avery, "The King of the Pirates" (1719), as well as his "A Brief Historical Account of the Lives of Six Notorious Street Robbers Executed at Kingston" (1726). As these two titles by Defoe indicate, criminal literature of the eighteenth century moved not only from the pirate to the highwayman, but from the short individual biography to either the longer biography or the compendium of several criminals' lives. The impulse to collect the lives of the notorious into one volume began with Captain Alexander Smith's *The Complete History of the Lives and Robberies of the Most Notorious Highwaymen* in 1714. Smith has a reasonably picaresque view of criminals, but on the more somber side of these compendia are the numerous versions and editions of the *Newgate Calendar*. Although no one has closely examined the bibliography of the Newgate and Tyburn calendars, these collections of hundreds of admonitory biographies appeared well before 1764. Reverend John Villette, the prison Ordinary at Newgate, published one of the most famous, *The Annals of Newgate, or the Malefactor's Register* in 1776, and two attorneys heaved Newgate literature into the nineteenth century with their *Criminal Chronology, or New Newgate Calendar* (1809-10). Indeed, collected chronicles of criminals' lives continued to be written, often using the Newgate title, through the nineteenth century. This great mass of material about crime and criminals had a specific impact on the modern development of the detective story. Godwin and Lytton used criminal biographies of Dick Turpin, Jack Shepherd, and Eugene Aram for details in their works, and later detective writers often dipped into Newgate literature for inspiration or detail. Eighteenth-century criminal literature, however, is hardly reputable fiction. Gay and Fielding could only use it by adding a thick top-dressing of irony. All of the Newgate Calendar stuff is pseudo-journalism, homiletic preaching or snatches of picaresque adventures. It requires a great deal of modification and shaping before it can serve the needs of the standard novel or short story.

The other eighteenth-century form which has a love-hate relationship with the detective story is the gothic novel. Gothic novels aim to frighten their readers in order to remind them they do have emotions. They do this by using spooky atmosphere and macabre detail. Also, they seek to trap readers into emotion by showing the prolonged torture of a naive and virtuous heroine. The atmosphere business certainly develops from the gothic novel into crime literature. Lytton's *Paul Clifford* really does begin with the arch gothic sentence, "It was a dark and stormy night" (it would be remarkable if the night were not dark, but this is not playing the gothic game). Mainline gothic novels also find resolution for all of the scary shenanigans of the plot in some sort of supernatural conclusion. In Lewis' *The Monk*, for instance, the hero actually has made a pact with Satan and the Fiend carries him off at the end. There was, however, a sub-group of gothic novels called "Tales of Terror" which eschewed the supernatural conclusion and explained all of the weird goings-on in the story by rational means. In Ann Radcliffe's *The Mysteries of Udolpho* (1794), which represents the best of this school, the author builds episodes of tension and release by creating events which seem supernatural but are not. At the Castle of Udolpho, for instance, the robbers hear a strange voice in their chamber which seems to come from some sort of disembodied wraith, but later we learn that this was really DuPont speaking from a hitherto unrevealed secret passage. Radcliffe structures the whole novel upon several hidden relationships, which we would have known six hundred pages sooner except the heroine faints whenever she runs across evidence of them. All of these elements of the gothic novel influence the development of the detective story in slightly different ways. Developing concurrently with the regular detective story is the detective story with gothic additions, or the gothic with detective additions. From Godwin and Lytton, to the sensation novel of the mid-nineteenth century, to the ladies novels of Oppenheim and LeQueux, to DuMaurier and Holt, gothic furniture and the fate of an innocent and psychotic heroine manifest themselves frequently in mystery literature. On the other hand, from Poe onward detective stories make strong anti-gothic statements. Poe's best Dupin story, "The Purloined Letter," has virtually no gothic features and the rule writers of the nineteen-twenties and nineteen-thirties were outspoken in their condemnation not only of love and sentimentality, but also about ouija boards, secret passages, and denouements handed out by gross coincidence. The gothic novel, therefore, has little influence on the essentials of the detective story. When it does enter mystery literature, it enters because writers wish to broaden the appeal of their fiction to bring in readers addicted to the pure gothic or the love romance.

After having plodded through a couple of millennia of history and literature, we have arrived at the nineteenth century, not arguably but definitely the starting place for the detective story. With much of the older material I have waffled: Pseudo-crypto this and crypto-pseudo that. Some of the material which critics suggest has historical relevance to detective fiction is clearly hooey. If Herodotus got sold a pup with "The Story of Rhampsinitus' Treasure House," E.M. Wrong tries to sell us the dog when he claims that this narrative contains "the twin themes of detection and crime sketched in their essentials," and Dorothy L. Sayers puts a cross-bred Great Dane and Saint Bernard on the block when she would have us believe it exhibits "the psychological method of detection." The search for ancient and historical connections to and for the detective story carries with it the air of the B.B.C. documentary, with a leisure-suited James Burke standing before the walls of the Old Temple, then in the Valley of Kings, then in Syracuse, and after a dozen or so hops to other exotic and colorful places, winding up in front of the Poe House in Baltimore. All of this seems impressive and erudite, but it also seems too wide-screen. Not only wide-screen, but it also illustrates one function of detective writers and detective readers. Most of the material I have included above comes from writers of the nineteen-twenties: E.M. Wrong (1926), Dorothy L. Sayers (1929), and Regis Messac (1929). These people patched together a history for the detective story because of their own cultural inclinations. The impulse to invent a history for the detective story came first from these people's classical educations. For a neo-classicist, all types of human expression simply repeat the universals put into forms by the ancients. With this bias, there must be classical precedents for the detective story. The drive to find analogies for modern detective stories also stems from the vogue, inspired by T.S. Eliot and Jessie Weston, of hunting for archetypes of modern expression in the myths of diverse cultures. Looking for a lineage stretching back to Moses also illustrates the conscious inferiority felt by detective writers about their work. Finding the first detective tale in the Scriptures parallels the bogus claim that science fiction begins with Plato or Lucian of Samosata. Finally, too, dipping back into historical literature about crime figures not only in the authors' searches for new material, but in the drive on the part of detective readers to collect, hoard, and revel in the discovery and possession of bits of arcane lore and abstruse information.

The crux of the connections approach to history is that your choice of a final object colors and determines the backward course which you will trace. If, instead of ending up with plastics in general we chose to end with nylon, to trace the full history we would have to begin back in the year dot when men switched to trousers and women did not. The invention of marine insurance companies would not make that much difference. Tracing the history of the detective story provides the same problem. The way in which we define the detective story determines the history we create for it. Some critics start with the crime novel, the amorphous twentieth century term which embraces any work of fiction about crime, detection, police work, or even general problem solving. I am not going to take this view. For the purposes of this book, the detective story is the kind of fiction invented by Poe and matured by Collins, Gaboriau, Doyle, Christie, Sayers, and a host of others. This is the sort of fiction to which people refer when they say that they are reading a detective story. Further, this is the sort of fiction against which writers reacted when they invented the hard-boiled story, the psychological crime novel, and the police procedural. Forgetting about the mild euphoria we need to see all of the early material as detective fiction, this sort of detective fiction emerged because of several definite developments of the nineteenth century.

First of all, we do not get detective stories without detectives, and detectives do not occur until relatively recently. When little crime exists we need few policemen, and in an agrarian, village-oriented culture, again, there is little need for police and detectives because the society can handle its own problems. In some measure, the growth of large cities caused the need for policemen and detectives. In France we find the establishment of modern detective forces with Eugene Francois Vidocq's organization of the *Brigade de la Surete* in 1817. Sir Robert Peel modernized London's metropolitan police force in 1829 and, in part because of Vidocq's advertisement, plainclothes detectives became part of the Metropolitan Police in 1842. Once detective police existed, they became available as literary figures. The police detective, however, suffered a good many ups and downs in the nineteenth century and did not become an entirely acceptable hero for almost one hundred years. As we will see with Godwin and Lytton, the paid "spy" ranked low in public esteem, as did the old fashioned thief-taker and the bounty hunter in the United States. Although Dickens built his fiction and non-fiction detective pieces on his admiration for the detective police, British police detectives suffered many reverses in the last part of the nineteenth century. In 1867, Fenians attacked Clerkenwell Prison, in 1877 three police detectives were tried and convicted of abetting confidence men, and in 1888, of course, there was Jack the Ripper. A gap, therefore, developed between the ideal of honest, efficient policework and the actual conditions observable in society. As most literature occupies the space between perfection and damnation, so does the detective story. Were there no police or detectives, writers would find themselves compelled to concentrate on heavy lessons about morality and social order. Were the police and detectives perfect, there would be little crime and therefore little fiction about it. The presence of half-successful police in the late nineteenth century not only gave fiction writers a soap box from which to inveigh against blinkered officialdom and pig-ignorant policemen versus the amateur detective, but it also lessened the pressure to make the crime story into a moral tract.

This corresponded to a change in writers' views about crime and criminals. Much nineteenth century literature is about crime. Few French writers, from Hugo to Balzac, could stay far away from writing about crime and criminals, and the crime story formed the staple of French newspaper fiction. English publishers churned out Newgate literature and penny-dreadfuls for lower class readers and adolescents; middle-class English writers almost invariably wrote about crime, too. As part of the reforming fervor, Victorian authors like Lytton and Dickens portrayed prisons and characters caught up in crime, not only to prey upon the sentiments of their readers but also to try to ameliorate social conditions. They wanted to create an environment in which the true Victorian virtues, work, piety, benevolence, etc., would operate for all people, without prejudice and outmoded institutions weighing them down and destroying them. Yet crime as sensation or crime as a social concern did not contribute to the rise of the detective story. Classic detective works like *The Moonstone* express little concern for crime or criminals. Poe does not care one iota about the origins, natures, or fates of the guilty people in his tales. Doyle hardly tries to make readers think about prison reform or an unjust legal or social system. What we need before we can arrive at real detective stories is a new class of readers and a new class of writers who have a vague interest in crime as subject matter but who remain aloof from its serious moral and social implications. The Victorian age shows the emergence of several new classes of readers brought into being by universal education and the urge to self-improvement. The most important of these, however, was the middle-class male reader who long ago had the ability, but not the time, to read fiction. Unlike most earlier fiction which made its pitch to female readers, the new detective story aimed at entertaining what it perceived to be the middle-class male mind. This sort of reader got his politics from his party and his trade, his news from *The Times*, his sentiment from his home, and his entertainment from the detective story which did not want to poach too much on these other preserves. The fact that female readers, too, latched onto the detective story serves to demonstrate how wrong writers from Richardson onward were when they directed their books toward what they conceived to be female taste.

Here we return to the police detective. If readers in the early nineteenth century saw the police detective in literature and life as a lower-class creature who was either incompetent or corrupt, they increasingly saw, in literature if not in life, the genius as the hero. From the romantics, Englishmen received an extensive cast of heroic supermen trammelled by convention, prejudice, and their own greatness. From Faust to Childe Harold, writers insisted that this world was not a home fit for heroes. Victorians, thinking something like "if you're so smart, why aren't you rich?," adapted the genius from the tragic figure of the romantics to Carlyle's vision of the genius as the shaper of history and progress. Childe Harold, in effect, becomes president of IBM. Even the most serious reader, however, can tire of too much "onward and upward" literature, and Carlyle hardly fit the notion of a good read on the commuter train to the suburbs. Detective writers, therefore, invented the pocket genius. Poe domesticated the genius to serve his own romantic ends, but Victorian writers like Doyle soon shaped the genius to their own down-to-earth values. Thus the developing concept of the genius joined with a modest concern about the police, and both appealed to a readership which writers perceived differently. But we do not get to the detective story without one more element.

At its inception, the novel was a slow-paced and rambling form written for people of leisure. We amble along with Joseph and Parson Adams on their picaresque adventures, we jog down an odd series of crooked paths and cul-de-sacs with Tristram Shandy, and we drag along Pamela's rocky road to the altar. A few more episodes, letters, or digressions make little difference. From the prose romance, eighteenth-century writers like Fielding took the unexpected ending, like the astonishing revelation of someone's ancestry, as a tongue-in-cheek method of concluding their fictions. The use of this sort of structural mystery descended to Mrs. Radcliffe, then to Lytton and Dickens—although, to be sure, Dickens used it with a more consistent and surer hand than the others. The demands of serial publishing and the three volume format for novels almost insured that this was as far as mystery and suspense would go in the novel. The invention of the short story and the slimming down of novels changed all of this. Joined with this, we find a reaction against the loose structure patterned on the romance and a movement toward the well-ordered novel. Here we need to note that early in its development, with Poe and later with Doyle, the successful detective story is the short story. Because of its need for economy, compression, and consistency, the short story cannot afford the casualness of the romance. If the hero says at the end he saw or found something, it had better be there in the story. Writers often use short stories, because of their brevity, as testing grounds for new literary techniques, something impractical in the novel until the twentieth century. Finally, short stories usually depend on cleverness—the witty conclusion, the epigrammatic close, the final couplet. Mainly because of Poe, the short story established the requisite literary form which later writers would then apply to the detective novel. This formula includes: 1) the surprise ending, 2) the presentation within the body of the story of all or most of the facts which explain the surprise—or give the illusion of having done so, and 3) the manipulation of narrative elements— plot, point of view, tone, etc.—so as to obscure the facts and make the surprise possible. This is the pattern invented by Poe, domesticated by Doyle, applied to the triple-decker by Collins, and introduced to the twentieth century by E.C. Bentley. When we take this new literary arrangement and connect it with the changing attitudes towards the policeman and the criminal, connect it to the evolving concept of the genius, and connect it to a newly-perceived area of interest among readers, we get something new. We get the detective story.

# Chapter 2
# Godwin and Lytton

Before we get to Poe and the actual beginning of the detective story, we ought to take an excursion through the fiction of William Godwin and Edward Bulwer Lytton. Technically, I suppose we could avoid these writers since neither of them wrote detective stories. They wrote novels which occasionally grip and amuse readers, so this chapter is not a terribly hard penance. It is, though, a scholarly penance, because most discussions about the history of the detective story start in earnest with Godwin and Lytton. In these writers, we will see the Newgate literature of the eighteenth century transformed into what Julian Symons calls "crime literature." More important than this, however, we will see in Godwin and Lytton the sorts of books which Poe, and later Collins, reacted against when they wrote real detective stories.

If William Godwin (1756-1836) knew he would be included in histories of the detective story, he would have had apoplexy. To consider that, instead of reading books about radical, sexual, or political equality, people would devote their time to reinforcing their comfortable middle-class lives with bits of tame excitement, artificial surprise, and smug superiority, would have been too much for him. He did not intend *The Adventures of Caleb Williams* (1794) to do these things. But then again, who knows? Godwin varied his principles enough in his relations with his son-in-law, Shelley, and he at least acquiesced to several changes in not only the structure of *Caleb Williams* but also the way in which the public was expected to receive it.

Caleb Williams himself narrates the novel which bears his name. As it is a three volume novel, Godwin packaged Caleb's fortunes in three reasonably separate containers. The first book of the novel has little to do with the hero himself, but recounts the tragic misadventures of his employer, Mr. Falkland. Falkland is a sort of universal genius (a fact which Caleb admits even when he has cause to hate him), to whom Godwin gives the ability to speak well and to write poetry, but few other particulars in the genius line. Mainly, Falkland's qualities of mind and manners show through in contrast to his neolithic neighbor, Barnabas Tyrrel. Tyrrel's behavior is quite up to the standards of the stone age: he hounds a man out of his living because his son will not serve as the whipper-in at the Big House, and he plots the rape of his niece because she has made eyes at Falkland. Falkland, a sort of eighteenth-century Shane, stymies Tyrrel's plots and gives the neighboring gentry enough courage to blackball him from their assembly rooms. Tyrrel, no respecter of convention, bursts into a polite gathering and publicly thrashes Falkland. Several hours later, Tyrrel's corpse turns up in the street. Evidence appears at the lodging of Tyrrel's displaced tenants. The father confesses that he murdered Tyrrel, and he and his son are hanged. In the midst of this narrative, Godwin inserts an episode from Falkland's youthful European travels which illustrates his obsession with "chivalry" and reputation: the two things which Falkland defiled when he murdered Tyrrel and allowed the Hawkinses to suffer for in his stead. Except, we are not supposed to know this yet.

In the second book, we get to young Caleb himself. Though of humble origins, Caleb has spent his spare time reading and when his father dies, Falkland makes Caleb his secretary. Just as Falkland's obsession is reputation, Caleb becomes overcome with the notion that Falkland murdered Tyrrel. Without particularly longing for justice, and certainly not intending to turn him in, Caleb snoops around and pesters Falkland with insinuations until his master confesses his guilt to him. Here Godwin causes Falkland to gloss over the proof which hanged Hawkins: "Whence came the circumstantial evidence against him, the broken knife and the blood, I am unable to tell. I suppose by some miraculous accident..." At any rate, from this point onward the social contract is broken, for Falkland feels that Caleb's knowledge puts him at risk. He consequently subjects the hero to such oppressive surveillance that Caleb determines to quit Falkland's employ. But that would be too easy. Falkland plants some jewels in Caleb's luggage and has him arrested as a thief. To make matters worse, Caleb has the gall to accuse his master of framing him. He is thrown into jail, and things look black for him at the next assizes. Caleb's imprisonment gave Godwin the chance to expatiate on the disgusting conditions of prisons as well as the law's corruption and delay. In prison, Caleb exercises his mechanical aptitude and, much in the manner of Jack Shepherd, he twice escapes from jail. With his second escape he becomes, in a way, a free man.

Book three of *Caleb Williams* follows the vicissitudes of the hero's escape from the law and then from Falkland's private paranoia. After successfully breaking jail, Caleb falls victim to a group of highwaymen led by the vicious Gines, but then Mr. Raymond, the chief brigand, rescues him and allows him to hide in the gang's headquarters. Escaping from the vengeance of Gines and his clique, Caleb runs through a series of disguises (Irish beggar, Jewish journalist, and crippled watchmaker) and eventually ends up in London. Here Gines, who has become a police spy, apprehends the hero and takes him once again to prison, only to discover that Falkland has dropped the charges against Caleb. Seeking only obscurity and quiet, Caleb settles in Wales as a free man. In this retreat, Godwin draws Caleb as the fugitive Eugene Aram, showing him studying the origins of the British language. Working through Gines, Falkland blasts this rural happiness, and after being on the receiving end of several choice bits of persecution, Caleb decides to openly accuse Falkland of Tyrrel's murder. He does so. Falkland confesses in court and then more or less spontaneously dies. Caleb ends his memoir vindicated and free but psychically wasted by having ruined Falkland, whom he still believes to be a great man.

Godwin did not originally entitle this book *The Adventures of Caleb Williams*; he called it *Things As They Are*. In his initial version, he intended to have Caleb fail to expose Falkland, to be driven insane, and finally to be poisoned by Falkland. In the published version, he altered the ending to show justice vindicated but at a terrible cost. By 1831 Godwin also changed the title of the book to *The Adventures of Caleb Williams*, thereby lessening its political impact and heightening its adventure and psychological sides. In 1831, Godwin also wrote an account of his conception of the novel, and since it comes up frequently in histories of detective fiction, I will quote a sizeable portion of it here. Godwin says that

I formed a conception of a book of fictitious adventures, that should in some way be distinguished by a very powerful interest. Pursuing this idea, I invented the third volume of my tale, then the second, and last of all the first. I bent myself to the conception of a series of adventures of flight and pursuit; the fugitive in perpetual apprehension of being overwhelmed with the worst calamities, and the pursuer, by his ingenuity and resources keeping his victim in a state of the most fearful alarm....

I was next called upon to conceive a dramatic and impressive situation adequate to account for the impulse that the pursuer should feel.... This I apprehended could best be effected by a secret murder, to the investigation of which the innocent victim should be impelled by an unconquerable spirit of curiosity....

The subject of the first volume was still to be invented. To account for the fearful events of the third it was necessary that the pursuer should be invested with every advantage of fortune.... Nor could my purpose of giving an overpowering interest to my tale be answered, without his appearing to have been originally endowed with a mighty store of amiable dispositions and virtues, so that his being driven to the first act of murder should be judged worthy of the deepest regret, and should be seen in some measure to have arisen out of his virtues themselves.

Allowing for the fact that here Godwin writes about something that happened thirty-seven years earlier, does this statement make *Caleb Williams*, in its conception at least, a detective story?

Brought up as a Calvinist, Godwin based *Caleb Williams* on one of the numerous Biblical examples of God's vengeance on sinners—Jeremiah 16:16 is as good a guess as any. Over this, he layered his own political radicalism which he had outlined the previous year in his *Enquiry Concerning the Principles of Political Justice*. Thus we find him shifting the Lord's vengeance upon sinners to the lord's vengeance on someone socially inferior. As *Caleb Williams* grew into multiple volumes, however, Godwin began to develop the tragic potential of his protagonist and his antagonist: Falkland's crime, as Godwin makes clear in his account of the book, derives from his virtue, his genius, benevolence, and concern for honor. Caleb, likewise, brings persecution on himself by a virtue magnified until it becomes a vice: his intellectual curiosity becomes nosiness. In *Caleb Williams*, Godwin aimed at the creation of something like classical tragedy.

Insofar as *Caleb Williams* deals with law enforcement, Godwin is against it. He portrays Gines, the thief turned thief-taker, as an utter degenerate, and the two agents whom Caleb bribes in book three are beneath contempt. Ian Ousby in *Bloodhounds of Heaven* points out Godwin's own fears of government agents spying on him because of his politics. Godwin's own feelings about police spies also show up in *Caleb Williams*. Caleb's diseased curiosity and eventual impeachment of his master deprive him of the readers' admiration, and in the end rob him of his own peace of mind and enjoyment of justice. Rather than being inspired by police or detectives, *Caleb Williams* drew somewhat upon eighteenth-century crime literature. As he also tells us in his account of the novel, Godwin steeped himself in Newgate literature and lives of pirates while he composed *Caleb Williams*. Caleb's escape from prison clearly comes from one of the numerous accounts of Jack Shepherd, who specialized in escapes from prison, including one which progressed through six strong rooms and over the walls of Newgate prison. Unlike Lytton, who would later curb them to Victorian taste, Godwin had only a passing narrative interest in highwaymen. In the novel, Caleb only spends four short chapters with Raymond and his crew. Prisons occupy a good deal more of the author's attention. Here Godwin called not only upon Newgate literature and other material he had read, but also upon the testimony of friends who had visited Newgate. As his footnotes in the prison chapters attest, he interested himself in the emotional power of the prison scenes, but he especially wanted them to be accurate.

But is *Caleb Williams* a detective novel? No, it is not even close to being one. In spite of some historians dubbing it a detective work, *Caleb Williams* just does not fit. Certainly Godwin never proposed to write what we would now call a detective novel, although in his more commercial moments he probably would have admitted to sharing some of John Buchan's conception of the thriller. If we want to call what Caleb does "detection," we then need to label *Caleb Williams* as an anti-detective novel. Objectively,

Caleb's sense of evidence might even be inadmissible at the *auto-da-fe*. He falls into a sick prejudice that Falkland is a murderer. This he works into proof by observing Falkland's answers to questions about Alexander the Great, his reactions at a murder trial, and other sorts of miscellaneous behavior. As a magistrate later tells him, Caleb has no real evidence against Falkland. Godwin, if he wished to, could have invented evidence; he does, after all, mention a broken knife and other material clues. But he did not wish to. As a detective, Caleb is a complete chucklehead. He is just a lucky guesser. Indeed, only Godwin's notion that the guilty go funny all over when confronted with their crimes, coupled with his decisions to give Falkland a final, magnanimous gesture, enable Caleb to win in the end. This, surely, is not detective business. Godwin never intends us to see or value Caleb's minuscule deductive and inductive talents at work. He created Caleb to be a persecuted man. He wanted to make us value his sufferings, empathize with his need for freedom, and marvel at his skill at escape and disguise. During Caleb's residence in Wales, Godwin parallels his hero with Eugene Aram (about whom we will hear more shortly), again emphasizing the waste and pathos, if not tragedy, which the criminal justice system produced.

In structure, likewise, *Caleb Williams* has little affinity to the detective novel. Getting back to Godwin's account of the conception of the novel, people have made a good deal of his reverse conception of the plot—imagining book three and then books two and one. Backward construction surely is a mark of the detective story. Writers typically work from the clever solution to the events leading to it. But Godwin did not work this way. As he says in his account of the novel, he created three separate plots he joined not with a mystery or plot surprise but with continuing characters. In terms of mystery or suspense, part three of *Caleb Williams* does not add any new facts about Tyrrel's death and, in fact, Godwin pays little attention to playing up mystery or suspense connected to the crime. In the space of about thirty pages in part two, Godwin moves from the assumption of Falkland's innocence, to Caleb's doubts, to the conviction that Falkland is a murderer, to Falkland's confession to Caleb. Thus, before the real story of Caleb's struggle with Falkland is thirty pages old, we know as much as we ever will about the murder. This sort of technique has little effect on the development of the detective story, even if it did have an impact on psychological adventure fiction.

Godwin does, however, present us with two bits of detective technique in *Caleb Williams*. At the start of book two, after Caleb has reiterated Mr. Collins' account of Falkland's formative years, the narrator tells us this:

I have stated the narrative of Mr. Collins, interspersed with such other information as I was able to collect, with all the exactness that my memory, assisted by certain memorandums I made at the time will afford. *I do not pretend to warrant the authenticity of any part of these memoirs, except so much as fell under my own knowledge,* and that part shall be stated with the same simplicity and accuracy, that I would observe toward a court.... The same scrupulous fidelity restrains me from altering the manner of Mr. Collins' narrative to adapt it to the precepts of my own taste; and *it will soon be perceived how essential that narrative is.* [my italics]

Here we see Godwin fudging his narrative point of view: he decided to use the first person narration of Caleb for the whole book but realized that parts of Falkland's past lay outside the knowledge of an obscure country boy, and so he did some fancy footwork here to make the whole consistent. Furthermore, with the last sentence, Godwin is protesting too much. Although book one presents interesting and affecting material, most of it does not bear on Caleb's history. The author does not even do much with the implicit parallel between Tyrrel and Falkland. Thus, Godwin's telling us about the essential importance of book one is merely an attempt to patch up what he perceived to be an aesthetic weakness in his plot. By accident, however, Godwin stumbled upon two important techniques of the detective story: the warning to the reader and the careful presentation of documentary evidence. The implications of these techniques were not lost on another Mr. Collins, who, seventy-four years later, used them in *The Moonstone.* They were, however, lost to Godwin's immediate successors.

Edward Bulwer Lytton carried on some of Godwin's concern for dealing with crime and criminals in fiction. He, however, strained Godwin's romanticism through the sieve of his own Victorian consciousness, weakening Godwin's psychological focus to substitute the work ethic, and ignoring Godwin's oblique hints for structuring the mystery novel to maintain older methods of novel-building. Lytton admirably illustrates the transition from the eighteenth-century novels of Fielding and Sterne to the Victorian novels of Dickens, but he kills off the vague movement toward the detective novel latent in *Caleb Williams.* If readers today know Lytton at all, it is through *The Last Days of Pompeii* (1834), but he did write four novels which illustrate the state of crime and detection in early Victorian literature.

*Pelham: or the Adventures of a Gentleman* (1828) seems a long way from Godwin's crime literature. Here Lytton combines description of manners and the growth theme with a dash of Godwin. The narrator of the novel, Lord Pelham, presents us with a picture of fashionable life in Regency England. We eavesdrop in countless salons and assembly rooms, noting fashion and epicurism (even seeing Beau Brummel), but also learning about wit and wisdom. Lytton mostly works with the character sketch, one of his favorite building blocks, showing us a succession of bucks, fops, dandies, wits, and beauties of the period. In the first part of the novel, the hero,

Pelham, mostly proves that he is the acme of fashion, able to handle *bon mots* and classical scraps with the best of them. The hero, however, needs to lead a useful life, so in the second part of the book he becomes a ward healer for a party leader. But politics is a whited sepulcher, full of back-stabbing and mendacity, and even though Pelham makes a grand gesture of sacrificing his ambition to his ideals, he needs something else. Lytton provides this by making Pelham uncover the truth about a mystery which has bubbled to the surface of the plot several times. Throughout the book, Sir Reginald Glanville, Pelham's boyhood friend, periodically enters and acts melancholy and mysterious, usually in the company of a blackguard named Thornton and in association with Sir James Tyrrell. Tyrrell's name bounces us back to Godwin, but Lytton here gives Godwin a sentimental twist. Just when Pelham needs a dose of some object in life, he discovers Tyrrell's corpse and circumstantial evidence pointing to Glanville as the murderer. After several occasions of mutual moodiness, Glanville relates to his friend how Tyrrell raped his beloved, but also protests his innocence of Tyrrell's death. With the help of a friendly pick-pocket, Pelham brings the murder home to Thornton. Glanville is thus freed to die of a wasting sickness, and Pelham can now marry and participate in life.

Partly because he wanted to publicize the need for prison reform and partly because he thought that gangsters were cute, Lytton wrote *Paul Clifford* (1830). To produce his desired effects, he turned not only to Newgate literature, but also to Gay's *Beggar's Opera*. *Paul Clifford* ostensibly tells the story of an innocent youth forced to take up a life of crime. His mother dying in a run-down pot house, Paul becomes the ward of Gammer Lobkins, hostess of "The Mug." She does her best for him, going as far as having him tutored in the classics, but the youth naively falls in with a fast set and is arrested for one of their crimes. Imprisoned in Bridewell, Paul meets Augustus Tomlinson who, as a rationale for his estate, has worked out an elaborate parallel (based on Gay) between "honest" society and the society of thieves. After their escape from Bridewell, Tomlinson introduces Paul to the society of highwaymen. This segment of the society is open to merit, and Paul quickly becomes their leader. When these merry Hells Angels are not singing (Lytton includes numerous lyrics in the text), they are staging amusing stick-ups, robbing the rich and succoring the poor. During one of the gang's robberies, Paul meets and falls in love with Lucy Brandon. Here Lytton leaves the picaresque and concentrates the rest of the novel on Paul's struggles toward conversion and Lucy's struggles to fend off the geriatric but lecherous Lord Mauleverer. When Paul begins to set off on a new life as a worker, one of his gang impeaches his fellows and Paul falls into the hands of the law while trying to rescue his comrades. Just as Lucy's uncle, Judge Brandon, puts on the black cap to sentence Paul to the gallows, he discovers that the youth is his own long-lost son. Before Brandon dies of another one of those mysterious Victorian illnesses, he helps to have Paul's sentence commuted to transportation. At the end of the novel we find Paul and Lucy living in America and working hard to make everyone's life pleasant.

In 1832, Lytton jammed together motifs from *Pelham* and *Paul Clifford* and combined them with a reworking of Godwin to give us a sentimental but optimistic version of *Caleb Williams* in *Eugene Aram*. Godwin used some background of Eugene Aram's life in *Caleb Williams* and intended to write a separate novel about him. We will never know what Godwin would have made of them, but the facts of Eugene Aram's career are these. The real Eugene Aram attracted a good bit of attention from the English romantics. Aram rose from modest circumstances to become, in potential at least, an original and important student of languages. His projected *Comparative Lexicon of the English, Latin, Greek, Hebrew and Celtic Languages* might have established the Indo-European origins of European languages a generation before C.J. Pritchard did it. But Aram had trouble. His wife, whom he deserted to take up residence in Lynn in Norfolk, began to gossip about her husband's involvement with the disappearance of Daniel Clark. Her chattering led to the arrest of a man named Houseman who testified he had witnessed Aram and another man murdering Clark. Although the second man disappeared, Aram was arrested, tried, and convicted of Clark's murder. In his confession, Aram justified the crime by claiming an illicit relationship between Clark and his wife. It was all rather sordid: a wife causing her husband's arrest, sexual infidelity, and two men stomping a third to death. So Lytton changed it. He eliminates Aram's wife, invents a serious and virginal fiancee, makes Clark the ravisher of an innocent child, and says Aram was an onlooker and not a participant in the murder. He also spruces up Aram's character by moving him away from dreary philology and connecting him with vaguely scientific pursuits. One part of Lytton's *Eugene Aram* combines *Faust* with Godwin's picture of the suffering genius. Thus, the satanic Houseman, Lytton would have it, tempted Aram to crime, and even though Aram engaged in crime for the best of motives, punishing a rapist, he will forever suffer for it. Aram's crisis comes when he falls in love with Madeline Lester, for in giving in to love, Aram runs his neck into the noose, with the aid of perverse circumstance. The parallel plot, the Caleb plot, starts with the picaresque wanderings of Walter Lester who, in the company of Corporal Bunting, vaguely has in mind that he is looking for his lost father. Through a series of coincidences, Walter discovers that Aram was involved in the murder of his father, who was using the pseudonym of Clark. Walter brings Aram to justice, but, as in Godwin, poisons his own happiness. His cousin, Aram's fiancee, dies of what can only be called an epidemic of mysterious illnesses in Lytton. Walter cannot stand the scenes of his youth and goes off to Prussia to fight with Frederick the Great's army. He returns a wiser and more useful man, just in time to marry his other cousin.

*Night and Morning* (1841) replays *Paul Clifford* with its scenes from the Newgate world and adds the heavy sentiment and sentimentality of *Eugene Aram*. The novel begins with the evil Robert Beaufort stealing his dead brother's estate from his widow and children. Once again, Lytton organizes the early portions of the book around the depressingly picaresque adventures of Beaufort's eldest nephew, Philip. After a series of melancholy attempts to start his life, Philip joins up with Gawtrey, whom misfortune and the animus of a wastrel peer have turned from gentleman to criminal. In Paris, Philip and Gawtrey run up against a policeman named M. Favart, whom Lytton compares to Vidocq. On the evening that Philip finally realizes that Gawtrey is a crook and determines to leave his company, Favart raids Gawtrey's secret counterfeiting factory, and circumstances cause the young man to take it on the lam. With the aid of a French noblewoman, however, Philip departs for India where he gains respectability in the army. Returning to London, Philip witnesses his uncle's avarice, but in the course of saving Gawtrey's ward from the lecherous embraces of an obnoxious peer, he finds the documents which establish his right to his father's estate. At the close of the novel, Philip lets his reptilian uncle keep part of his father's estate, and he resigns his beloved to his younger brother. After another of Lytton's mystery illnesses, Philip marries Gawtrey's ward, an industrious and intellectual woman, and proceeds to lead a useful and fulfilling life.

None of these four novels is a detective novel, or even a crime novel for that matter. The nature of the early Victorian novel precluded this. First of all, as with Godwin, the very size of these novels prevents the kind of tight construction requisite to the detective novel. Until late in the nineteenth century, writers, readers, and publishers accepted that novels had to be long: the three volume novel, the triple-decker, was the standard. To fill up the multiple volumes, Lytton typically includes twin plots and frequently stops to dilate moral points far beyond any sort of effectiveness. Further, Lytton consciously wrote for an upper-class female audience, and this often caused him to pull back from making Godwinian points about crime or even human nature. Thus, he gives us plenty of "fair readers," and in a footnote in *Paul Clifford*, Lytton tells his readers that "The author need not, he hopes, observe that these sentiments [the legitimacy of warring against unjust laws] are Mr. Paul Clifford's, not his." Acceding to his readers' expectations about the form of the novel and aiming his books at his conception of the moral and ethical fragility of upper-class women went a long way toward preventing Lytton from creating either a detective or a crime novel.

Another fact which prevented Lytton from arriving at the detective novel was his devotion to eighteenth, century novelists. Perhaps the most graphic example of this is his inclusion in *Paul Clifford* of a chapter consisting entirely of exclamation points. As this takes us back to *Tristram Shandy*, the travels of Walter Lester and Corporal Bunting in *Eugene Aram* come pretty clearly from Tom Jones' travels with Partridge. The fact that half of each of these novels follows the picaresque adventures of the hero points to Lytton's affection for Fielding and Sterne. Most importantly, Lytton uses mystery in his novels the same way that writers of the Enlightenment used it. In *Paul Clifford* and *Night and Morning*, Lytton introduces the loss of some sort of papers which will alleviate the suffering of the heroes. At the end of the books, this material accidentally, or providentially, turns up and resolves their fates. This is precisely the sort of *deus ex machina* which Fielding uses to conclude *Tom Jones*. The fact that every novel except *Pelham* depends upon the unravelling of paternity—finding the lost father—ties Lytton to the old structure of the romance rather than to the new structure of the detective story.

In terms of criminals, too, Lytton adheres to old-fashioned ideas rather than to the modern attitudes which gave rise to the detective story. Lytton gives us four classes of criminals in his books. First, there are the highwaymen. Here Lytton draws on Robin Hood legends, Newgate literature, Godwin, and John Gay. The young Paul Clifford cuts his teeth on a biography of Dick Turpin, rather than on the classical learning which Dame Lobkins paid for. Lytton, like Godwin, presents us with gentlemen highwaymen, intelligent, educated, honorable, and jovial. Part of his reason for doing this lay in his desire to emphasize the hypocrisy of "honest society." But part of it rested on Lytton's fascination with thieves' cant. Thus in *Pelham* and *Paul Clifford*, he gives us patches of gangster patois, along with footnotes telling us what "tobymen" are (highwaymen), and what "doing a panny" is (being transported). For his second class of criminal, Lytton goes back to Godwin and gives us the genius. Glanville, in *Pelham*, and Eugene Aram are both geniuses whom momentary weakness, allied with virtue and conjoined with perverse circumstance, make criminals. Glanville almost becomes a criminal (in actuality instead of intent) because he did not marry his lover, because of his mother's illness which took him away to France, and because of his just rage at Tyrrell's rape of Gertrude. Precisely the same thing happens to Eugene Aram, although he goes along to become an accessory to the crime. For Lytton, the wonderful thing about geniuses is the nobility of their sufferings. Instead of focusing on the detection of crime or the criminal's fear of arrest, Lytton shows us the exquisite sentiments and soul-inspiring melancholy of the genius. At the opposite end of the spectrum, Lytton gives us the naturally vicious man the genetically inclined thug, murderer, cheat, or lecher. Thornton and Houseman fall into this group, but it exists in the upper classes, too, with men like Tyrrell and Beaufort. Finally, Lytton gives us the criminal who is not a criminal. As much as he satirizes classical education, Lytton teaches that if you have such an education and if your parents are gentlefolk, you cannot become a real criminal. Neither Paul Clifford nor Philip Beaufort can become a real criminal because of the genetic inheritance from their parents. They naturally respect virtue and shrink from vice. Their natures prove themselves when circumstance flings the heroes among criminal companions, but Lytton also needs to doubly prove their virtue for his readers and so gives them gilt-edged birth certificates at the end of the novels. For Lytton it is, ultimately, as absurd to suppose that the son of gentle parents can become a conscienceless criminal as it would be for Dickens to imagine Oliver fire-bombing constables and looting television shops.

Essential Victorianism prevents Lytton from truly writing either crime novels or detective novels. He cannot admit as Godwin did that anyone can be a criminal. He treats the subject of crime because it is comic or sentimental, but also because he wants to help make it disappear. Of course, he intends a social message about prisons and early environment, but he has no real interest in crime or its detection. His detectives, like the Bow Street Runners and the fictionalized Vidocq, are still contemptible people. When his heroes uncover crimes, as they do in *Pelham* and *Eugene Aram*, they do so by chance and accident rather than by insight or acumen. For Lytton, crime and criminals only provide fuel for his larger arguments about usefulness, work, and hero worship. In every case, involvement with crime forms part of the hero's conversion from a frivolous to a useful life. It gives the final push toward adulthood not only to Pelham, but also to Paul Clifford, Walter Lester, and Philip Beaumont. After his contact with crime, each man goes on to employment and benevolence. In the case of geniuses like Glanville or Aram, crime distracts the genius from his real job, and Lytton builds on the pathos of this. Lytton, though, gives the positive side of genius in Paul Clifford's attempted, and Walter Lester's actual, travels to Prussia to fight for a real genius, Frederick the Great, one of Carlyle's heroes, who effectively changed the world for the better. Here is real genius, but, of course, Frederick the Great had little to do with Dupin, Lecoq, or Poirot.

With *Caleb Williams* and Lytton's novels, we can see the uses of crime, criminals, and detectives before the advent of the detective story. Both writers use crime as part of a larger argument about social justice, and they use traditional forms to accomplish both their educational and diversionary objectives. Caught by the size and shape of the multiple-volume novel, they exhibit little compactness and much imprecision in unfolding their plots and characters. For both Godwin and Lytton, the character of the genius stood at the pinnacle of human development and aspiration, but their genius characters either become mired in circumstance and tragic dilemmas or they accomplish things outside of the realm of the ordinary mortal. Although their works remain amusing, interesting, and occasionally gripping, Lytton and Godwin contributed little to the development of the detective story.

People who read them, however, did. In the 1840s, an American reviewer appraised Lytton this way:

We have long learned to reverence the fine intellect of Bulwer. We take up any production of his pen with a positive certainty that, in reading it, the wildest passions of our nature, the most profound of our thoughts, the brightest visions of our fancy...will...be enkindled within us.... Viewing him as a novelist—a point of view exceedingly unfavorable (if we hold to the common acception of "the novel") for a proper contemplation of his genius—he is unsurpassed by any writer living or dead.

This American reviewer was Edgar Allan Poe.

# Chapter 3
# Poe

In March of 1841, *Graham's Magazine* of Philadelphia published the first genuine detective story, "The Murders in the Rue Morgue." Over the next four years its author, Edgar Allan Poe, wrote four other detective tales— or tales of ratiocination as he called them—and taken together they provide the conventions of character and the narrative formats which would power detective fiction for the next hundred years. Collins, Gaboriau, Doyle, and countless other writers depended upon Poe for inspiration. In one sense, Poe's detective tales resulted from certain historical and literary developments which made some kind of crime fiction inevitable. Poe, never terribly original in creating plot details, borrowed freely from other writers in his detective tales. Voltaire's *Zadig* and Vidocq's *Memoires* contributed to Poe's detective tales, and even seemingly original details like the use of ballistics in "Thou Art the Man" were not really new.

Like early moralistic stories of crime and detection, Poe's tales first appeared in popular magazines. It seems strange today to consider that one of the more grisly tales, "Thou Art the Man," appeared first in *Godey's Ladies Book*, a journal for middle-class women. Although they were relatively popular, often reprinted, and quickly translated, Poe did not write his tales for mass appeal. In part, this was due to the fact that the spread of literacy and the revolution in technology lay forty years in the future. Doyle, for instance, could depend on a much larger audience than Poe could. Poe, moreover, never intended his detective tales to have mass appeal. They began as explorations of certain tenets of his own romanticism. Poe, in fact, does not develop according to the historical scenario. For all of the ink spent on tracing the historical attitudes toward criminals and detectives, Poe ignores almost entirely the issues of justice and cares little about the social or psychic causes of crime. The success of his detective tales comes not from the tramp of progress toward efficient law enforcement or the humane treatment of criminals. It comes from his ability to combine old scraps into new garments, certainly, but most of all Poe's achievement rests upon his invention of new ways of telling stories.

In the winter of 1841, when he wrote "The Murders in the Rue Morgue," Poe obviously did not think about composing a detective story. I suspect he thought he was writing something halfway between a treatise on genius and a joke. "The Murders in the Rue Morgue" is, of course, a macabre narrative about an orangutan killing Mme. L'Espanaye and her daughter. The sensational material in the story, the shocking surprise of the disposition of the bodies and the furniture of gore, comes pretty directly from the gothic tradition. This, however, occupies only the smallest part of the tale. Remove it and we find that "The Murders in the Rue Morgue" mostly deals with mental things. Even before he came to write the detective tales, Poe saw himself, to use the trendy redundancy, as an investigative reporter, able to observe more closely, to ask more insightful questions, and to reason better than mere hacks. In "Maelzel's Chess-Player," which he wrote for *The Southern Literary Messenger* in 1836, he tries to display these qualities. In this piece, he anatomizes a contrivance which Maelzel tried to pass off on a gullible public as a chess playing automaton. Poe saw through the whole thing (or almost did), and in his article he argues against a Baltimore newspaper's theory and for his own—there was enough room for a boy to fit inside the chess-player. Given his bent of mind, Poe naturally appreciated the demonstration of close observation and reason in Voltaire's *Zadig* (1748). In this tale, which Voltaire may or may not have borrowed from de Mailly's *Le Voyage et les aventures des trois Princes de Serendip*, a Gallic Natty Bumppo infers the nature of a particular dog, and later a horse, from the evidence which he reads along the roadside. If we add one more source, we ought to be able to arrive at the background of reasoning in "The Murders in the Rue Morgue." Poe, we know, had read the *Memoires* of Eugene Francois Vidocq, published in Paris in 1829 and translated into English in the following year. Vidocq, an odd combination of con man and genius, founded France's first official detective force, the *Brigade de la Surete*, in 1812, and when he was nudged out of government employment in 1838, he began the Information Bureau, the first private detective agency. Now if Poe had wanted to create a fictional detective who had quick wits—there being little in the way of subtlety in Vidocq—as well as one who battled ignorant officials and travelled incognito so as to pick up the secrets of the underworld, Vidocq would have been very useful. On one level, we can couple Voltaire and Vidocq and Poe's inclination to be a real detective and we get Dupin. But Poe did not quite work that way. Poe was, certainly, interested in close observation and fighting with blinkered officialdom, but only as a petty exercise or as a superficial sign of genius.

Poe was most interested in the gap between fact and conclusion. Almost any simpleton, he held, could master a physical environment. In "Instinct and Reason" (1840), Poe recounts how his cat has solved the mechanical problem of how to open a thumb-latch on a door. The first thing we need to remember, then, is that the enigmatic conditions at the Rue Morgue present only a trivial problem for Dupin—James Beard or Elizabeth David mixing up a batch of Kool-aid, if you will. Poe is really devoted to drawing Dupin as the genius for whom men wear windows in their shirt-fronts and for whom the world is largely routine and tedious. Dupin's shuttered mansion represents a removal from the mundane rather than anti-social misanthropy, and the trance-like states which the narrator describes clearly represent Dupin's removal into a higher world. Thus, instead of coming from a scientific urge to master the physical environment by reading its material signs, Poe's detective connects with the romantic urge to understand perception in order to come to terms with imagination and to look for the ideal which exists behind material things. Dupin's reading of the narrator's mind in "The Murders in the Rue Morgue," thinking about the association of ideas, comes more from Hartley, Wordsworth, and Coleridge than from Voltaire. Further, Dupin's personality depends not on the flamboyant and self-aggrandizing Vidocq, but on the Byronic conception of the exiled genius and on Poe's own concoction (for himself and for his Roderick Usher) of the legend of the genius spurned by society. In creating Dupin, Poe had no notion that he would become the original eccentric detective who stuns the incompetent police with a brilliant, if obvious, solution. He wanted to show Dupin off as a genius.

In order to put Dupin across as a genius, Poe included lots of theoretical discussion in "The Murders in the Rue Morgue." When dealing with the murder mystery, he contrived a number of story-telling tricks which enhance the character's superiority. "The Murders in the Rue Morgue" is really a pretty sorry detective situation—Raymond Chandler should have taken on Poe instead of A.A. Milne. A close look at the scene of the crime reveals a tuft of orangutan hair, a sailor's ribbon, and a broken window fastener. We would have to be pretty dense not to draw the proper conclusions from these things. For this tale, however, Poe puts things together to make them complicated. In effect, he arranges the plot materials so as to trick the readers. He tricks us to provide surprise, and the surprise adds to our estimation of Dupin's genius. "The Murders in the Rue Morgue," like most of Poe's tales, was conceived and constructed backward. He thought up the orangutan and the locked room before he thought up the evidence leading to them. Also, like numberless later detective stories, "The Murders in the Rue Morgue" unfolds in an unusual way: it proceeds not from beginning to middle to end, as Aristotle would have it, but from middle (the finding of the bodies) to end (the orangutan did it) to beginning. If Poe had stuck to telling the story in normal time, he would have engaged his readers far less and forfeited the surprise so essential to detective stories. Along these same lines, Poe tosses the readers a bone by providing a problem that they can, to some degree, solve. He lets us figure out, by overlapping the testimony of the witnesses, that the intruder in the L'Espanaye apartment spoke neither French, English, Spanish, nor Russian, Our acumen in adding these things up brings us, however, only an illusory triumph—it does not lead us to the conclusion that the intruder spoke ape—but it is still a triumph. Also, as another way of fooling his readers and enhancing Dupin's triumph, Poe withholds essential evidence—the tuft of hair—until the unravelling at the end. Finally, in "The Murders in the Rue Morgue," Poe invents the limited narrator, whose main job is to ignore the critical, to state the obvious, and to advertise to us the unapproachable genius of the detective. In theme, therefore, "The Murders in the Rue Morgue" presents a general thesis on genius along with an example of it in action, while in structure it aims to hoax and to diddle the reader into accepting something which, as Poe admits in the beginning of the tale, is "little susceptible of analysis."

"The Murders in the Rue Morgue" was immediately popular. In France, two separate writers translated and published it as their own work, and the authorship became the subject of a court case. The tale was also widely read in America, and to capitalize upon its success (if $40.00 or $50.00, the prices Poe quoted to editors, can be considered capitalizing) Poe wrote "The Mystery of Marie Roget" as a sequel to "The Murders in the Rue Morgue." After being declined by several journals, "Marie Roget" was finally serialized in *Snowden's Ladies" Companion* from November 1842 to February 1843. This tale carries all of the marks of the typical sequel: loss of energy, long-windedness, and confusion of purpose. "Marie Roget" uses as its source the actual case of Mary Cecillia Rogers, whose corpse bobbed up in the Hudson River on July 28, 1841 (in 1844, Poe would go on to use another actual crime as the basis for "The Oblong Box," but it is hardly a detective tale). Using an actual crime as the basis for his fiction set the pattern for later detective writers who turned to real criminal cases for inspiration for their plots, but it proved to be a disaster for Poe. Poe had the whole murder figured out, pointing to a secret lover as the murderer of Mary Rogers, and two of the three installments had been printed when evidence appeared that Mary Rogers had died as the result of a botched abortion. Consequently, he had to modify the last installment to avoid being labelled an incompetent. If "Marie Roget" fails as a comment on actuality, it succeeds, insofar as it does, because of its narrative structure. "Marie Roget" contains several detective story "firsts." It is the first armchair detective story, in that Dupin scarcely leaves his rooms but still solves the case, and it is an embryo documentary narrative with Poe reprinting large portions of the newspaper accounts of Mary Rogers' death. Perhaps more importantly, this tale points us toward another of Poe's non-traditional sources for his detective tales. As a magazine writer and editor, Poe did lots of reviews and, in fact, was no mean literary critic. He prided himself on being knowledgeable and acute enough to detect inconsistencies and plagiarism in other writers. He also believed the essence of reviewing and criticism for the analyst was to see through the printed word to the author's ideas. Indeed, in May of 1841, Poe semi-accurately predicted the outcome of Dickens' *Barnaby Rudge* before the appearance of the last installment. As a consequence of this, Poe made "Marie Roget" into a somewhat windy demonstration of literary criticism, with Dupin glossing the newspaper passages, pointing out cases of their ineptness, ignorance, illogic, and self-contradiction, and then applying his superior knowledge of men and the world (Dupin knows, for instance, all about the effects of water on decomposing bodies) to come to the truth. Here, as in "Murders in the Rue Morgue," mere knowledge is not enough to handle a true intellectual problem. Just as he defined genius as the faculty of combination *and* novelty, Poe again has his detective bring in an unsuspected culprit, the naval officer, who has been ignored by everyone else. This demonstrates the *"recherche"* movement unique to the true analyst.

Perhaps because circumstances made a mess out of "The Mystery of Marie Roget," or perhaps because he felt that Dupin as the amateur detective solving concrete crimes was not quite sufficient to make his points about the intellect, Poe moved away from crime and detection with his next tale of ratiocination, "The Gold Bug." Written some time in 1842, "The Gold Bug" first appeared in Philadelphia's *The Dollar Newspaper* on June 21, 1843. We can argue about whether "The Gold Bug" is, in fact, a detective story in the first place. It does not deal with crime or the detection of it, but recounts the search for buried treasure. We can reply with the fact that later writers involve their detectives in non-criminal treasure hunts (see Sayers' "Uncle Meleager's Will") and that cryptography became a convention in the detective novel of the 1920s, but this misses the point. In conception, "The Gold Bug" came from the same impulses which caused Poe to write "The Murders in the Rue Morgue." The year before he wrote "The Murders in the Rue Morgue," Poe conducted what can only be called a cryptography contest in *Alexander's Messenger*. Here, he promised to decipher any code which his readers could invent. In July 1841, four months after "The Murders in the Rue Morgue," Poe published an article on cryptography in *Graham's*. His cryptography articles, thus, chronologically bracket his first detective tale. In fact, in both the detective tales and the cryptography articles, Poe tries to do the same thing, to examine the human intellect and especially that part which operates non-mechanically. The following passage will make this clear:

...It may be roundly asserted that human ingenuity cannot concoct a cipher which human ingenuity cannot resolve. In the facility with which such writing is deciphered, however, there exist very remarkable differences in different intellects. Often, in the case of two individuals of acknowledged equality as regards to ordinary mental efforts, it will be found that, while one cannot unriddle the commonest cipher, the other will scarcely be puzzled by the most abstruse. It may be observed generally that in such investigations the analytic ability is very forcibly called into action.\*...The analytical power should not be confounded with simple ingenuity; for while the analyst is necessarily ingenious, the ingenious man is often remarkably incapable of analysis.... Between ingenuity and the analytic ability there exists a difference far greater, indeed, than that between fancy and the imagination, but of a character very strictly analogous.

What I have given here is an authentic but artificial passage by Poe. The first part (to the asterisk) comes from the beginning of "Cryptography," and the second part comes from the opening of "The Murders in the Rue Morgue." Both parts probe the same idea, and together they argue the same point: in the cryptographer and in the detective we see the superior mental powers of the genius in action. In turning to "The Gold Bug" on code-breaking, therefore, Poe wishes to illustrate the same mental capacity as in Dupin's crime-solving. The connection between these two tales shows clearly in the fact that Poe draws Legrand (note that name!), the hero of "The Gold Bug," as a southern—fried Dupin. Like Dupin, he is a ruined aristocratic genius who has retired from society, in this case to Sullivan's Island instead of to a spooky shuttered mansion in the Faubourg Saint Germain. Both characters choose to exist outside of time and are subject to reveries which further detach them from this world. As in the Dupin tales, Poe chooses to describe characters and events from the point of view of a narrator who is normal but whose main response to the genius is awe and adulation. Although "The Gold Bug" illustrates the same mental points as Poe's earlier detective tales, it is much better fiction. Professor Mabbot suggests that Poe came upon his more or less universal point for "The Gold Bug" when he reviewed Warren's *Ten Thousand a Year* and wrote

A main source of the interest which this book possesses for the mass, is to be referred to the pecuniary nature of its theme...it is an affair of pounds, shillings, and pence— a topic which comes at least as immediately to the bosoms...of mankind, as any which could be selected

If Poe had written "The Gold Bug" as he had written "The Murders in the Rue Morgue," though, he would have befogged the fictional presentation of even the most universal theme. But he did not. "The Gold Bug" sloughs off the argumentative casing of the earlier tale and presents the action more directly. Correspondingly, in "The Gold Bug," Poe moves from the puns and ingrown humor of "The Murders in the Rue Morgue" to the broad racist farce found in Jupiter. In the transition from "The Murders in the Rue Morgue" to "The Gold Bug," Poe may have been making the same points, but he was also moving from the essay with illustrations toward pure fiction.

In 1844, Poe published the last of the Dupin tales, "The Purloined Letter." It appeared in a publication designed to catch a host of customers, *The Gift: a Christmas, New Year and Birthday Present.* "The Purloined Letter" is the best of the Dupin stories for several reasons. Like "The Gold Bug," this tale centers on a universal human motif. In choosing Minister D—'s obvious hiding place for the purloined letter, Poe happened upon something which every reader empathies, having searched for spectacles, keys, books, or papers only to find them where they ought to be. Again, Poe intends his detective tale as an illustration of genius, but his example of Dupin thinking what Minister D— thinks instead of what D— thinks the detective will think is a much cleverer instance of his mental power, as well as being less haughty than Dupin's tricks and boasts in the other tales. Just as "The Gold Bug" involves a good bit of action, Dupin acts a lot more in "The Purloined Letter" than in the other tales. Not only does he rouse himself to visit Minister D—'s flat, but he returns, exposing himself to danger, to retrieve the letter when he could have simply told the police where to look in their diurnal shake-down of D—'s rooms. Finally, this tale succeeds because it introduces real competition for the detective. From Vidocq, Poe probably got the idea of the great detective versus the imbecile policeman. This background plays a reasonably important role in all of the Dupin tales. It is, however, not much challenge to put something over on the police force of Penzance. For "The Purloined Letter," therefore, Poe creates a worthy antagonist for Dupin, so worthy that some would have it that D—is Dupin's double. Much of the verve of this tale rests on the competition rather than on the mundane stuff of crime detection.

Poe's last detective tale, "Thou Art the Man," came out in *Godey's Ladies Book* in November of 1844. In many ways, this tale succeeds as fiction (as opposed to its worth as social or intellectual comment) far better than any of the earlier tales. Here Poe moves away from the lengthy passages of theoretical and technical material which clog the plots of the earlier tales, and contents himself with telling a story. "Thou Art the Man" recounts how the narrator saved an innocent man from the gallows and exposed the guilty person by means of a gruesome trick. Even if Poe relishes too much the putrefaction of Shuttleworthy's corpse as it springs out of the wine case, in this tale he sorts out and expertly uses the techniques which he had developed earlier. He begins the tale by calling the business "the Rattleborough enigma," tying it back to "The Murders in the Rue Morgue" which insisted that the analyst "is fond of enigmas, of conundrums, of hieroglyphics..." The narrative point of view, too, uses and builds on the same motives as does the point of view in the Dupin stories. In the Dupin stories, Poe covered up facts by employing an obtuse narrator, and here he covers up material by using the sardonic humor of the detective's narration. The Narrator in "Thou Art the Man" clearly despises Old Charley, but he covers this with fulsome praise of the villain. As in "The Murders in the Rue Morgue," Poe gives the readers a clue which they ought to be able to remember and interpret. Early on, he tells us that Shuttleworthy's riderless horse returned to the village "...all bloody from a *pistol* shot, that had gone clean through the poor animal's chest," and later he has Old Charley discover a rifle ball in the horse's chest. He wants us, I think, to have forgotten about the initial mention of the wound, but even if we do recall it, we do not have much in the way of evidence. The point, of course, ramifies in other directions (How does the narrator know it is a pistol shot? Could two bullets have made the same entry wound?), but mainly because we have been conditioned by the quiddities of later detective writers. At any rate, Old Charley Poe draws on "The Purloined Letter" and gives his detective a worthy opponent, but this time he also sets the pattern for subsequent fictions by keeping the villain's identity, if not secret, at least less than obvious. Old Charley manipulates the material evidence which the detective must interpret, but interpretation of the evidence will not, by itself, bring victory to the analyst. For this, the detective needs to make a "recherche move," something unexpected which will decisively defeat the criminal. Here we get recherche with a vengeance, with the narrator's construction of a jack-in-the-box out of Shuttleworthy's moldering corpse. Finally, in this tale Poe does something which he had not done before. In the Dupin tales, the narration and the character of the detective, and the message tend to place readers in something like the first row of a slow class. In "Thou Art the Man," Poe places the readers more surely and gently. Although we are not on a par with the detective, we are superior to the world of the story. From the second sentence ("I will expound to *you*— as I alone can—the secret of the enginery that effected the Rattleborough miracle..."), we realize that the narrator sees us as superior to the citizens of Rattleborough; he never tells them how he extorted Charley's confession (they think that it is a miracle), but he gives the secret to us as an afterword. This peculiar equilibrium, suspending readers between the helpless and moronic world of the story and the acute and often awesome intelligence of the detective, was to become the standard in later detective writers.

With his detective tales, Poe set the machine going. The tales gained immediate popularity in France and then England. Poe directly influenced all the detective writers of the next generation, from Collins to Doyle. Critics outdo one another in classifying the detective story conventions which Poe invented, with one recent list numbering thirty-two separate elements which Poe contributed to later detective fiction. Of course, he introduces the amateur detective to fiction. Sure, Dupin's genius begot Holmes and Thorndyke. Yes, he popularizes the locked-room mystery, ballistics, and blood tests. If he had not done these things, however, someone else, probably a Frenchman drawing on Vidocq, would have. But this hypothetical other writer would not have been the same, and the mystery story, if one existed, would be far different. Poe's distinctness, rather than resting on details, rests upon his creation of new ways of telling stories. You can take plenty of details out of Poe's stories and they still work, but if you alter their narrative structure they fail. "Once upon a time an orangutan killed two women" is a far cry from "The Murders in the Rue Morgue." Here Poe's new arrangement of telling the story backward ranks high, but his manipulation of point of view ranks higher. Poe also takes us out of the world of sentimental drivel, where to cover up a mystery, writers make their characters take refuge only in vague and artificial statements. Poe took the detective story away from moralists who told stories about people who were born bad, achieved badness, or had badness thrust upon them. Leaving behind the English conception of the genius as a titanic loser, Poe began to explore some of the more attractive features of the story about the genius as a winner. He put the detective story into the hands of the storyteller.

Poe's particular brand of storytelling, moreover, differed from the traditional sort in another way. As the detective loves enigmas and conundrums, Poe loved jokes. Two months before he put "The Murders in the Rue Morgue" in *Graham's*, he wrote an article about handwriting analysis called "Autography." This was a straight version of a series of joke articles which Poe had done for *The Southern Literary Messenger* in 1836. Between "The Gold Bug" and "The Purloined Letter," Poe perpetrated "The Balloon Hoax." Almost in the way of summary of his joking inclination, Poe wrote in 1843 that "man is an animal that diddles, and there is *no* animal that diddles *but* man." In his detective tales, therefore, we can almost say that Poe contributed structures to diddle his readers, and that detective fiction began with this impulse. For Poe, diddling outlasted his theoretical blather on genius, and it overcame his need to mire his plots in treatises and digressions. For later writers, too, diddling became the heart of the detective story. Indeed, we can see the whole subsequent development of the detective story as a history of diddling, both by those writers who want to provide a clever entertainment for their readers and by those who want to wrench us back to a serious consideration of moral, ethical, psychological, or social issues. It all began with Poe.

# Chapter 4
# Dickens

Charles Dickens (1812-1870) does not need to be seen as a detective story writer. From *Pickwick Papers* (1836-7) onward, his novels draw upon a number of traditions and appeal to a variety of sentiments which have little connection to the detective story. Still, Dickens did participate in the school of Godwin and Lytton. From *Pickwick Papers* to *Oliver Twist* (1837-8) to *Little Dorrit* (1857-8) and *Great Expectations* (1860-1), Dickens makes plenty of strenuous observations about crime and punishment and the police. He obviously wants to convince his readers that prison conditions stink, that honest people can be defiled by unwholesome social conditions, and that the machinery of law and law enforcement leave much to be desired.

The fact that the Bow Street Runners in *Great Expectations* falsely accuse Joe of having maimed his wife is only one of Dickens' many comments on the deplorable state of affairs in society. Most of Dickens' novels, however, do not center on detective problems, and they do not quite use detective story technique even when they do deal with crime and criminals. Nevertheless, Dickens did write four novels which almost do these things: *Barnaby Rudge* (1841), *Martin Chuzzlewit* (1843-4), *Bleak House* (1852-3), and *The Mystery of Edwin Drood* (1870). Each of these novels does contain a murder mystery and develops one or more detective characters. Following Dickens' progress through these four novels, we can see that he changed his portrayal of crime and detection a good bit. We cannot, however, see quite as easily whether, and to what extent, he consciously developed the techniques of telling the detective story. Since many of the devices used by later detective writers grew out of the standard tools of the serial novelist, and since Dickens was both a serial novelist and, to some extent, a detective writer, it is hard to tell where the one stops and the other starts. In manipulating his sentimental surprises, his surprises of coincidence, and his flabbergasting surprises, Dickens began occasionally to tempt his readers with the same sort of playful baits which typify the narrative angling of the detective story. Because he was stuck in the serial novel, and the three-volume serial novel at that, Dickens never felt sure enough of his relationship with his readership to go all of the way over to detective technique. He never completed a novel which centered on crime and detection.

With *Barnaby Rudge*, Dickens carries on and elaborates the social concerns of Godwin, develops the portrait of the criminal more fully than did Lytton, and uses a murder mystery as one of the structural elements of his novel. In almost every way, *Barnaby Rudge* is an advance from *Caleb Williams* and *Paul Clifford*, but in his handling of the murder mystery Dickens still adheres to gothic formulas rather than the new techniques invented by Poe the year before.

Wishing to escape from the picaresque novel and to write a historical novel in the vein of Walter Scott, Dickens based *Barnaby Rudge* on the anti-Catholic riots of 1780 combined with the repercussions of a generation-old murder. That he would eventually redo this novel in *A Tale of Two Cities* (1859) shows Dickens' principal interest in political, social, and historical points. *Barnaby Rudge*, however, does have specific connections with crime and criminals. Dickens portrays the riots as a holiday for crime and criminals, and, separate from this, he continues to campaign for the reform of the criminal justice system which not only punishes but creates criminals. Barnaby and Mrs. Rudge's persecution by a boorish country magistrate and the execution of Hugh's mother for stealing food serve as vivid indictments of the system. With Hugh the wild man in *Barnaby Rudge*, Dickens develops the same sociological point which he would show in Magwitch in *Great Expectations*: by its harshness, prejudice, and unconcern, society conditions people to become criminals to then be caught in the net of unequal and inhumane justice. Here Dickens supersedes Godwin, who bogged down in the contemplation of tragedy and universal guilt, and surpasses Lytton, whose orphans receive the benefits of classical educations. In *Barnaby Rudge*, as elsewhere, Dickens stands firmly on the platform that most criminals need not be criminals. Social abuse, sheep-headed authority, and draconian law create most evil.

But governments and laws do not create all criminals. Some men and women turn to crime because of the blight on their hearts and the abscesses of their souls. Dickens needed to make this distinction between types of criminals or he could never approach the detective figure as other than the agent of bloody law and oppressive government. For his portrait of the murderer in *Barnaby Rudge*, therefore, Dickens set aside the social arguments and clothed Old Rudge with the cerecloth of the gothic tradition and weighted him down with Christian guilt. Old Rudge is the nightstalker, the terror lurking in the graveyard, the bogey to all good people, and the warning that the fruit of sin is the death of the soul. Dickens loads down Old Rudge with all sorts of gothic accoutrements. At the beginning of the novel, the hayseeds at "The Maypole" scare each other with a ghost story about Reuben

Haredale's murder. Old Rudge is the "ghost" with which Dickens resolves, in typical gothic fashion, the ghost story. When we realize that the unnamed highwayman who appears throughout the novel is really Old Rudge, we can see Dickens describing the criminal's guilty conscience. Early in the novel the highwayman, Old Rudge, appears as a forceful and larger-than-life figure, the terror both to innocent people and to the denizens of the underworld. In chapter one, he sits through the retelling of Haredale's murder without turning a hair. Later, though, he becomes a tool of the sinister Blind Man, he starts wandering around in graveyards, and finally he allows himself to be captured when the sound of the bell at the Warren turns him to pudding. The heart has its own vengeance with Old Rudge. If Dickens shows the deterioration of Old Rudge, he can also conceive of the villain without a conscience. John Chester in *Barnaby Rudge* is one, and Tulkinghorn in *Bleak House* is another. These people are exempt from guilt or conversion since one needs a conscience in order to feel and they have none. Dickens, therefore, favored criminals like Old Rudge in whom he could combine the agony of guilt with gothic dress.

*Barnaby Rudge* shows that, at this stage at least, Dickens was of two minds about crime prevention, crime detection, and the maintenance of civil order—the police. Set in the 1780s, this novel shows scenes from the bad old days. London, in the novel, is a sump of crime and a breeding ground for dark deeds: "It is no wonder that...street robberies, often accompanied by cruel wounds, and not infrequently by loss of life, should have been of nightly occurrence in the very heart of London." Villains waylay innocent citizens and rioters trash the property of respectable citizens, while there are no policemen and few magistrates to keep the peace. Civil authorities in *Barnaby Rudge* have no choice but to call in the army and to establish martial law to quell the riots, and Dickens realized the dangers of this. He also knew, writing in the 1840s, about the uses of the Metropolitan Police, but in *Barnaby Rudge* he adheres to many of the traditional English prejudices about police agents. Dennis, the rioter turned thief-taker in *Barnaby Rudge*, could have been spawned by Godwin's Gines. Dickens clearly views Chester's use of Hugh as an informer as scandalous. Finally, as punishment for the amphibian-toady Gashford, Dickens invents for him the most degrading future and it makes him become a police spy; Gashford "...procured an appointment in the honorable corps of spies and eavesdroppers employed by the government." It is partly, moreover, the onus attached to the police and detectives which prevents Dickens from detailing the spying and prying which his heroes assuredly do in order to win. Joe Willet sneaks among the rioters in disguise and weasels his way into Dennis' confidence in order to save Dolly and Emma, but here Dickens concentrates on ends rather than means. Shortly after fortuitously discovering his brother's murderer, Geoffrey

Haredale retires to a monastery, in part because of his duel with Chester, but also because of the role which he played as a detective.

Because *Barnaby Rudge* was a serial publication, Dickens introduced a wide variety of material into the novel in order to maintain readers' interest. There is the satire of John Chester and his Regency manners, the historical account of the Gordon riots, the sentimental love stories of Dolly and Emma, and the gothic account of the threatened rape of the heroines. Out of the conventions of the gothic novel, Dickens also built the story of the capture of Reuben Haredale's murderer. We find, therefore, that he attaches the ghost story in chapter one to the murder, something which he may have been going to do in *The Mystery of Edwin Drood*, too. The murder mystery in *Barnaby Rudge* is based on events which occurred twenty years earlier, but Dickens does not handle parts of the Haredale business in the manner of a detective story. At the start of the novel, Dickens causes the timerous Solomon Daisy to tell the story of Haredale's murder, thereby not only justifying the gothic aura fixed to the event, but also cleverly avoiding the obligation of naming Old Rudge as the murderer. Daisy tells us that Reuben Haredale was killed along with his steward, Mr. Rudge, "...whose body— scarcely to be recognized by his clothes and the watch and the ring he wore— was found, months afterwards..." The murderer seems to be the absconding gardener. Case Closed. Suddenly Dickens introduces the terrible, unnamed highwayman. The fact that he does not name him, however, signifies little in terms of detective technique, since it takes several chapters for Dickens to name many characters. When Haredale goes to visit the burned-out ruins of his house, he catches a lurking stranger and, to the surprise and amazement of the readers, he is Old Rudge. Fate, circumstance, and the criminal's guilt bring him to justice, there is no detective work about it. Likewise, even though Dickens began with the equivocating description of the second corpse, he does not sustain his deviousness because, principally, he wants to shock his readers.

Even though Dickens seeded a murder mystery into *Barnaby Rudge*, he did not develop it as a detective plot. He had not yet examined the character of the detective, and he was too attached to the crude jolts of gothic plotting. Still, in this novel Dickens betrayed an inkling of an insight about detective plotting. When he discusses the topic of charlatanism in connection with Gashford and Gordon, Dickens works at a definition of mystery:

> To surround anything, however monstrous or ridiculous, with an air of mystery is to invest it with a secret charm, and a power of attraction which to the crowd is irresistible...Curiosity is, and has been from the creation of the world, a master passion. To awaken it, to gratify it by slight degrees, and yet leave something always in suspense, is to establish the surest hold that can be had...

Dickens knew well that he was describing the methods not only of fakirs and snake oil merchants like Gordon and Gashford, but also of the serial writer. All that we need to do is to add the idea of playing with readers' curiosity, and we get detective technique. Dickens did not make this connection here. *Barnaby Rudge* relegates the detective problem to gothic cliches, preferring to excite and gratify its readers solely with the problems of people, society and history.

*Martin Chuzzlewit* repeats some of the same murder mystery elements which Dickens used in *Barnaby Rudge*. Once again the murder subplot has a loose relationship to the main plot, and Jonas Chuzzlewit repeats some of the same notions about murderers found in Old Rudge. The murder business in *Martin Chuzzlewit*, however, shows Dickens adding some new material to his depiction of crime and detection, material which at least approximates that of the detective story. His portrait of the detective has changed significantly here, and Dickens feels less embarrassed in making normal people search for answers to a mystery. Separate from his characterization, Dickens introduces a twist in the mystery plot in *Martin Chuzzlewit* which comes close to the practice of the detective story.

*Martin Chuzzlewit* mainly deals with the development and exposure of humbug and hypocrisy in Mr. Pecksniff and with the presentation of Dickens' jaundiced viewed of America in young Martin's travels in the New World. As a minor plot, Dickens depicts the household of Anthony Chuzzlewit, merchant and miser. Anthony's mean and sterile family includes his son, Jonas, in whom Anthony has built a meaner, more sadistic, cunning, and mercenary model of himself. Dickens takes us through Anthony's death, showing a temporary revolution in Jonas' character, but after the funeral the son reverts to type. In the last third of the novel, Jonas falls afoul of Montague Tigg and his fraudulent Anglo-Bengalee Disinterested Loan and Life Assurance Company. Tigg blackmails Jonas into investing heavily in the Anglo-Bengalee. Finding this intolerable, Jonas determines to murder Tigg, and at this point Dickens tars him with the archetypal brush:

> Did no man passing through the dim streets shrink without knowing why, when he came stealing up behind them? As he glided on, had no child in its sleep an indistinct perception of a guilty shadow falling on its bed, that troubled its rest...? When he looked back, across his shoulder, was it to see if his quick footsteps still fell dry upon the dusty pavement, or were already moist and clogged with the red mire that stained the feet of Cain?

Dickens then goes on to describe with the same rhetorical fervor Jonas' murder of Tigg. But this is just the end of the treatment. Long before the murder of Tigg, Dickens leads readers to believe that Jonas had murdered his own father. Thus, he gives us Jonas' changed behavior at Anthony's funeral, his increased jumpiness, his accelerated brutality to his wife, as well as his susceptibility to Tigg's blackmail. In terms of character, though, Dickens does the same thing with Jonas that he did with Old Rudge. Murderers, he says, carry the mark of Cain, they suffer psychological torment from fear of discovery, and they obdurately refuse repentance, preferring the cesspool of self. This part of the murder mystery in *Martin Chuzzlewit* has changed very little; the character of the detective and the nature of the narration, however, have changed a great deal.

*Martin Chuzzlewit*, like *Barnaby Rudge*, depicts thief-takers, both amateur and professional. As we have seen, Dickens handles them rather gingerly in the earlier novel: detection and police work seem degrading, and Dickens even glosses over Joe Willet's adventures, which are potentially exciting and heroic. In *Martin Chuzzlewit*, Dickens changed his mind about this. With John Westlock and young Martin, Dickens goes part way toward creating the amateur detective hero. First of all, he brings their detective work out into the open. Through the double operations of benevolence and circumstance, Westlock comes to the aid of a young man suffering from want, disease, and the psychological effects of guilt. After regaining his health, this fellow, Lewsome, tells Westlock that the first step on his road to ruin was selling poison to Jonas Chuzzlewit shortly before the death of Anthony. So far, this comes straight from the pot-boiler, but the heroes' reaction to it does not. Convinced that there is something to investigate, Westlock and young Martin seek out Anthony's old clerk, Chuffey, having first "... satisfied themselves that no communication had ever taken place between Lewsome and Mr. Chuffey." With the aid of Mrs. Gamp, the amateur detectives, along with Mark and old Martin, descend on Jonas and confront him with their facts. Here the heroes' concern for unspotted evidence moves them a notch above the investigators of the mere pot-boiler. The amateur detectives also highlight one of the chief impediments to the development of the real detective hero: they care almost as much for family honor as they do for law. Not only is Westlock especially delicate in acquainting young Martin with Lewsome's story, but they call not upon the police or a magistrate, but upon the head of the family, old Martin, to charge Jonas with his misdeeds. When the family finally does turn Jonas over to the police, Dickens keeps it within the family context by introducing cousin Slyme, now a policeman, who allows Jonas to commit suicide.

Family considerations aside, Dickens does introduce into *Martin Chuzzlewit* his first real detective. As it turns out, Westlock and young Martin are wrong in their interpretation of Jonas' actions, and it takes Mr. Nadgett to get the goods on the criminal. Dickens evolves Nadgett out of the ethical swamp of the thief turned thief-taker. He is a private investigator for Tigg's Anglo-Bengalee scam, and this should cover him with all of the muck associated with the shady traditions of the thief-taker. But Dickens chooses not to present him this way. Instead, Dickens introduces Nadgett in a chapter entitled "Secret Service," and builds around him a variety of impressive mysteriousness (he describes Nadgett as the "man of mystery of the Anglo-Bengalee...."). Vital to this sense of mystery is Nadgett's omniscience, and Dickens tells us that "...every button on his coat might have been an eye; he saw so much." He is also a good lurker—people ignore his presence and there is no telling where he will turn up next. It is Nadgett who supplies Tigg with the circumstantial evidence that Jonas murdered his father, and in the end, it is Nadgett who supplies the proof that Jonas murdered Tigg. Although Nadgett supplies the goods, Dickens does not develop him very much. Perhaps because he was to be the *deus ex machina* in the Jonas plot, Dickens keeps him in the background, showing only that he is sinister and efficient. Thus, even though in this novel Dickens moved a few steps away from the cliches of the thief-taker, he still primarily operated in the conventions of character, mood, and technique derived from the gothic novel.

If, in its use of the detective character *Martin Chuzzlewit* makes a tentative move toward the detective story, its plotting moves more boldly in that direction. Through most of the novel, Dickens leads us to believe that Jonas Chuzzlewit murdered his father. After witnessing his guilty behavior, hearing Chuffey's mumbling, observing Tigg's blackmail, and then learning Lewsome's story about the poison, we are fully convinced that Dickens is going to tell us that Jonas poisoned his father. That is, we expect the same sort of confirming surprise based on sentiment that we anticipate with Pecksniff, young Martin, and his grandfather. But then Dickens pulls a fast one. When Chuffey finally wheezes out his secret, it is that Jonas did not, in fact, murder his father. He intended to do it, but Anthony died of a broken heart when he discovered Jonas meant to poison him. Dickens here uses the reversal of expectations. He leads readers, through legitimate evidence, to believe that Jonas killed his father, then shows that he did not poison Anthony, but ends by showing Jonas guilty by intent and conviction. This all happens consistently and plausibly, as we can see when we review what we really saw in the novel. Technique like this lifts Dickens' plotting out of the conventions of the tale of terror, as well as those of the popular serial. It embodies the sort of playfulness fundamental to the detective story, and, therefore, the murder mystery in *Martin Chuzzlewit* comes much closer to being a real detective story. Still, the Jonas plot suffers from Dickens' overwrought picture of the criminal and his half-formed notions about the detective character. In his next fictional treatment of a murder mystery, Dickens would correct these things.

Between *Martin Chuzzlewit* and *Bleak House*, Dickens recognized and made journalistic hay out of England's police reforms, which had been going on since the 1820s. He and W.H. Wills, Dickens' co-editor at *Household Words*, wrote a number of articles about the Detective Police for their magazine. Dickens developed an almost boyish admiration for the new detectives, and in 1851 he had the whole force over to the *Household Words* office and then described the affair in "A Detective Police Party." The next year saw "On Duty with Inspector Field," which describes a nocturnal jaunt through London which Dickens took with Field. In 1853, he spent the night with the Thames River Police, and this eventually appeared in *Household Words* as "Down the Tide." These articles betoken a new attitude on Dickens' part toward a profession which he had reviled. With the detectives, especially, Dickens discovered a government bureau which actually worked in spite of government's tendencies to spawn departments like the Circumlocution Office. Dickens found that the detective force is "...so well chosen and trained, proceeds so systematically and quietly, does its business in such a workmanlike manner, and is always so calmly and steadily engaged in the service of the public, that the public really do not know enough of it, to know a tithe of its usefulness." Dickens then carried this adulation for the Detective Police into *Bleak House.*

Dickens brought his personal and journalistic interest to *Bleak House,* and one part of this very big book is more or less straight advocacy for police and detectives. Before *Bleak House,* Dickens makes his policemen from the likes of Gashford and Slyme, morally degraded and deplorable men. In *Bleak House* Dickens has seen the light. When Esther uncovers yet another good cause in the orphans of Coavinses, the officer who had earlier arrested Skinpole for debt, John Jarndyce, gives us a lecture on public attitudes toward officers of the law:

The man was necessary...If we make such men necessary by our faults and follies, or by our want of worldly knowledge, or by our misfortune, we must not revenge ourselves on them. There was no harm in his trade. He maintained his children. One would like to know more of this.

We do not, in point of fact, learn more of this. Dickens still tends to see constables as the agents of oppression, like the one who continually moves Jo along. But here Dickens does admit that the officer of the law is not entirely to be despised, and this is an advance over characters like Gashford and Slyme. He was, though, much higher on the Detective Police, and he shows this mainly through Bucket. Thus, during Bucket's pursuit of Lady Deadlock, Dickens gives his readers one picture of the detective in a police station and another of him at a River Police depot. In both locales, the neatness, the organization, and the efficiency of the police in contact with a detective officer are supposed to be impressive. This made even more of an impression on Victorian readers, who prided themselves on their neatness, organization, efficiency, and delicacy.

More important than Dickens' brief spot of propaganda for the police is his development of the detectives in *Bleak House*. First of all, he engages more characters in the detective business in this novel than in the earlier books. There is, of course, Inspector Bucket, Dickens' first official detective, but plenty of other people in this novel work at unravelling mysteries. In this respect, lawyer Tulkinghorn plays a major role in gathering and evaluating mysterious information. But there is also Guppy and the Smallweeds, too, who act as detectives as they rummage through the debris of Krock's junk shop. Indeed, in Snagsby, Dickens drew a man obsessed with the process of uncovering mysteries, and with this character he forecasts Betteredge's "detective fever" in *The Moonstone*. With Allan Woodcourt, Dickens even anticipates the sort of detective flourish which made Joe Bell and Sherlock Holmes famous. When Woodcourt happens upon Lizz, out of the blue he says

"So your husband is a bricklayer?"

"How did you know that, sir?" asked the woman astonished.

"Why, I suppose so, from the color of the clay upon your bag and on your dress. And I know brick-makers go about working at piece-work in different places. And I am sorry to say I have known them cruel to be to their wives."

In spite of antedating "You have been in Afghanistan, I perceive" by thirty-five years, Dickens does not make Woodcourt into a functioning detective because he is a good man. Dickens will not have the good characters in *Bleak House* act like or as detectives. The novel states firmly that snooping around for information about other people's lives is either selfish, prurient, or downright evil. With the private individuals who act as detectives, Dickens works down the scale from Snagsby's innocent obsession with mysteries (which his wife mistakes for sexual infidelity), to the hypocritical self-interest of Guppy, to the sliminess of the Smallweeds, to the absolute evil of Tulkinghorn. Although Dickens does invest most of these people with comic traits, he finds nothing that is comic in Tulkinghorn. Tulkinghorn combines the blackmailing bent of Tigg and the sinister omniscience of Nadgett, and in the lawyer Dickens creates a very bad man who extorts and hoards information for the onanistic pleasure of having secret power over people.

Since none of the main characters can be sullied by dabbling around in the sewer inhabited by Tulkinghorn, Dickens invents a new character who can solve the book's problem without tainting himself: Mr. Bucket of the Detective Police. Although today we have trouble viewing Bucket as an officer of the law (in the novel he first works for Tulkinghorn and then for the reward offered by Sir Leister Deadlock), Dickens did create Bucket to counter the dark side of detection and to act as an anti-Tulkinghorn.

Reputedly based on the real Inspector Field, Bucket emphasizes that duty stands behind all of his acts. Bucket also stresses the fact that above all things he is discreet. Countering public fears about police spies in the wainscot, and specifically contrasted to Tulkinghorn's vicious use of his knowledge of other people's intimate lives, Bucket tells Sir Leister Deadlock to

> "...let me beg of you not to trouble your mind for a moment, as to anything having come to *my* knowledge. I know so much about so many characters high and low, that a piece of information more or less don't signify a straw."

His exertions in the novel all prove he stifles all unnecessary scandal. Thus, he kidnaps Jo from Bleak House to keep him from spreading rumors about Lady Deadlock, and in his unravelling of the mystery, he carefully unfolds Lady Deadlock's past to Sir Leister in order to deprive Hortense of the opportunity of using her information to shock the old man.

In many ways, Bucket is a new development for Dickens. His earlier detectives were either men like Haredale in *Barnaby Rudge*, for whom detection becomes a corrosive obsession, thief-takers like Gashford, who are beneath readers' contempt, or sinister men of mystery like Nadgett, who may uncover the truth but who also ooze terror and potentially destructive power. From Nadgett, Dickens gave Bucket those things which he considered to be the key traits of the detective: the capacity to appear and disappear without attracting notice and virtual omniscience. Bucket, in spite of the tone of some of his early appearances, is not a bogeyman. Toward the end of *Bleak House*, Dickens brings the detective into the mainstream of his world by characterizing Bucket the same way that he vivifies his other minor characters. Thus we find Dickens highlighting Bucket's roving forefinger, his amiability to the people whom he arrests, his linguistic quirk of repeating "Sir Leister Deadlock, Baronet," and his lower-middle-class background. That Dickens provides a companionable and acute Mrs. Bucket signifies, too, his desire to grant Bucket citizenship in the sunlit world.

Having banished gothic creepiness from the detective, Dickens adds two highly significant new elements to Bucket's character. These complete the renovation of the detective character and tie Dickens to Poe, who invented these things a decade earlier. First of all, Dickens establishes Bucket as a game player: the fittest metaphors which Dickens can find for the detective come from games. Before Bucket unravels Tulkinghorn's murder, Dickens says that "...from the expression on his face, he might be a famous whist-player for a large stake..." Also, in his description of Bucket's explanation of the Tulkinghorn case and later in his pursuit of Lady Deadlock, Dickens compares the detective's maneuvers to moves on a game board. Dickens, then, makes his first real detective out of the same material that Poe used to create the first detective. Either Dickens copied the whist and the game board (chess and checkers) analogies from "The Murders in the Rue Morgue," or something built into the idea of the detective brought these two writers to the same metaphor. By comparing Bucket to the game player, Dickens has found a way of not only giving his detective ingenuity and analytic ability, but also a means of keeping him pleasant and even jolly at the same time. Here Dickens has gone a step beyond Poe, whose gamester humor remained pretty ingrown.

Dickens could also have drawn Bucket's other characteristic detective traits from Poe's detective tales, particularly their narrative technique. Bucket deliberately plays games with his listeners when he explains things to them. As he puts his case to Leister Deadlock, Bucket squashed old Smallweed, who is about to anticipate him, by saying "I am damned if I am going to have my case spoiled, or interfered with, or anticipated by so much as half a second of time by any human being in creation." Bucket wants to tell the story his own way, and he wants to revel in narrative misdirection and surprise. In presenting his case, therefore, Bucket leads his hearers to suppose that Lady Deadlock killed Tulkinghorn, only to spring (the title of the chapter is "Springing a Mine") Hortense at the last moment. Likewise, during his pursuit of Lady Deadlock, Bucket allows Esther to believe they are following Lizz, the brickmaker's wife, and only reveals at the last minute he knows Lady Deadlock has changed clothes with Lizz. This sort of misleading and withholding of facts in order to create first surprise and then suspense lies at the heart of the detective story.

In the main, however, *Bleak House* is not a detective story. Like all of his previous novels, *Bleak House* hangs on several different classes of questions. The most important question of the novel concerns the parentage of the heroine, Esther Summerson. Here Dickens introduces little suspense. From Guppy's entrance in chapter seven, we know Lady Deadlock is Esther's mother, and shortly thereafter we know Hawdon (Nemo) was her father. By stringing the Chancery suit of Jarndyce versus Jarndyce through the novel, Dickens clearly indicates that answers to questions about the past of human relationships will bring only grief, and people would do better to forget them and to cultivate sympathy and effective compassion. Underneath the big question, Dickens, because of the demands of the serial, inserts small questions which have little thematic importance. In *Bleak House*, for instance, Dickens brings up the question of the whereabouts of Mrs. Rouncewell's son and answers it with George at the shooting gallery. This kind of question Dickens answers through coincidence and the use of outside agencies. Neither the big thematic question nor the serial questions have the sort of presentation requisite for the detective story. Dickens' handling of Tulkinghorn's murder in *Bleak House*, however, does approximate detective technique. Early on, Dickens establishes Hortense's vengeful and passionate nature and brings her into conflict with Tulkinghorn. Then, he goes on to drag a herring across the path. As he did in *Martin Chuzzlewit*, Dickens misdirects curious readers into believing that Lady Deadlock is the murderer. The portrait of Lady Deadlock's emotional state coupled with the truncated description of her walking out into the night suggests her guilt, as does Bucket's teasing summary of the case. Then Dickens springs Hortense back in on his readers, providing the detective surprise—presenting something which seems startling but which is consistent with certain previous events. This technique works much more effectively in *Bleak House*, primarily because Dickens has loosened up on his passionate reaction to the criminal's guilt. Although Hortense wins no prizes, Dickens does not brand her with the mark of Cain. When nature reacts to the impending murder, Dickens would have it warn the victim instead of hounding the murderer. This diminution of the moral lesson of murder, combined with the surprise and the readers' attachment for Bucket, make this part of *Bleak House* a real detective story. That Dickens placed most of the detective material in five chapters instead of stringing it out over the entire novel, as he had done in *Barnaby Rudge* and *Martin Chuzzlewit*, serves to demonstrate that Dickens may have begun to view the detective story as a separate entity instead of simply one more arrow in his quiver of serial techniques.

We will never know whether Dickens intended to sharpen the detective story technique of *Bleak House* in his last novel, because he never finished it. He completed only six installments of *The Mystery of Edwin Drood* before he died. Yet, *The Mystery of Edwin Drood* contains so many suggestive elements that it has become the pet of people interested in detective fiction. All sorts of writers think they know what Dickens had in mind for the last half of the novel, and a fair number have, in fact, finished *The Mystery of Edwin Drood* for him. It is, of course, very tempting to do this. Extrapolating Dickens' characters and techniques from the earlier novels and the fragment of *Edwin Drood* can be infectious. The whole game becomes doubly fascinating when we consider that, in 1868, Dickens' friend, Wilkie Collins, published *The Moonstone* in Dickens' *All the Year Round*. When we read the completed chapters of *Edwin Drood*, all sorts of tantalizing questions arise: does Dickens intend to use Jasper's opium as Collins used opium in *The Moonstone*? What happened to Drood? Who is going to be the criminal? Who is going to be the detective? Why has Jasper been sneaking around the cathedral? I can answer these questions to my own satisfaction, but, given that we have only half of the novel, nobody can absolutely say what Dickens intended. We can, however, say that *Edwin Drood* contains several instances of what look like the purposeful obfuscation of detective plotting.

In chapter fourteen of *Edwin Drood*, John Jasper enters and announces that his nephew, Edwin has disappeared. There is a great stir in Cloisterham: the authorities question Neville Landless, Jasper has circulars printed up, and then Mr. Crisparkle discovers Edwin's watch and pin in the water near the Cloisterham weir. We will never find out what happened to Edwin Drood, whether he is dead or kidnapped or has absconded. But we can note that Dickens handles the narrative leading up to Edwin's disappearance with the sort of technique which typifies the detective story. From the beginning of the novel, he builds up a triangle of animosity, passion, and pique between Jasper, Landless, and Drood. Prior to Edwin's disappearance, they plan to have a dinner party to patch up their differences. Dickens goes as far as describing each of the participants as they walk up the postern stairs of Jasper's lodgings. We never see the dinner; Dickens cuts away to a description of the storm which tears at Cloisterham that evening. When day breaks, Dickens plunges us into the fact of Edwin's disappearance with Jasper clamoring "Where is my nephew?" at Mr. Crisparkle's window. This sort of narrative jump is, in fact, one of the principal methods in the extant portions of *Edwin Drood*. What has Jasper been doing in the crypt while Durdles lays asleep? It is questions like this, generated by hops, skips, and leaps in the narration, which drive the plot of the novel. These posers, however, give us a hard time when we try to classify them as gothic, serial, or detective devices. We really cannot tag them until we know how Dickens was going to prepare for and furnish the answers, which, except for hidden papers in someone's junk room, we never will. We can, however, class at least one of the implicit questions in *Edwin Drood*. Dickens puts great emphasis on Rosa's mother's ring. Mr. Grewgious gives Edwin a solemn talk about it, and Edwin thinks a good bit about the ring in his pocket when he breaks off his engagement to Rosa. Then, when Mr. Crisparkle probes the river bottom at the Cloisterham weir, he finds Edwin's watch and pin, but not the ring. Nobody mentions the ring, and with this small device Dickens does two things. He arranges things so as to force his readers to ask the question "what happened to the ring?", and he gives them knowledge superior to that of the people in the book. At this point, neither item profits us much, and it is moot to argue whether our knowledge would have profited us if Dickens had finished the novel. Yet this treatment of the readers in this part of *Edwin Drood* relies on detective story assumptions, rather than those of the gothic or the serial novel.

Amid all of the imponderables in *Edwin Drood*, there is one other item which bears on the detective story. When Rosa ponders Edwin's disappearance, Dickens inserts a parenthesis on the criminal mind which reads

...what could she know of the criminal intellect, which its own professed students perpetually misread, because they persist in trying to reconcile with the average intellect of average men, instead of identifying it as a horrible wonder apart.

This attitude, continuing in Dickens from his first to last books, at once permitted him to view the detective as a worthy character and almost disqualified him from writing detective stories. Basically, Dickens holds that the world, man and nature, ought to respond in a palpable way to evil. The fallen world, however, does not respond to man's crimes, but the narrator of Dickens' novels does. In graphing these reactions, we can witness Dickens' belief become mellowed, or shackled, by technique. When Jonas Chuzzlewit sets out to murder Tigg, the narrator would have all of life shrink from the approach of the murderer. In *Bleak House*, however, the narrator would only have London warn the victim, Tulkinghorn, not to return to his chambers. Finally, *Edwin Drood* moves away from specific identification of the criminal or victim and gives instead the storm which follows the dinner at Jasper's rooms, indicating symbolically the turbulence in the human heart, but withholding identification of whose heart because of the demands of mystery organization.

That Dickens chose to attach the term "mystery" to the title of his last novel may indicate that he was at last going to write a full-fledged detective novel. We will never know. The character of the detective and the special techniques of surprise necessary for the detective story nevertheless, did play an important role in Dickens' work. With detectives, Dickens gradually accepted their social worth and became an advocate of the real Detective Police. He took the detective out of the garbage dump of the thief-taker, converted him into the sinister genius, and finally raised him to the level of the jovial and acute Inspector Bucket. In terms of criminals, Dickens learned to gag his sense of moral repugnance in order to work more effectively upon the curiosity of his readers, rather than upon their sentiments. Finally, Dickens moved from exclusively using the brainless conventions of gothic and serial plotting toward combining them with the more logical and playful techniques which would eventually become the conventional narrative devices of the detective story. He went from the crude sentimental surprise to the motivated but devious surprise of the detective story. Still, Dickens never arrived at the complete detective novel. He wrote triple-deckers which needed to be filled up, and he wrote for a heterogenous audience which was not quite ready for the detective story.

It would be presumptuous to suggest that Dickens failed to capitalize on the bits and pieces of the detective story that he discovered while writing his novels. Certainly he was interested in making plots which surprised readers, but he was more interested in manipulating characters and events so as to touch people's hearts. He saw crime and its solution as one method of adding structure to his fiction, but he realized the structural value of, among other things, images. He became fascinated with the character of the detective, but he was more interested in the differences between self and selflessness. Dickens played a major role in forming the detective hero of the sensation novelists; after *Bleak House,* pale versions of Bucket began to turn up in their works. Nevertheless, most people who read *Martin Chuzzlewit* or *Bleak House* do not recognize Dickens' tinkering with the detective story, yet still come away from these novels with a high degree of satisfaction.

# Chapter 5

# Collins and the Sensation Writers

While Dickens slowly moved away from the openly sentimental treatment and the loose romance-like presentation of crime, criminals, and detectives in his novels, his young friend Wilkie Collins (1824-1889) busied himself with modifying and inventing literary attitudes and techniques which would later provide the basic materials for the modern detective story. Indeed, many critics believe that Dickens' reading of Collins' novels played a major role in his new respect for structure and consistency, which we can see in his later novels. Although Collins certainly knew about Poe (having written a short story entitled "The Stolen Letter"), he did not consciously set out to participate in the development of the detective story. It just so happens that certain techniques which Collins created to forward his sensation novels admirably fit the aims and purposes of the detective story, and it just so happens that Collins' attitudes toward detectives, crime, and the author's relationship with his readers contributed to what would become the fully-developed, consciously written detective story.

After writing his obligatory historical novel, *Antonia, or the Fall of Rome* (1850), in the vein of Lytton, Collins turned to novels of contemporary life. Some of these apprentice works, like *Hide and Seek* (1854), involve a bit of detection, and some of Collins' journalistic pieces for *All the Year Round* look at crime, but his first substantial step toward the detective story was *The Woman in White*. Dickens ran his friend's novel in *All the Year Round* from November 1859 to August 1860. In its forty episodes, *The Woman in White* established the subject matter, the form, and the fashion for the sensation novel. Writers from Mrs. Henry Wood to Miss Braddon depended on Collins' lead when they came to manufacture their novels. *The Woman in White* also contained the first Master Criminal in the person of Count Fosco. Collins' combination of Napoleonic elements with a "feminine nature," cultural sophistication, bizarre habits, good humor, and frank ruthlessness goes a long way toward generating FuManchu and the whole gang of Master Criminals so important to the thriller of the twentieth century.

Several episodes in *The Woman in White* also display some interest in detection. But most importantly, *The Woman in White* provided Collins with the ideas for and practice in the techniques which he would later use in *The Moonstone*.

*The Woman in White* tells of the harrowing experiences of Laura Fairlie, a typical Victorian heroine possessed of determination in matters of principle but susceptible to disorders common to exquisite Victorian female sensibilities. Because of a promise to her dying father, Laura marries Sir Percival Glyde, thus foregoing her attractions to her true love, Walter Hartright. Sir Percival, in spite of his initial suaveness, proves to be a rotter who married Laura only for her money. He and his mentor in evil, Count Fosco, try to trick Laura into giving up control of her money. When they fail in this attempt, Fosco comes up with the idea of involving the person of Anne Catherick, a mentally defective young woman who has some sort of mysterious connection with Sir Percival's past, and who also bears a striking resemblance to Laura. When Anne dies of heart disease, Fosco registers her death as Laura's and has the heroine locked up in an asylum as Anne Catherick. At this juncture, Laura's half-sister, Miriam Halcombe, and her true love, Walter Hartright, team up to prove that the dazed and bewildered Laura is, in fact, alive and the victim of a monstrous conspiracy. Walter noses about, doing a bit of detective work here and there. He discovers the fact that Sir Percival was a bastard and had forged his parents' marriage entry in order to inherit his father's estate. Also, he discovers that Anne Catherick's amazing likeness to Laura came from the fact that Anne was the illegitimate daughter of Philip Fairlie, Laura's father. As surprising and interesting as these discoveries may be, they get Walter no further in the legal resuscitation of Laura; they, in fact, set him back because Sir Percival dies in the fire that he kindles to destroy the evidence of his forgery. Walter's only recourse, now, is Count Fosco, but Fosco is a tougher proposition than Walter can handle by himself. Help arrives in the person of Professor Pesca, a political exile from Italy who, in his youth, had been mixed up in the *Carbonari*. Fosco, it seems, was also a member of the secret society, but turned traitor. Knowing this, Walter forces a confession out of Fosco which outlines the switching of Anne and Laura. Fosco then decamps for Paris where he is assassinated by a *Carbonari* hit man. Laura's identity is returned and she and Walter go about the business of marriage and prosperity.

*The Woman in White*, then, gives readers plenty of melodrama and sentiment and little in the way of detection. The novel does, however, have connections to the detective story which we can see when we look at some of its sources and when we examine some of the techniques which Collins used to tell the story. In the first place, *The Woman in White* grew, in part, from Newgate literature. In 1877, Collins told an interviewer that he got the idea for *The Woman in White* when

...he received a letter asking him to take up some case of real or supposed wrongful incarceration in a lunatic asylum. His thoughts being directed in this groove, he next came upon an old French trial turning on a question of substitution of persons.

This "old French trial" Collins found in Maurice Mejan's *Recueil des Causes Celebres* (1804-14), which Collins himself called "a sort of French Newgate Calendar." More important than either the letter asking for help or the old trial proceedings, Collins gained a good bit of inspiration for *The Woman in White* from Godwin's *Caleb Williams*. Juxtaposing these two novels, we find both tell the story of a powerful aristocrat who tyrannizes someone without power. Caleb becomes the object of his master's persecution because he knows Falkland's secret just as Anne's troubles begin when she claims that she knows Sir Percival's secret. Collins then proceeds to portion out the action of *The Woman in White* the same way Godwin organized his novel. For three-quarters of both novels, the tyrants hold all of the cards and there is little that the heroes can do but try to avoid the more blatant threats. In the last section of both books, the hero wins, but victory does not come from his own exertions. Thus in Collins, Walter Hartright gains power over Sir Percival, but then he doubts whether he could have used the knowledge to defeat the villain if Sir Percival had not defeated himself. As similar as these things seem, sixty-odd years of cultural change have severely modified the impact of the persecution story: Collins hopelessly sentimentalizes those characters and events which have tragic potential in Godwin. He starts *The Woman in White* with the thesis that the narrative will show "What a Woman's patience can endure, and what a Man's resolution can achieve." Instead of creating his conclusion out of the reason and action of his characters, Collins resolves events with coincidence and the machinery of providence. He also fluffs up the sentiment of the persecution story by transforming Godwin's male lead into the weak and pathetic figures of Anne and Laura. He insists on the sentimental side by naming his heroine Fairlie and his hero Hartright. These things, of course, fit the aims and devices of the sensation novel, but they do deprive the persecution story of some of the austere vigor which we find in *Caleb Williams*.

Collins, however, was a better writer than Godwin. More important than the similarity of plot and character patterns in *Caleb Williams* and *The Woman in White* is the fact that Collins got part of the inspiration for his technique in *The Woman in White* from Godwin, and in this he improves on Godwin almost as much as he degrades the moral force of *Caleb Williams*. As stated in the Preface to his novel, Collins felt that the most remarkable technique of *The Woman in White* was its narrative technique. The novel presents readers with separate narratives of seven individuals in which they describe those things which they personally witnessed in the affair of Laura Fairlie: as Collins says, "Thus, the story here presented will be told by more than one pen, as the story of an offense against the laws is told in court by more than one witness." This method of telling a story, he goes on to say, is an experiment "which has not (so far as I know) been hitherto tried in fiction." This claim, of course, cannot stand up, and even contemporary reviewers were quick to point out the origins of Collins' technique in the epistolary novel. Indeed, his own novel *Basil—A Story of Modern Life* (1852) uses the private records of several characters. But the point of view in *The Woman in White* is not quite the same as that in the novel narrated by letters or as that in his own earlier book. *The Woman in White* purposely and specifically sets the readers up as a court, whereas in the epistolary novel readers merely snoop into someone else's private life. Further, Collins' method of narration in this novel and later in *The Moonstone* has some importance for the development of the novel. What Collins, ultimately, does is to take the narrative quirks of the eighteenth-century novel—the letters in Richardson, the asides in Fielding, and the psychological sign posts in Sterne—and apply them to the carefully-constructed novel instead of to the loose and digressive romance. Collins began to make this contribution with his construction of the point of view in *The Woman in White*. But where did he get the idea for a novel in quasi-judicial form? Collins was trained as a lawyer and could have developed the idea from his legal apprenticeship. More probably, however, he derived his new point of view from his reading of Godwin. Early in *Caleb Williams*, the narrator tells his readers that

> I do not pretend to warrant the authenticity of any part of these memoirs, except so much as fell under my own knowledge, and that part shall be stated with the same simplicity and accuracy, that I would observe *toward a court* . . . The same scrupulous fidelity restrains me from altering the manner of *Mr. Collins'* narrative. [my italics]

Here, Collins found the idea of the semi-judicial form progressing through the testimony of separate witnesses. This passage is even more striking when, in *The Woman in White*, Walter comments on how much the accidental occurrence of one's name captures the attention. I, at least, take it as proved that Collins developed part of his narrative technique from this hint in Godwin. But does narrative technique a detective story make, and, indeed, is *The Woman in White* a detective story in the first place?

To answer the second question first, no, in its main plot *The Woman in White* is not a detective story. First of all, Collins does not hide the fact that Glyde and Fosco are villains, he does not obscure the fact that they switched women in order to filch Laura's inheritance, and Walter Hartright does not establish Laura's identity through the collection of evidence. In short, there is no detection because, with the central problem at least, there is nothing to detect. Also, providence does too much in this novel. Even though Count Fosco has a significant speech refuting sentimental concepts of justice like "murder will out," the hand of God surely seizes Sir Percival, who is immolated while burgling a church, and Fosco himself becomes the victim not of logic or reason, but of his own turpitude. Collins, in fact, felt a bit queasy about the way he finished Fosco off, and he apologized to his readers for reintroducing Professor Pesca, the unconscious agent of Fosco's defeat and death, after forgetting about him for thirty-odd episodes. Throughout the novel, Collins demonstrates the workings of time, instead of his stated purpose of showing what "Man's resolution can achieve." Hartright and his counselors periodically insist upon waiting for events to take their course, and Collins frequently uses the word "clew" in its original sense—that of a ball of magic thread followed to find the way out of the labyrinth—to explain the development of the action rather than explaining it as the accumulation and use of knowledge. At the end, the specific evidence which proves that Laura is Laura comes not from any sort of investigation, but from the confession which Walter extorts from Fosco. All of this Collins chose to do: he chose to ignore the detectival implications of his own plot, for *The Woman in White* does have the makings of a detective story. The story contains evidence which could have been used to establish at least a decent case against Fosco: several people knew of Fosco's visits to Anne in the country, several people knew both Laura and Anne, and several people, including a physician, knew of Anne's heart disease. Yet Collins preferred not to take this approach, in large measure because following through on the detective implications of the plot would have robbed him of too many chances to purvey sensation to his readers.

In spite of its general direction toward sentiment and sensation, Collins does develop detective elements in some of the subsidiary action of *The Woman in White*. The first of these episodes is Walter's discovery of Sir Percival's secret, and the second is his inductive leap concerning the identity of Anne Catherick's father. Both episodes occur late in the novel, between installments thirty and thirty-seven. In this section of *The Woman in White*, in fact, Hartright thinks of himself as doing detective work. He recognizes that "this was the first step forward in my investigation." After collecting some facts from Anne's guardian, Walter goes to Old Welmingham to find evidence to support his vague notion that Sir Percival was Anne's father and that once he has evidence of this he will be able to force a confession out of Laura's husband. He interviews Mrs. Catherick, but comes away with an impression of her emotions and no facts. Then he examines the church register and observes there is something vaguely fishy about the entry for Sir Percival's parents' marriage. Without hoping for much, he walks to Knowlesbury to check the duplicate register kept by Mr. Wansborough. Here he discovers Sir Percival's secret: his parents never married and he forged the marriage entry in an accidentally generous margin of the register. Shortly after this, Walter also gathers some circumstantial evidence (Philip Fairlie and Mrs. Catherick were at the same place at the same time) that Anne was the illegitimate daughter of Laura's father. In both of these instances, Collins handles the material in the manner of the detective story. Hartright makes the discoveries by purposeful investigation and not by accident. Further, Collins manipulates his characters and facts so both discoveries evoke surprise: he defeats the expectations which he had developed, but, at the same time, remains consistent with facts and events which he described earlier.

Collins considered surprise to be perhaps the most important element in *The Woman in White*. In the Preface to the 1860 edition, he took the unusual step of asking reviewers to praise or damn his novel without summarizing the plot or revealing the ending. To reveal the ending, he says, will destroy the "two main elements in the attraction of all stories— the interest of curiosity, and the element of surprise." Reviewers, to their credit, went along with Collins, and established a continuing convention of reviewing mysteries. But, as far as *The Woman in White* is concerned, Collins was off the mark. The main plot of the novel may evoke curiosity, but it contains no surprises. Readers, as I have said, know early on that Glyde and Fosco switched women, and only the most obdurately naive readers can progress very far in *The Woman in White* without knowing that Walter Hartright and Laura Fairlie will end up happily ever after. Guessing the ending of this novel does no substantial damage to readers' enjoyment. Collins was, nevertheless, absolutely right about the implications of his techniques, developed for *The Woman in White*, when he extended them into *The Moonstone*.

Of all of the techniques which he employed in *The Woman in White*, two have special importance for *The Moonstone* and for later developments of the detective story and novel. The flashiest of these is Collins' use of multiple points of view. This, as we already know, Collins intended to use in order to put his readers in the position of a jury at a trial. Multiple points of view in *The Woman in White*, however, have little to do with making this novel a detective story. First of all, *The Woman in White*, by and large, tells a single, continuous story. And, although the separate narratives may be flashbacks, they do not overlap to provide contradicting observations or opinions. Further, although Walter asks us to in the beginning, the whole novel does not really push its readers to judge guilt or innocence or to certify information as true or false. *The Woman in White* simply asks us to judge the propriety of Walter Hartright's actions, not his conclusions. Thus, there is little unreliable narration in *The Woman in White*, and there is little recapitulation—the constant review of one situation which becomes so important to *The Moonstone*. Collins' chief motive for employing multiple points of view in *The Woman in White* is to facilitate his development of eccentric characters—hence the narratives of Fairlie, Mrs. Michelson (Miss Clack in germ), Hester Pinhorn, and Count Fosco. Notably, the most significant developments in the novel occur in the extract from Miriam's diary, which soon ceases to be very diaretic, and in Hartright's narratives. These sections are pretty much in the same style and they tell the story in a reasonably conventional manner.

Far more technically important, for the detective story and for the novel in general, is Collins' construction of *The Woman in White*. Like Godwin's ballyhooed construction of *Caleb Williams*, Collins wrote *The Woman in White* backwards: he finished most of the third volume before he wrote the opening sections. This, moreover, means much more with Collins than it does with other writers because he was so meticulous. Working from the conclusion to the beginning not only enabled Collins to develop his action and characters consistently, it also meant that he could create details of description and dialogue so they responded both to the moment and, often in another sense, to later developments in the plot. Thus, for instance, when Walter meets Anne Catherick in the churchyard early in the novel, he muses on the resemblance between Anne and Laura, ending with "Although I hated myself even for thinking such a thing, still, while I looked at the woman before me, the idea would force itself into my mind that one sad change, in the future, was all that was wanting to make the likeness complete." Here Walter responds to what he sees, and Collins also prepares us for the switch of Laura and Anne after Laura's suffering and illness. Thus, Collins has taken the technique of premonition from the gothic tradition, stripped it of its association with dreams and mysticism, and turned it into a method of construction. This same technique eventually was to become the narrative "I told you so" which plays such a large role in the growth of the detective story. Collins' manipulation of small but significant facts may have had something to do with his legal training and the lawyer's awareness of the importance of fine print. Much of this, however, comes to naught in *The Woman in White* because Collins' motives were so mixed in the creation of the novel. He, therefore, not only provided secularized and sanitized premonitions like the one cited above, but he also provided real prophetic dreams which are the typical stuff of the sensation novel. While crime and detection lay confined to the sensation novel, they could only move part of the way to the detective novel.

Between *The Woman in White* and *The Moonstone*, the motifs of the detective story became a standard part of the sensation novel. I have been bandying this term about for a good bit, and it is about time to define it. The sensation novel was a beast with many parents. As it existed in Collins and his followers, it was, first of all, a new manifestation of the gothic novel. Like the gothic novel, the sensation novel intended to stir up the readers' emotions to remind them of the non-rational parts of their beings. It derived much of its impetus not from British writers like Walpole or Monk Lewis, but from Nathaniel Hawthorne's gloomy New England fictions. Sensation novels also follow the rational gothic patterns of Mrs. Radcliffe: no mysticism, *per se*, comes into them. The sensation novel, along with reducing Satanic evil to domestic crime, does not wish to terrify its readers, and, therefore, substitutes pity and sentimentality for terror and fear. Thus it responds not only to the gothic tradition, but also to the more mundane developments of early Victorian melodrama. Sensation fiction, further, sprouted up as a revolt against the historical novel: sensation writers wished to end the reign of Scott and Lytton and to deal with the contemporary world. Finally, the sensation novel corresponds to the Pre-Raphaelite movement in art. It attempts to fuse meticulous attention to surface detail with emotionally evocative subject matter. In short, it wants to do the same things which Holman Hunt describes in *Pre-Raphaelitism and the Pre-Raphaelite Brotherhood*:

It has been seen how in a quite child-like way we at the beginning set ourselves to illustrate themes which we consciously persuaded ourselves to be connected with the pathetic, the honest, the laudable, the sublime interests of humanity. When we treated of vicious power triumphant, it was to excite honest pity for the victims, and indignation toward arrogant vice.

This statement pretty much describes *The Woman in White* and its progeny. But so much for objective description. In reality, sensation novels are unreadable concoctions of pseudo-realism, and diseased emotionalism, and maudlin portraits of virtue which give Victorian novels such a bad name. They do, however, treat detective themes and detectives. This was not altogether a welcome development. Mrs. Oliphant saw the detective as a character "whom we [do not] welcome with any pleasure into the republic of letters. His appearance is neither favorable to taste or morals." This did not deter sensation writers, and official detectives enter sensation novels like Mrs. Henry Wood's (1814-1887) *Mrs. Halliburton's Troubles* (1862) and Mary Braddon's (1837-1915) *Henry Dunbar* (1864). We must, therefore, take a brief look at a sample of sensation novels if we are going to follow through on the development of detective story motifs and are to properly gauge Collins' achievement in *The Moonstone*.

After Collins set up the features of the sensation novel in *The Woman in White*, Mrs. Henry Wood dabbled with crime in her immensely popular novel, *East Lynne, or the Earl's Daughter* (1861). *East Lynne* mostly lectures female readers on the importance of marital fidelity. The main plot shows how Lady Isabel, the aforesaid Earl's daughter, leaves her husband, Mr. Carlyle, and her children to run off to the Continent with Sir Francis Levison.

Levison deserts her, her face is mangled in a train wreck, and she penitently returns to East Lynne as a governess to her own children. She, of course, suffers and, after a protracted series of miseries, dies. There is no detection here. In the sub-plot, however, Mrs. Wood does introduce a thread of crime, discovery, and punishment. Before the opening of the novel, Old Hallijohn has been murdered by one of the young men mooning about after his daughter. Suspicion falls on Richard Hare. Almost every seventy-five pages, Richard drifts into the novel, his mother has premonitions in dreams, and Mr. Carlyle gets mixed up in the inquiry. No one, however, can discover the true identity of the man who really committed the murder. Finally, Richard sees Levison, identifies him as Thorn the murderer, and Levison is condemned. Mrs. Wood introduces little detection into this sub-plot: either accident or providence uncovers the truth, and it takes its time doing it. With *East Lynne*, then, the sensation novel had not fastened on to detection. Rather, it used crime as an occasion for the suffering of innocents, as proof that evil people commit not only immoralities but illegalities as well, and, finally, as an acceptable and semi-realistic means of punishing bad people.

Mary Elizabeth Braddon comes much closer to the detective story with her sensation novel *Lady Audley's Secret* (1862). Some enthusiasts, in fact, view this book as a detective story. Let us see about this. Lady Audley has a past. The daughter of a feeble-willed naval officer, Helen, the title character, marries a good-hearted soldier, George Talboys. Disinherited by his hard-hearted father, George deserts his wife and infant son to go to Australia to make his fortune. Helen, depressed by her narrow existence, leaves her son with her father and goes off to find a better life. After Helen teaches school and governesses for a country doctor, old Sir Michael Audley falls in love with her and she marries him. Then George Talboys returns from the Antipodes and Lady Audley has to do some fancy footwork to cover her past. In a ploy admittedly taken from *The Woman in White*, Lady Audley has another woman buried as Helen Talboys in order to keep George off of her bigamistic track. Accidentally, George meets an old school chum, Robert Audley, and they visit his uncle's estate. After some near misses, George sees Helen, and Bradon leads us to believe she knocks him down a disused well. Robert Audley, missing his friend, starts to investigate. He gives several set pieces of circumstantial evidence and compiles a list of suspicious items connected with George's disappearance. Although Robert lacks the first requisite of a corpse, most of the novel involves his ferreting into Lady Audley's past. Finally Robert confronts her with evidence of her perfidy, she confesses and is bundled off to an asylum on the Continent. Then, in walks George Talboys who had clawed his way out of the well and returned to Australia. *Lady Audley's Secret* would have been a detective story but for the fact that Braddon made it a sensation novel. The novel does possess some of the elements of detective stories: there is a substantial surprise at the end, the hero, Robert Audley, spends most of his time investigating, and there are passages discussing the nature and use of evidence. But *Lady Audley's Secret* paints over these things with the lurid cast of sensation. First of all, Robert Audley may act as a detective, but he acts as one out of the old mold. The role of detective is distasteful and only brings him to the tragic realization of the conflict between truth and revenge, along with the realization that his acts will soil his name and break his uncle's heart. Lady Audley, too, comes out of the old mold. Not only do readers know everything about her from the start of the novel, but Braddon cannot describe her without stirring up readers' feelings of moral revulsion. Lady Audley's features act like liquid crystal registering guilt and fear at the same time Braddon calls her a consciousless criminal. We can see Braddon's drift away from detection in the fact that the title refers not to the fact that Lady Audley is a bigamist, murderer, and incendiary, but to her closely-guarded secret that her mother was insane. *Lady Audley's Secret*, in spite of its detective features, remains in the realm of the sensation novel. It uses detection merely as a means of developing Lady Audley's madness, Robert's conversion, and providence's organization of a happy ending.

Joseph Sheridan LeFanu (1814-1873) uses even less detection and more sensation in his novel *Uncle Silas* (1864). Here, as in *The Woman in White*, readers derive most of their pleasure from witnessing the persecution and torture of an innocent young woman by a very nasty old man. Uncle Silas and his agents spend most of the novel inventing ways of terrorizing the virginal, and rich, Maud Ruthyn. At the end of the book, Silas and his doltish son, Dudley, try to murder Maud, but she escapes to marry a lord whom LeFanu conveniently stations in the neighborhood. Unless one construes waiting around to be murdered to be detection, *Uncle Silas* contains very little detection. As in *East Lynne*, LeFanu uses an old crime as a minor structural element in his novel. Years ago, a man named Clarke died in a locked room in Silas' house; although no one can prove Silas a murderer, tongues in the county wag. At the end of the novel, Silas confines Maud in the same room. In three sentences, LeFanu explains the trick window through which one can enter the room which is ostensibly locked. This comes as no surprise and LeFanu expresses little technical interest in the solution. LeFanu intends little beyond the pity and fear evoked by the heroine and the villains.

As it stood in the late 1860s, the sensation novel routinely treated crime, criminals, and detection. Crime provided a gloss of realism as well as offering writers a structural device to hold together occasions for what Mrs. Oliphant called "sensation incidents." The chief aim of the sensation novelist lay in manipulating not the readers' curiosity or intellect but their emotional response to the victim and the villain. Detectives and detection, therefore, were useful chiefly for their melodramatic potential as well as for their link with the traditional themes of tragedy and social propriety. Further, sensation writers accomplished their aims largely by using conventional technique in telling their stories. Because of their preoccupation with hysteria and their use of old-fashioned, if somewhat meticulous, technique, most sensation novels settle into the lowest reaches of mid-Victorian fiction. It is, therefore, a tribute to Collins that in *The Moonstone* he turned the sensation novel toward something more like the real detective story.

The development of the detective story owes a great deal to the fact that Dickens ran *The Moonstone* in his magazine *All the Year Round* between January 4 and August 8, 1868. Almost anyone with even a nodding acquaintance with English letters knows something of this novel, which T.S. Eliot called "the first, the longest, and the best of modern English detective novels." Now Eliot may not have been exactly right about this pronouncement—people have taken offense at his calling *The Moonstone* "the first" and there are certainly longer detective novels—but almost everyone agrees that *The Moonstone* is a very important book. In this novel, Collins tells the story of the Moonstone, a fabulous jewel from India, which John Herncastle stole and bequeathed to his niece, Rachel Verinder, as a sadistic practical joke. The night of Rachel's birthday, the Moonstone disappears, and no one can discover how it vanished. Superintendent Seegraves, the clumsy local policeman, investigates but finds nothing. Even the celebrated London detective, Sergeant Cuff, can come up with little besides the outlandish notion that Rachel took her own diamond to pay secret debts. In the year that elapses between the beginning and the end of *The Moonstone*, Rachel undergoes extensive emotional travail. She unaccountably jilts her true love, Franklin Blake, her mother dies, she engages herself to Godfrey Ablewhite, and then, again unaccountably, she jilts him too. Blake, determined to win her back, digs into the disappearance of the diamond only to uncover incontrovertible evidence that he himself took it. After this jolt to his central nervous system, Blake, with the help of the Byronic Ezra Jennings, discovers that Mr. Candy slipped opium into his drink the night of Rachel's party, and that he abstracted the jewel in a drug-induced trance. Still, nobody knows just how the Moonstone wound up in the vault of Mr. Luker's bankers in London. The only course left to the party of amateur detectives—now including Rachel and the family lawyer along with Blake—is to watch the bank to discover to whom Luker will deliver the Moonstone. The watchers lose track of the gem at the bank, but they pick it up the next day when they get on the trail of a suspicious sailor who was mooching about the bank. They find him murdered in his bed, and upon removing a wig and fake beard they discover that the sailor was Godfrey Ablewhite, the evangelical do-gooder who lifted the Moonstone from the drugged Blake. The novel closes as we learn that Franklin and Rachel have busied themselves peopling the world with Blakes, and the Moonstone has been returned to the forehead of its idol.

Whether or not it shows from this synopsis, *The Moonstone* began as a redressing of *The Woman in White*. As in the earlier novel, Collins uses a number of narrators to tell the story of the stolen diamond. Franklin Blake repeats certain elements of Walter Hartright: both fall in love over the paintbox and both pursue the central investigation in the novels to achieve happiness in love. Rachel Verinder is a muscular version of Laura Fairlie— or a combination of Laura and her brainy and determined half-sister, Miriam. The heroines, in both cases, offer to sacrifice their real loves to their principles. Rachel's reaction to Ablewhite's proposal and his response to this come pretty clearly from Laura's revelation of the truth to Sir Percival early in *The Woman in White*. In Rosanna Spearman and Limping Lucy from *The Moonstone*, we can find echoes of Anne Catherick, and Godfrey Ablewhite is the same sort of hypocrite found in Sir Percival. Finally, although the machinery is more consistent in *The Moonstone*, Collins resolves the problems of both novels by using foreign agents to kill off the villains.

If *The Moonstone* were, however, simply a recapitulation of *The Woman in White*, it would have contributed little to the development of the detective story. Using similar plot materials, as well as similar technique, Collins makes modifications, major and minor, which move *The Moonstone* away from the sensation novel and closer to being a detective novel. Perhaps the most significant of the changes which Collins made in *The Moonstone* was with his villain. As original, energetic, and magnetic as Fosco is in *The Woman in White*, he is also a grossly melodramatic figure, and Collins' manipulation of the audience's fear and fascination with him lessens the "curiosity and surprise" which he said he aimed at in the novel. Collins realized he could not manage curiosity and surprise with his villain on center stage, so in *The Moonstone* he opted for the hidden culprit. In *The Moonstone*, therefore, Collins dispensed with villains who seem like figures out of Edward Gorey and substituted Godfrey Ablewhite. Since here, as in the earlier novel, Collins tends to use suggestive names (Mr. Luker for the money lender, Betteredge for the Verinders' sanguine servant), he makes the first step in obscuring his villain by combining four symbolically pure terms in his name. Not only does Rachel seem to clear him of suspicion in the middle of the novel (begetting the guilty—innocent—guilty technique beloved of Christie), but readers even grow almost to like him in proportion to Miss Clack's disillusionment with Ablewhite as the "Christian hero." Since we see little of him in the novel, readers tend to appraise him as someone who is merely insipid, rather than someone with origins in Napoleon or Cain. Doing this, changing the emphasis on the villain, was absolutely necessary for a break with the sensation novel. It was a break which Collins alone was willing to make.

The other significant character change between *The Woman in White* and *The Moonstone* was Collins' introduction of an official detective in the later novel. Just as he used some French judicial proceedings for details in *The Woman in White*, Collins used legal records for details in *The Moonstone*—those involving the arrest and trial of Constance Kent for the Road murder of 1860. Constance Kent was tracked down and apprehended by Inspector Jonsthan Whitcher, who then became famous when the courts acquitted Constance Kent only to have her confess, five years later, that Whitcher was right. In addition to using some details from the investigation of the Road murder, Collins founded his Sergeant Cuff on the real-life Whitcher. But there is more to Cuff than this. With Cuff, Collins had to deal with some of the same prejudices which Dickens struggled with in his creation of Bucket. Foremost, he had to overcome public doubts about the discretion of detectives: over and over again Cuff must assure other characters that "I have put the muzzle on worse family difficulties than this, in my time." Unlike Dickens, however, Collins pays more attention to the impact of dealing with crime upon the detective's personality. Cuff, therefore, announces that his professional experiences have dragged him "along the dirtiest ways of this dirty little world," and as a release from human depravity, Collins gives his detective an absorbing interest in and a retirement among roses. We need to be aware, however, that Collins made Cuff as both the typical and the anti-typical detective officer. Although Betteredge and Blake both come to think of Cuff as unbeatable, he is not. Granted, Cuff understands servants better than Seegraves does, and Collins allows him a certain facility in making predictions. But he does err. He makes fools out of the local police not because he is right—Seegraves, in fact, is right about the jewel being in the house—but because he is obsequious to parlor maids and kitchen help. Further, when Cuff gives the case up, he firmly believes that Rachel took her own diamond with the aid of Rosanna Spearman's underworld expertise, and this is dead wrong. Although Collins does permit Cuff's assistant to summarize events near the close of the novel, he does this in part to remove his major characters from the sullying effects of crime. Collins wanted to create in Cuff an unconventional portrait of the detective to match the unconventional surprise at the close of the mystery. He acknowledges this in the novel. Rather than being one of the first detective heroes, Cuff acts as antidote to conventional portraits of detectives, for, as he says, "it's only in books that the officers of the detective force are superior to the weakness of making a mistake." At least as important as this, Collins purposely altered the relationship between his major characters and his detective. Almost everyone, at first, approaches Cuff with social prejudice and fear: social propriety preoccupies them. Then, against their wills, they become wrapped up in and fascinated by the search for the truth. They all catch what Betteredge, the butler, so aptly calls "detective fever." In *The*

*Moonstone,* Collins intended to raise this infection to epidemic proportions. It spreads from Betteredge to Blake to Rachel to Mr. Buff and, ultimately, to his readers. With this, he effectively achieved the "curiosity and surprise" which he aimed for in *The Woman in White.*

But Collins could have done this without Cuff, because he effects most of his purposes through technique. It is principally the writer who makes the detective story, not the characters. As in *The Woman in White,* Collins uses his pseudo-epistolary technique in *The Moonstone,* revealing the story through the narration of twelve characters—five of whom are very minor. Once again, Collins' use of these narratives stems from his desire to speak in the voices of peculiar characters more than from any intent to create quasi-legal testimony. Thus Betteredge's garrulousness, detective fever, and addiction to *Robinson Crusoe* claim more of Collins' attention than any attempt to produce a narrow slice of perception or to portray an unreliable narrator. In a legal sense, Collins frequently skips the best evidence (like Penelope Betteredge's diary and Luker's confession) for hearsay in order to stick to his scheme of using idiosyncratic narrators. Unlike *The Woman in White,* however, *The Moonstone* does not pretend to be a legal or quasi-legal document. Franklin Blake's motive for collecting the narratives is not to present them to a court or even to the court of public opinion. He collects them for future generations of Blakes, and the narrative exists to explain facts about a past scandal. This shift from quasi-legal to family document presented Collins with some problems. Without the judicial framework, some of the reasons for withholding the solution disappear. He solved this by making Franklin Blake, the editor, into a semi-tyrannical controller who enjoins his social inferiors Betteredge and Miss Clack (both of whom want to tell us what really happened) from revealing everything they have heard.

As with the earlier novel, *The Moonstone* rests on Collins' careful planning and writing. He does, for example, mention that Dr. Candy sneaks away from the table during the birthday party in order to make the beginning consistent with the revelation at the end that Dr. Candy drugged Franklin Blake. In *The Moonstone,* however, Collins does this sort of seeding more extensively and meticulously than in *The Woman in White.* He also constructs *The Moonstone* in such a manner that his seeding and reaping of facts has more effect than it did in the earlier book. First of all, Collins concentrates things in *The Moonstone.* This novel covers one year and travels, basically, between Fizinghall, London, and Brighton. But in large measure, *The Moonstone* focuses on the few days surrounding Rachel Verinder's birthday. Thus, one of Collins' major devices in the narrative is recapitulation. He repeatedly takes us back to the events surrounding the disappearance of the diamond. Rosanna Speaman's letter, Jenning's experiments, and Cuff's investigations all lap back over events which readers have seen before. Coupled with this, moreover, Collins warns his readers about what he is doing. Early in the novel, he causes Betteredge to say

> Here follows the substance of what I said, written out entirely for your benefit. Pay attention to it, or you will be all abroad, when we get deeper into the story. Clear your mind of children, or the dinner, or the new bonnet, or what not. Try if you can't forget politics, horses, prices in the City, and grievances at the club. I hope you won't take this freedom on my part amiss; it's only a way I have of appealing to the gentle reader. Lord! haven't I seen you with the greatest authors in your hands, and don't I know how ready your attention is to wander when it's a book that asks for it, instead of a person?

Here we have not only an address to an audience of men and women, something, in itself, important to the development of the novel and the detective story, but we also have the warning to the reader to pay attention to everything. This sort of admonition eventually would play a major role in the articulation of the fully-developed detective story. Along these same lines, Collins peppers the later sections of the novel with I told you so's. At numerous points in the narrative, Franklin Blake tells readers to flip back to specific parts of Betteredge's narrative to verify the truth of elements in his own account of events and persons. This, too, would become a standard device of detective story writers.

For all of this, is *The Moonstone* a detective story? Well, it is more of a detective story than *The Woman in White*. We can see this in those techniques which I have just described, and we can see it in Collins' handling of the detective and the villain, and in his adroit shifting of suspicion from one person to the next. *The Moonstone's* chief claim to detective story status lies in Collins' purposeful use of surprise—that Blake himself took the diamond, and that in turn Ablewhite took it from him. In typical detective story fashion, these surprises come out of the blue, but upon careful consideration they are also consistent with inconspicuous facts which undeniably occur in the novel. Here Collins moves past the pure sensation of *The Woman in White* and toward the purposeful construction of the detective story. *The Moonstone* also surpasses the earlier novel in presenting instances of characters solving problems through the use of evidence and reason. Among others, Ezra Jennings' reading of Dr. Candy's delirium, smacking as it does of cryptography, falls into this category. Further, in the manner of the detective writer, Collins not only asks his readers to pay attention, he also asks them to form opinions instead of gliding along with the notions of the current narrator. Thus Betteredge tells us that

> If you desert me, and side with the Sergeant, on the evidence before you—if the only rational explanation you can see is, that Miss Rachel and Mr. Luker must have got together, and that the Moonstone must be now in pledge in the money-lender's house— I own I can't blame you for arriving at that conclusion.

He gives but he also takes away. Collins urges his readers on to form conclusions, but he arranges things so these conclusions will be wrong. This, too, is fundamental detective story technique.

Collins, then, takes a substantial step toward the detective story in his treatment of his readers. His playfulness and use of detective fever make the conventional concepts of justice and the sentimental ramifications of crime less obtrusive than in the sensation novel, but convention and sentiment still play a fairly large role in *The Moonstone*. It remains at its core a sensation novel and not a detective story. Thus Collins' controlling metaphor for the detective action is the word "clew." Clew, however, does not evoke its modern sense but rather ties back to the myth of Theseus following the magic thread out of the labyrinth. Collins' detectives, then, follow a preordained path provided not by their own logic or activity, but by an agency outside of the novel. Consequently, every time the investigation balks, as it does after Blake's receipt of Rosanna Spearman's letter, either coincidence bumps things back on the right track, or the characters must wait for the fullness of time. From the very beginning of the novel, we know this is, essentially, a murder-will-out story, for the Prologue announces "that crime brings its own fatality with it." Collins, however, with typical Victorian secularizing, moves the hand of God and the operations of providence into the background. He also moves sentiment into the background, but it is there nonetheless. Victorian readers, when approaching *The Moonstone*, valued things like the pathos of the Indians returning the Moonstone to their god far more than they appreciated the detective machinery of the novel—at least they said they did. Further, Collins did not conclude *The Moonstone* with the detectives' solution to the mystery. Instead, he ends the novel with Betteredge telling us about the propagation of Blakes and with Mr. Murthwaite's narrative of the return of the diamond. Throughout the novel, in fact, Collins busies himself with displaying sentiment. As much as it is about tracing the Moonstone, this novel concerns a woman with a tragic secret. In fact, Collins invented much of what would later be seen as detective machinery for the purpose of highlighting emotion rather than observation or ratiocination. Blake may give us asides telling readers to check back with Betteredge's narrative, but he does this so they can savor emotion. Thus, he says things like "A glance back at the sixteenth and seventeenth chapters of Betteredge's Narrative will show that there really was a reason for my sparing myself, at a time when my fortitude had been cruelly tried."

It is, finally, to Collins' credit that readers of the next generation could overlook the sentiment in *The Moonstone* and view it as a detective novel instead of a sensation novel. Collins did not consider it a detective novel or, if he did, he quickly lost interest in detection. After *The Moonstone*,

Collins turned to novels of social comment, a move which prompted Swinburn's couplet

What brought good Wilkie's genius nigh perdition?
Some demon whispered—"Wilkie, have a mission."

In the 1870s, in fact, major sensation writers left off their treatment of crime and detection. LeFanu, of course, died in 1873, but Mrs. Wood and Miss Braddon consciously switched to other subjects. Readers in the 1870s and 1880s who wanted to read about crime and detection, therefore, had to switch to foreign imports. They had to switch to the novels of Emile Gaboriau.

# Chapter 6
# Gaboriau

In the 1870s and 1880s, when the sensation novel was slowly dying, what did people interested in crime fiction read? Arthur Conan Doyle, reviewing his own reading in the mid-1880s, noted that "I have read Gaboriau's *Lecoq the Detective*, *The Gilded Clique*, and a story concerning the murder of an old woman, the name of which I forget [it was *The Widow Lerouge*]. All very good. Wilkie Collins, but more so." Like Doyle, many people read Emile Gaboriau (1833-1873). Although he is hardly "Wilkie Collins, but more so," Gaboriau did contribute a great deal to the development of the detective story. His novels about Pere Tabaret and M. Lecoq summarize earlier writers' characterizations of the detective hero, and Gaboriau invented one way to construct a detective novel. Both his detective heroes and his structural pattern influenced detective writers of the 1880s and 1890s, including Doyle. Even though Gaboriau can still, at times, catch readers' interest with his detectives, the conventions of publishing and the standards of taste to which he conformed virtually assured that his books would not last much beyond his own century. This makes him Wilkie Collins, but less so.

Before we get to Gaboriau, however, we need to do some backtracking to fill in the history of crime fiction in nineteenth-century France. Crime and detectives, of course, existed outside of Great Britain and the United States. In fact, the first significant modern detective was a Frenchman, Eugene Francois Vidocq. And, in a sense, all modern detective literature starts with him. Poe, as we have seen, alludes to Vidocq, as does Lytton; both writers knew about him because they had read his *Memoires* (1828). Vidocq's *Memoires* may have been ghost written for him (there is some controversy over this), but it was certainly an influential book. This influence, however, came mainly from the book's novelty, for in retrospect *Memoires* seems hardly worth getting excited about. Roughly picaresque in nature, the first part of the book recounts Vidocq's seemingly endless series of prison breaks. Vidocq began his life in the provincial town of Arras and quickly became an accomplished juvenile delinquent. For most of his youth and young manhood, Vidocq got himself into one scrape after another as he floated through the anarchy of the Revolution, the persecutions of the Terror, and the domestic social jumble caused by Napoleon's military adventures. Vidocq's frequent prison breaks testify not only to his own native cunning, but also to the fact that dotards and incompetents ran most of the jails in France. As he approached middle age, Vidocq tired of the picaresque life, boosted his way into a job as a police informer, and eventually, with the aid of one M. Henry, became a secret agent for the police and a thief-taker. He even worked his way up to chief of the *Surete*. The second part of *Memoires*, therefore, presents a disorganized flood of Vidocq's cases. He seems, by his own account, to have been a crackerjack detective. He says he succeeded as a detective for several rudimentary reasons. First, unlike the rest of the former convicts on the police payroll, he was honest and refused to make police work into an occasion for larceny. Second, he possessed some talent as an actor, and after it became known he was a police agent, he could disguise himself and mingle with potential felons. Third, he knew a great deal about criminals—who they were and what ploys they habitually used. He had, after all, shared accommodations with them. Vidocq also succeeded, he suggests, because M. Henry liked him, and because he always took the trouble to butter him up. Finally, he became an eminent detective because, as he acknowledges, criminals were and are basically stupid people. Vidocq was, then, fortunate in that he was a policeman when generations of non-existent or incompetent law enforcement served to allow criminals to be even stupider.

From the historical point of view, Vidocq's *Memories* is a mine of information about the development of law enforcement. But from the point of view of literature, the book has only minimal value. As a mental giant, Poe was correct in describing the detective of the *Memories* as a bungler. The book presents little which a combination of sheer plodding joined with a pinch of intelligence could not accomplish. It does, however, provide several character motifs upon which later fiction writers built. Vidocq, first of all, displays an almost Homeric capacity for self-assertion, or, if you will, hyperbole. According to Vidocq, once he joined the force, the denizens of the underworld became so intimidated by him that the mere mention of his name was enough to make even the most hardened crook drop his jimmy and dark lantern. Vidocq the detective never for a moment lets us forget his immense accomplishments: he says things like "not a day passed that I did not make important discoveries. No crime was committed or was about to be committed that I did not learn all of the circumstances." This sort of statement is either epic or a lie. Along with his constant vanity, the *Memoires* presents us with a man in the grip of paranoia, a condition based on fact but raised by Vidocq to the level of real mental disorder. Because he was honest, because he had energy, and because his police colleagues were lazy, dishonest, and inept, other policemen frequently tried to discredit him. Vidocq, however, turned the tables on them by avoiding their traps and by continuing to be more efficient than they. From these two motifs in Vidocq's *Memoires*, Poe, Gaboriau, and then Doyle built the conventional contest between the police force and the detective as well as the convention of the detective's justifiable vanity.

As art, Vidocq's *Memoires* makes no direct contribution to detective fiction. The book may provide a couple of character points, but Vidocq's narrative both rambles too much and presents too little detail to have much impact on the detective story. The material had to be cut, restructured, and altered before it would contribute to detective fiction. In the United States, of course, Poe did this, but the process also went on in France. It began with a Vidocq craze and eventually ended with Gaboriau. Vidocq's *Memories* was immediately and immensely successful, and inspired a number of pseudo Vidocq books from *The Biography of the Founder of the Surete, 1812-1827* (1829) to *A Convict's Memoirs* (1829), in which Vidocq pursues the protagonist. Jumping from this kind of work, which patently took advantage of Vidocq's celebrity, lots of big names in French fiction took an interest in Vidocq and incorporated him into their works. Balzac in part based his three Vautrin novels, beginning with *Pere Goriot* (1834), on Vidocq. Sue, in *Les Mysteres de Paris* (1843), echoed Vidocq's opinions on criminal justice. Dumas, in *Crimes Celebres* (1841), reported on some of his cases. And Hugo, in *Les Miserables* (1862), depends on Vidocq's expressed views of prison reform and criminal justice. Mixed up with the careers of all of these writers and with the history of French crime literature is the rise of popular journalism in France. In 1836, with the publication of *La Presse*, modern commercial journalism began. *La Presse* and other papers, called *feuilletons* started the sort of aggression against the consumer which we take for granted today. These new papers attacked readers' purses by carrying advertisements which, in turn, enabled them to cut their prices and thereby appeal to a larger market. Lured into the newspaper by low prices, readers were then hooked by sensational serial fiction, *romans feuilleton*, so they would continue to buy the paper and, naturally, see the ads. Almost all of the major writers of fiction in mid-nineteenth century France, Sue, Dumas, etc., were *feuilletonists*. Part of the reason for all of the crime, melodrama, suspense, and sensation in their work, therefore, derived from the necessity of appealing to and riveting a large reading public. *Romans feuilleton*, however, had little focused detective business in them in spite of their frequent connection with Vidocq. This changed in the 1860s. During this decade, Alexis de Ponson (1829-1871), with his Rocambole stories, helped to bring detective work to the *roman feuilleton*, but it was really Emile Gaboriau who put the *policier* in the *roman policier*.

Ex-attorney, ex-soldier Gaboriau started out in the *feuilleton* trade as an apprentice to Paul Feval in 1860. Over the next thirteen years, he dutifully manufactured a dozen or so novels, most of which, in one way or another, touch upon crime. The most significant of these, the detective novels, are *L'Affaire Lerouge* (1865), *Le Crime d'Orcival* (1867), *Le Dossier No. 113* (1867), *Monsieur Lecoq* (1868), and *Les Esclaves de Paris* (1868). In these, he introduced his principal detective characters and pioneered one way of writing detective novels.

Gaboriau presents us with a reasonably good study of the metamorphosis of the detective character in the nineteenth century. In *L'Affaire Lerouge*, he introduces his readers first to a convict turned thief-taker in the young and eager M. Lecoq. Then he introduces the principal detective, Pere Tabaret. Tabaret, nicknamed "Tirauclair" because of his habit of saying "*Il Faut que cela se tire au clair,*" is a self-made man who has worked his way up from pawnbroker's clerk to plutocrat. He "has taken to the business of the police, as others do painting or music, for entertainment." Papa Tabaret, moreover, needs his alias because if others of his class knew about his hobby his "oldest friends will refuse to take [his] hand, as if it were not an honor to serve justice." Here, in quick succession, we find the Vidocq background in Lecoq as well as the prejudice against detectives so common to nineteenth-century literature. There is also the amateur detective whom we can trace to Poe. As it turns out, Tabaret is not a bad detective. He is unequalled in the book as an observer of material facts, and he certainly answers questions which stump the police. Gaboriau, however, wrote *L'Affaire Lerouge* as an anti-detective book. First, the author plays with the word "clair." Claire, the fiancee of the falsely accused male lead, sees more clearly using the evidence of the heart than does Tirauclair who, at first, fails to get to the bottom of things. Throughout the novel, Gaboriau treats the detective alternately as a genius and a buffoon, and he ends on a serious note when he describes Tirauclair giving up his hobby of detecting:

> The old amateur detective doubted the existence of crime, and believed that the evidence of one's senses proved nothing. He circulated a petition for the abolition of capital punishment, and organized a society for aiding the poor and innocent accused.

Gaboriau, granted, based these sentiments on details from Vidocq's later life, but they do steer away from, rather than toward, the detective story.

Although *L'Affaire Lerouge* looks as if it is going to be Tabaret's last case, it became a hot item. It not only ran in its initial appearance in *Le Pays*, but was reprinted two years later in *Le Soleil*. Because of this success, Gaboriau changed his mind. He set about remodeling his detective hero. He got rid of the old-fashioned convict thief-taker background, and he dropped the pessimism of the end of *L'Affaire Lerouge*. The result was a new model M. Lecoq. In *Le Dossier No. 113, Le Crime d'Orcival*, and *Monsieur Lecoq*, therefore, the detective is observant, acute, energetic, and heroic. Finally, in 1868 with *Les Esclaves du Paris*, Gaboriau worked himself back out of the detective hero. He returned most of the action to the laity, the non-detective characters, and moved Lecoq upstairs into the upper reaches of police officialdom, reserving for him only the role of the *deus ex machina*.

In the characters of Tirauclair and, to a greater extent, Lecoq, Gaboriau reshapes, enlarges, and transmits certain particular and peculiar features of the detective hero. To a small extent with Tirauclair and in large measure with Lecoq, he uses the detective as an argument that the law and the men who enforce it deserve greater respect. We can see this when Gaboriau touches on Tirauclair's embarrassment about helping the police. We can also see it in the fact that Gaboriau includes speeches in most of the novels which bewail the low public esteem of the police coupled with documentary evidence that the police are good, honest, discreet fellows. As Dickens and Collins both stress the detective's ability to keep his mouth shut about what he knows, so Gaboriau stresses this side of police behavior. Thus, he says of Goudar, the detective in *La Corde au Cou* (1873), he "was one of those men who have heard in their lives more confessions than ten priests, ten lawyers, and ten doctors all together. You could tell him everything." Added to this sort of reassurance, Gaboriau attempts to still public fears about the police by describing their routines. He recognizes that people for whom he wrote had never seen the inside of a police station—to say nothing of the inside of a prison—and he set out to fill this gap not only as an appeal to the exotic tastes of his readers, but also to present quasi-real information to elevate the public's opinion of the police agent. Gaboriau certainly shows his readers how the police collect evidence, but mostly he got this from Poe, or at least he repeats Poe's attitude toward physical evidence. He also exhibits the particularly French use of psychological evidence in the attention the police give to statements made at the arrest, as well as their use of the judas window to secretly observe prisoners' behavior. Newer sorts of police information occur in Gaboriau's attempt to describe some of the techniques used in the streets to combat crime. Several times, for example, he recounts the way plainclothesmen provoke fights with criminals whom they cannot arrest on legitimate grounds in order to charge them with mayhem and get them safely into cells while other agents look for evidence to convict them on graver charges. Along with this sympathetically rendered information about the police, Gaboriau tries to simulate realism in other ways. He was very fond of facsimiles and statistics. *L'Argent des Autres* (1873), for instance, gives us two and one half pages from a trial record supposedly reproduced from the *Police Gazette*. All of his realistic equipage ostensibly lends support to Gaboriau's arguments, enhancing the public's view of the individual police agent. In this respect, he uniquely forecasts the personal themes of the police procedural story of the 1960s. Not only does he bemoan the typical lack of respect for the police, he also pictures the complications made for policemen by meddling magistrates, the debilitating effects of inter-departmental rivalries, the personal dangers which policemen confront, and even, in *La Corde au Cou*, the devastating power of police work on a marriage. Almost all of this grew from Gaboriau's desire to make the policeman a sympathetic character, and here we can see a more distinct and sustained—if less successful—effort in this direction than we find with Dickens' humanization of Bucket or Collins' portrait of Cuff.

Now, if you are French and you are going to produce a detective hero, the first model to come to mind is Vidocq. Naming his second detective hero, M. Lecoq points readers in this direction, even if Gaboriau did make the cock M. Lecoq's emblem. Although Gaboriau did eventually change Lecoq's background, when he first appears he is, like Vidocq, a thief turned thief-taker. Even though he did forget about this and create a new past for Lecoq in *Le Dossier No. 113*, Gaboriau built other resemblances of Vidocq into both of his detective heroes. Thus Tirauclair and Lecoq both run into bull-headed and occasionally corrupt colleagues who, with their Beta Minus brains, cannot appreciate the real superiority of the true detective's discoveries and insights. Almost all of Lecoq's disguising, and there is a great deal of it, comes from Vidocq. Finally, Gaboriau borrowed Vidocq's vanity and terrifying reputation and included it in his creation of the later Lecoq. In the books, all Lecoq has to do is to announce himself and even reasonably honest people get goose bumps. The only problem in this connection is that Gaboriau pictures Lecoq's vanity and ambition as admirable and, at the same time, he commits himself to showing that vanity and ambition create social evil and lead to crime. Either Gaboriau had not read his deTocqueville or he did not care about contradictions.

As Poe discovered some twenty years earlier, Vidocq may suggest some items of interest to the detective writer, but he certainly gives few hints of how to use these things in fiction. Poe, therefore, added features to the detective hero which particularized and intellectualized him. So did Gaboriau. Vidocq's *Memoires* details little about collecting physical evidence—and why should it since most real crime and detection does not depend on minute physical evidence? So Poe, and following him Gaboriau, starts his detective's job with close observation of the physical surroundings, and, in turn, makes a fundamental character point out of the fact that the detective looks harder and better than the ordinary mortal. Thus Gaboriau's Tirauclair reads the minuscule signs of human passage in the Widow Lerouge's cottage, the signs which others have missed. Lecoq finds and interprets footprints, fibers, and other tiny records of human activity which Gervol, the ham-fisted policeman, misses. Much of Gaboriau's motive for portraying the detective's ocular prowess came, no doubt, from Poe. A bit more of it came from reading

Feval's *Les Couteau d'Or* (1856) which features an Indian tracker and his dog Mohican. A lot of it came from the fact that Feval, Gaboriau, and many Frenchmen were obsessed with James Fenimore Cooper. Thus, whenever Gaboriau starts his detective on the scent of a criminal, he introduces the comparison of a bloodhound, and he also couples this with a comparison of the detective to "the savages of Cooper [who] pursue their enemies in the depths of the American forest."

Gaboriau, then, took one part of his detective's character from Cooper's indians looking for wilted leaves, as well as from Dupin's observation of particulars. More important than this, Gaboriau built the core of his detectives' characters around what he perceived to be Poe's advocacy of science and mechanical logic. He emphasizes the detective's genius and stresses it belongs to a particular type. Just as Dupin brings up a comparison of the detective and the work of the naturalist Cuvier, Gaboriau has Tirauclair say he will "reconstruct all the scenes of an assassination, as a savant who from a single bone reconstructs an ante-deluvian animal." This is, however, window dressing, and neither Poe nor Gaboriau takes the naturalist-detective analogy too far. The thing upon which Gaboriau really fastened was Poe's mention of mathematics and logic, and here Gaboriau helped Poe pull off what is probably his grandest hoax. In all of the Dupin tales, Poe tosses the term mathematics around pretty freely. Minister D—is a mathematician, and Dupin often mentions mathematics too. "The Mystery of Marie Roget" seems to contain all sorts of mathematical ramifications when Poe introduces the term "calculus of probabilities." Poe, however, did not mean anything abstruse or difficult by this. Dupin succeeds as a detective because he is a genius and not because he can compute. Most of the mathematical business in Poe, in fact, came from his experience playing cards and the lower mathematics which he read about in *Hoyle's Games Improved* (like how to figure the odds while counting tricks at whist). Gaboriau, of course, knew nothing of this, and finding the terms "mathematics" and "calculus" in Poe, built for his detectives a fancy structure of mathematics and academic logic. In this connection, it is significant that Gaboriau developed for Lecoq a second past as a mathematician's assistant after he dropped the thief-taker tie with Vidocq. His detectives, in fact, more often speak like academicians than like gumshoes. They approach reason as a machine which will produce the criminal: vacuum the material evidence into the nozzle and the inevitability of logic takes over. It is almost Baconian. Listen to the sort of thing Tirauclair thinks in *L'Affaire Lerouge*:

Rapidly he analyzed the situation. Had he been deceived in his investigations? No. Had his calculations of probabilities been erroneous? No. He had started from a positive fact, the murder. He had discovered the particulars; his inferences were correct, and must inevitably point to a criminal as he had indicated.

We know where Gaboriau got "calculations of probabilities;" here, however, he extends it into a whole process of induction, consciously, methodically, and carefully done. Poe would have thought this very funny, but later writers did not. They simply adopted it for their detective heroes, and it took up to sixty years before detective writers could loosen up enough to acknowledge that other parts of human intelligence worked as well or better than pure reason and that reason could not be understood by reference to mechanical analogies.

While Gaboriau derived the substance of the detective's intellectual processes from his reinterpretation of hints in Poe, from the very beginning he perceived that to be a popular literary character, the detective needed not only intelligence but also attractive humanizing traits. He realized Dupin's mental qualities might be able to impress readers, but they lacked points of contact with ordinary life which so often draw readers to literary creations. So with Tirauclair, Gaboriau tried to compensate for the over-intellectual bias of the genius by coupling it with sentiment and semi-comic absent-mindedness. Thus, in *L'Affaire Lerouge*, we witness not only the detective's mechanical logic, but also his impatience, comic abstraction, and intense depression when logic leads him to identify as a criminal a man whom he loved as a son. In *Le Crime d'Orcival*, Gaboriau made a concerted attempt to give his detective, Lecoq, a Dickensian coloring. As Inspector Bucket in *Bleak House* holds dialogues with his forefinger in the way of an amusing idiosyncrasy, here Lecoq periodically communes with the portrait of a "very homely, well-dressed woman" on the lid of the comfit box that he carries with him. Much later in the same novel, we discover that Lecoq's housekeeper, Janouille, is a former convict who possesses so much brawn that she is capable of strangling an assassin disguised as a porter who tries to insinuate himself into Lecoq's headquarters. She sounds a good bit like Jaggers' servant, Molly, in *Great Expectations*. Echoing his obsession with sentiment in his non-detective characters, Gaboriau adds to these derivative bits of whimsey Lecoq's alluring but headstrong mistress, Nina Gypsy. Finally, in order to heighten the suspense quotient in his novels, Gaboriau creates for Lecoq his own headquarters from which he directs his corps of agents and changes into his myriad disguises, and which his enemies try to penetrate in order to do him dirty.

Along with establishing certain features of the detective hero, Gaboriau had something to do with the change in attitude toward crime and criminals which made the detective story possible. As we have seen, Dickens struggled with his moral outrage in his presentation of villains. When someone commits a crime, the heavens lower and conscience pricks the soul of the offender. Collins moves away from moral outrage in two directions. First, he uses the criminal hero in Count Fosco, and then in *The Moonstone*, he obscures the culprit and thereby disposes of any need to deal with his conscience. In his treatment of villains, Gaboriau resembles Collins rather than Dickens. He, in fact, combines the Master Criminal and the obscured culprit, a coupling which is not and cannot be altogether happy. At any rate, Gaboriau's villains commit their outrages without turning a hair. They have a real spark of genius about them which we can see in their construction of crimes which almost baffle the genius detective. Two social developments in France brought Gaboriau to portray this new kind of character. The first was Gaboriau's attitude, and his public's attitude, toward the old aristocracy. Many of Gaboriau's villains are aristocrats gone wrong. When an aristocrat goes bad, he tells his readers, he brings with him the self-confidence and effrontery which has been drummed into noblemen for so long it virtually alters their genes. Thus the aristocrat, or usually the aristocrat's younger brother, can survive police tricks designed to cow peasants. This provides one line to Gaboriau's conscienceless criminals. The other line came from the Bourse. Gaboriau, like other Frenchmen in the mid-nineteenth century, saw the constant bursting of financial bubbles. He knew all about wheeler-dealers setting up bogus companies and absconding with other people's money. Unlike others, however, Gaboriau could do something about this. He could write about it, and he made the financial manipulator into the second type of major villain in his novels. Often he joins the banker and the blackmailer, transforming the swindler into a new sort of villain—one who can, at the same time, ruin you and go to your club. All of this ups the ante of crime fiction. Gaboriau's novels sometimes pit innocent victims against seemingly gigantic foes, and they consequently deal with the detective's uncovering of some sort of grand coup with millions upon millions of francs at stake. All of this moves away from the English obsession, voiced in the sensation novel, with the idea that women cannot handle either money or circumstance and become easy prey to conscienceless villains. With this sort of villain, Gaboriau brings us to the brink of the story centering on the detective's prevention of the villain's well-laid schemes, as well as uncovering his past crimes.

It all sounds as if it should be pretty thrilling fare. Here is Gaboriau with an attractive, energetic, and brilliant detective hero, with atmosphere which gives the feel of the *Palais de Justice* and isolation cells, and with all of the makings of the hidden culprit as well as the Master Criminal. But Gaboriau's novels are not thrilling. For modern readers, his books are tedious in the extreme. This seems all the more strange when we recall that Gaboriau was a serial writer. Serial writing, however, did not mean the same thing to Gaboriau as it did to Dickens or Collins. The English writers possessed a collection of techniques, large and small, to provoke interest, to create suspense, and to shift suspicion from one character to another. Gaboriau, on the other hand, used only a few larger, structural methods for generating interest and semi-intellectual involvement on the part of his readers. Further, his most important detective novels develop from middle to beginning to end, and this kind of organization, especially when coupled with Gaboriau's absorption in sentiment, fails when compared to the pattern of middle, end, beginning which became the standard for the detective story.

At the opening and closing of his novels, Gaboriau essentially wrote detective stories. This was something of a revolution in long fiction. To a large extent, earlier writers like Lytton and Dickens used detective materials chiefly to supply secondary plots for novels which had purposes other than the depiction of detection. Thus they embedded detective episodes in the bodies of their novels, and these provide neither the beginning nor the ending of the major narrative. The fate of Jonas Chuzzlewit does not begin or end *Martin Chuzzlewit*. Even *The Moonstone* does not quite end when the problem has been solved. Most earlier writers used detective material to make character points in the middle of their novels. Gaboriau, on the other hand, typically begins the story with the crime problem and the presentation of material facts connected with the crime. Usually, hayseed officials and mole-eyed policemen look at the scene of the crime and draw improper conclusions from insufficient evidence. The detective then enters and finds all of the clues, upon which he bases preliminary hypotheses which turn out, much later, to be correct. Here Gaboriau does the same thing as Poe by beginning the detective story in the middle of the chronology of the crime. With this kind of opening, however, Gaboriau needs to turn the plot somehow. If he does not tack the plot in another direction, he will end up with a short story and not a novel. In several cases, he strings out the detective story by inventing a conspiracy to stymie the detective and keep the truth hidden. Most often, however, he introduces a long, sentimental story which has only the most tenuous connection to the explanation of the facts in the detective plot. This inserted story usually treats the adolescence or exposes the youthful peccadilloes of an aristocrat. Here we have the beginning of the traditional story: the narrative which discusses the causes which lead to the crime. But Gaboriau invariably dwells far too long on this part of the narrative and thereby vitiates the force of his novels. After telling the inserted story—which is, in fact, the thematic core of his novels—Gaboriau gives his readers a surprise at the end spiced with a bit of physical danger involved in the capture of the criminal. This is the end of the normal narrative. Although Gaboriau alters the usual pattern of the detective story by the length of his inserted narratives, he does, nevertheless, save a surprise for the end of the plot. He is, in other words, a genuine detective story writer. For his surprises, however, Gaboriau too often depended on mistaken identity or upon the outrage of a cuckolded husband. His surprises grew out of decrepit romance formulas like the announcement that someone is, or is not, the lost child who caused all of the trouble. In all, Gaboriau did advance detective story plots. He made the detective short story of Poe into the detective novel. By splitting open Poe's detective tale, however, he not only moved the surprise from the three-quarter pole to the final chapters (an alteration which can actually help the movement of a detective story), but he also transplanted a gooey mass of palpitating tissue, in the form of the inserted story, to the central parts of the novel. Even though the next generation of detective writers had Collins' pattern to follow, it took the detective novel until the twentieth century to break away from the pattern of construction evolved by Gaboriau.

In spite of his weaknesses, Gaboriau made real contributions to the evolution of the detective story. He combined Poe, Vidocq, and Dickens to form a more complete version of the detective hero. He forecasted certain motifs of the police procedural novel and contributed to the complex history of the Master Criminal. Finally, he invented one way of making detective stories cover the distance of the novel. Gaboriau, of course, stimulated the growth of the detective story in France, but he also stimulated the development of the detective story in Britain and America. Between 1871 and 1886, almost all of his novels appeared in English translations. Fortuitously, this was the same period when the sensation writers ran out of steam. If, in the 1870s and 1880s, people wanted to read about crime and detectives, they had few alternatives other than Gaboriau. If people wanted to write about crime and detectives they, likewise, had to start with Gaboriau. Thus, when Fergus Hume set about to write his popular book, *The Mystery of a Hansom Cab* (1886)—a book which also served to summarize detective literature— he asked a "bookseller what style of book he sold most of. He replied the works of Gaboriau had a large sale." So Hume started from Gaboriau. Writers of dime novels in the United States also started from Gaboriau. More important than this, Arthur Conan Doyle set to work on Gaboriau, too. In 1887, therefore, when *Beeton's Christmas Annual* appeared, Doyle's creation eclipsed its source, and the world of detective fiction belonged to Sherlock Holmes.

# Chapter 7

# Doyle

When people read the Sherlock Holmes stories in the 1890s, they lived in a world radically different from that pictured by Collins, the sensation writers, or Gaboriau. In the old world, crime writers had to blush and apologize for introducing detectives, the crimes in fiction usually involved the rich and powerful, and the main concern of everyone involved was how to cover things up. Although a few atavistic twinges of these things remain in the Sherlock Holmes stories, Doyle wrote of a new world. In Doyle, people accept the fact that whenever a crime occurs, the police will be involved, and in the stories both the powerful and the humble seek out Holmes and Watson to air their problems before them. In Doyle, too, we get away from crime among the aristocrats. Holmes takes a high hand with the nabobs and robber barons who come to him and, in general, concentrates on the problems of the modest middle-class. Finally, Doyle, through his fictional narrator, takes it as a given that the public has a right to know about crime, criminals, policemen, and detectives.

These changes in detective fiction occurred because the world changed drastically between the 1860s and the 1890s. All sorts of technological innovations, such as electric lights and telephones, began to make life easier in Britain, and life also became more egalitarian and open. Part of this came about because of the reforms of the late Victorian era. Not only did mechanical innovations like the linotype revolutionize printing at the end of the nineteenth century, but labor laws and the Education Act of 1870 also broadened the reading public. Whereas in the 1860s, popular fiction and "best sellers" hardly existed, in the 1880s and 1890s they reshaped the world of publishing and the reading habits of millions. Add to this the facts that in the late 1880s Jack the Ripper was painting Whitechapel red and the Fenians were planting bombs even at Scotland Yard, and it is easy to see why the public asked not, why do we need snooping policemen, but, why aren't the police doing anything? Late in the 1880s, the public was ready for a new variety detective story and the editors were ready to publish anything which caught the public's fancy. It was, therefore, lucky that few people in Southsea chose to avail themselves of the medical services of young Arthur Conan Doyle (1859-1930).

Doyle always wanted to be a writer. Even during his medical apprenticeship, he began to write stories for the burgeoning Victorian periodical market. These started with "The Mystery of Sasassa Valley" (1879) in *Chambers*, and included pieces in *Cornhill Magazine* and *Boys' Own Paper*. By the time he opened his medical practice in Southsea, Doyle had written a novel, *The Firm of Girdlestone*, which publishers persisted in sending back to him. Then, in 1886, Doyle wrote a skimpy novel, or a hefty short story, entitled *A Study in Scarlet*. Because *A Study in Scarlet* introduced Sherlock Holmes, people endlessly asked the writer about its conception. In *The Westminster Gazette* of 13 December 1900, he emphasized plot:

> At the time I first thought of a detective...I had been reading detective stories, and it struck me what nonsense they were, to put it mildly, because for getting to the solution of the mystery, the authors always depended on some coincidence. This struck me as not a fair way of playing the game, because the detective ought really to depend for his successes on something in his own mind and not on merely adventitious circumstances which do not, by any means, always occur in real life.

Twenty-four years later, in his autobiography, *Memories and Adventures*, Doyle emphasized character as the motive for *A Study in Scarlet*:

> Gaboriau had rather attracted me by the neat dove-tailing of his plots, and Poe's masterful detective, M. Dupin, had from my boyhood been one of my heroes. But could I bring an addition of my own? I thought of my old teacher, Joe Bell, of his eagle face, of his curious ways, of his eerie trick of spotting details...It was all very well to say that a man is clever, but the reader wants to see examples as Bell gave us every day in the wards. The idea amused me. What should I call the fellow?...First it was Sherringford Holmes then it was Sherlock Holmes. He could not tell his own exploits, so he must have a commonplace comrade as a foil...A drab, quiet name for this unostentatious man. Watson would do. So I had my puppets and wrote my *Study in Scarlet*.

Whether Doyle got his idea for *A Study in Scarlet* as a reaction to story-telling or from his detective character, he wrote the book and began the soul-destroying job of sending it around to publishers. A handful sent it back to him until Mrs. G.T. Bettany recommended the manuscript to her husband. He recommended it to Ward, Lock & Company, which demurred at publishing the novel as a separate edition because of its brevity, but included it in the 1887 edition of the omnibus *Beeton's Christmas Annual*. Not many people noticed *Beeton's Christmas Annual*, and Doyle himself turned to writing historical novels, first *Micah Clarke* (1889) and then *The White Company* (1891). Meanwhile Stoddart, the American editor of *Lippincott's Magazine* (published in England by Ward, Lock), contracted with Doyle for another Sherlock Holmes novel. While working away at *The White*

*Company*, the author dashed off *The Sign of the Four* (1890). Appearing in *Lippincott's*, *The Sign of the Four*, like its predecessor, was not remarkable for its success.

Although Doyle held out great hopes for himself as a historical novelist, he continued to tinker with Sherlock Holmes and the detective story. Since his slim novels still ran counter to the accepted three-volume format, Doyle decided to change his vehicle. Early in 1891, he says

> It struck me that a single character running through...[a] series, if it engaged the attention of the reader, would bind that reader to that particular magazine...Clearly the compromise [to the serial novel] was a character which carried through, and yet installments which were each complete in themselves...I believe I was the first to realize this.

Of course, Poe realized this a long time before Doyle did, and so did Dickens. At this point, at any rate, Doyle decided to write short stories with Holmes as the hero. He wrote six Holmes stories, beginning with "A Scandal in Bohemia" (July 1891). His agent, A.P. Watt, sent them to Greenhough Smith, the editor of *The Strand Magazine*. Several things were in Doyle's favor here. First of all, in the 1890s the short story was a relatively new form in Britain. Second, Doyle hit the beginning of the rage for the popular illustrated magazine. *The Strand* was an aggressive magazine, fashioned to capture readers by including some kind of illustration on every page. Finally, Doyle was fortunate that Smith chose Sidney Paget to illustrate his stories. All of these things combined with Doyle's fusion and fission of detective story elements and made the first Holmes stories immensely successful. Naturally, *The Strand* knew they had a winner. As the first stories began to appear, Smith wrote to Doyle for more Holmes stories. Thinking himself as a historical novelist, Doyle at first declined but then asked *The Strand* for fifty pounds a story, a price he considered exorbitant. Smith, however, agreed and Doyle contracted to write six more stories, beginning with "The Blue Carbuncle" (January 1892), a Christmas piece. Originally, Doyle thought of killing Holmes off in the twelfth story: "I think," he wrote to his mother, "of slaying Holmes in the last and winding him up for good and all, He takes my mind from better things." This shocked his mother. "You won't! You can't! You mustn't!" she wrote to him, and she sent him a story idea which she cribbed from *The Woman in White* and which Doyle converted into "Copper Beeches" (June 1892).

*The Strand* ran the first twelve Sherlock Holmes stories from July 1891 to June 1892, and then George Newnes, the founder of the magazine, published them as *The Adventures of Sherlock Holmes* (1892). In February 1892, as the first series of Holmes stories was running out, *The Strand* began begging Doyle for more. He "offered to do a dozen more for a thousand pounds," but hoped this figure would put them off. It did not, and after

Doyle took a short break, "Silver Blaze" appeared in December 1892. At the end of these twelve stories, Doyle reduced Holmes and Moriarity to strawberry jam on the rocks of the Reichenbach Falls in "The Final Problem" (December 1893), so he could devote himself to other things. Newnes published the second twelve stories as *The Memoirs of Sherlock Holmes* (1894), but that did not help *The Strand*. The magazine wanted more Holmes tales, or lacking that, more detective stories. When their Holmes stories ran out, therefore, they put in this notice:

> There will be a temporary interval in the Sherlock Holmes stories. A new series will continue in an early number. Meanwhile, powerful detective stories will be contributed by other eminent writers.

Doyle's first twenty-four Sherlock Holmes stories created such a demand they turned people into detective story writers overnight, and started the continuing development of the detective story. Doyle, however, wanted nothing to do with it.

From 1894 until 1901, Doyle ignored Holmes and Watson. He fed *The Strand* stories about Brigadier Gerard, his continuing character from the Napoleonic wars; worked on plays and historical novels; travelled to America; and volunteered for service in the Boer War. Out of the last experience, he wrote *The Great War* (1900), and *The War in South Africa: its Causes and Conduct* (1902), which led to his knighthood in 1902. In 1901, because he picked up some provocative material about Dartmoor, he revived Holmes for his third detective novel, *The Hound of the Baskervilles* (August 1901 to April 1902). This got him back on the Holmes track, and, beginning with "The Adventure of the Empty House" (September 1903), thirteen new stories came out in *The Strand*, collected in *The Return of Sherlock Holmes* (1905). After the detective returned to life, Doyle wrote an occasional Holmes story for *The Strand* until the beginning of the Great War. During the war, he wrote *The Valley of Fear* (September 1914 to May 1915), based on shop talk with the American detective William J. Burns, and he also wrote "His Last Bow: the War Service of Sherlock Holmes" (September 1917). Between 1921 and 1927, he wrote twelve more stories for *The Strand* which became *The Case Book of Sherlock Holmes* (1927). There were no more stories about Holmes. Publishers wanted them, the public wanted them, but Doyle did not. He spent his last years thinking and writing about spiritualism, one of his life-long passions.

Just as the Sherlock Holmes stories mark the real beginning of the detective story as a continuing popular literary form, they also present real difficulties. First of all, Doyle wrote the Holmes tales over a period of forty years, from 1887 to 1927. During this span, human technology and social organization changed mightily. None of this affects the Holmes stories. Doyle is purposefully anachronistic and the stories written in the 1920s are set in the 1890s. For Holmes, the Russian revolution, the Great War (with one story excepted), manned flight, and myriad other changes in the culture never happened. Along with the world's transformation, the detective story changed too. Doyle began writing when Gaboriau was in vogue, and he continued to write Holmes stories well after Christie created Poirot, Sayers invented Wimsey, and American writers introduced the hard-boiled detective story. Further, even at his best, Doyle wrote very casually. After the first spurt of tales, he had to be bribed to continue writing detective stories. Doyle was, in fact, always sloppy about details—when he wrote "A Scandal in Bohemia," for example, he forgot he had named Holmes' landlady Mrs. Hudson—and cavalierly added and subtracted traits from Holmes as he progressed with the stories. Doyle's sloppiness, to be sure, has provided a lot of entertainment for Baker Street Irregulars and other Holmes fans, but it certainly stands in the way of a careful assessment of the Sherlock Holmes canon and the importance of Doyle's contribution to the development of the detective story.

The Sherlock Holmes stories start from Poe. Doyle freely and frequently acknowledged this and noted in one statement that he was not alone in his borrowings: "If every man who received a cheque for a story which owed its springs to Poe were to pay a tithe to a monument for the master, he would have a pyramid as big as that of Cheops." This being the case, Doyle would have had to finance a couple of courses of dressed stone near the base. As many people have recognized, the Holmes stories owed much of their popularity to the fact that they were short stories. This Doyle owed to Poe. But, he streamlines Poe's short stories. His essential Victorianism made him embarrassed about metaphysics, and his desire to be popular caused him to remove the abstruse. These things led him to eliminate Poe's lectures as well as his gropings for the great beyond and, as a consequence, Doyle brought the detective story closer to pure narrative than Poe's Dupin stories. Doyle also borrowed Poe's point of view. In the years between Poe and Doyle, with the exception of Collins, most detective writers used conventional third or first person points of view. Doyle, of course, realized the uses for plot and characterization of the detective's assistant as the narrator: the writer can use the narrator's ignorance to hide important facts and through him can praise the detective and keep him civilly reticent at the same time. Ever since Doyle introduced his narrator, this sort of figure in a detective story has been called a Watson, but, of course, Doyle borrowed the technique from Poe. Like this one, many motifs in the Holmes stories depend on Poe: the police versus the amateur, the detective's conceit, and so on. When Holmes interrupts Watson's thoughts, as he does in "The Cardboard Box" (January 1893) and "The Dancing Men" (December 1903), Doyle makes him acknowledge Dupin as the source of this dramatic but irritating bit of mental showmanship. Building Holmes on Poe's model, in fact, got Doyle tangled up in his own Victorianism. In Poe, we find a good bit of material on the Bi-Part Soul and the essential duality of genius, if not human nature. Dupin and Legrand both have spells, vital to the solution of the problems in the tales, where their eyes go blank and they go drifting off into other worlds and other seas. When Doyle introduced Holmes in *A Study in Scarlet*, he tried to come to grip with Holmes' genius in a chapter entitled "The Science of Deduction." Before mentioning that Holmes has written an article proving the observant person can reach conclusions "as infallible as so many propositions of Euclid" (thereby bringing in the coupling of math and deduction, itself derived from Poe), Doyle states that Holmes goes off into Dupin-like trances:

> ...for days on end he would lie upon the sofa in the sitting-room, hardly uttering a word or moving a muscle from morning to night. On occasions I have noticed such a dreamy, vacant expression in his eyes that I might have suspected him of being addicted to the use of some narcotic, had not the temperance and cleanliness of his whole life forbidden such a notion.

Doyle, however, immediately regretted this connection of Holmes with the inexplicable, ineffable, transcendent realm. He drew back from Poe's concept of genius, and in the second novel, *The Sign of the Four*, Doyle associated Holmes with the Decadents and made him a cocaine addict. Thereafter, Holmes' lassitude associates him with the Victorian theme of work, as well as with the Lotus Eaters, and moves away from the inexplicable realms hinted at by Poe's romanticism. Too late, Doyle realized the cocaine was a tactical error and he had to cure Holmes of his drug addiction by the time of the second set of stories.

If Doyle could not handle Poe's themes, he certainly could and did handle Poe's plot details. All of the cipher stories—"The Musgrave Ritual" (May 1893), "The Gloria Scott" (April 1893), and "The Dancing Men"— depend on "The Gold Bug." The treasure hunt business in "The Musgrave Ritual" likewise comes from Poe's tale. Holmes' device of inserting an ad in the newspaper and capturing the criminal who answers it (used in *A Study in Scarlet*, "Black Peter" [March 1904], "Abbey Grange" [September 1904], and elsewhere) goes directly back to Dupin's practice at the end of "The Murders in the Rue Morgue." More than anything else, Poe's signal importance for Doyle's detective stories is the fact that when he turned from the novel to the short story, he went immediately to "The Purloined Letter" for the plot of "A Scandal in Bohemia." Without Poe, Doyle might have given us Holmes in love as a contrast and sequel to Watson in love in *The Sign of the Four*. This, of course, is something we do not have to worry about. Doyle had absorbed enough Poe to be able to put the guts into his detective stories.

While Holmes grudgingly admits Dupin "had some analytical genius," in the next full paragraph of *A Study in Scarlet* he insists "Lecoq was a miserable bungler." He well may have been, but Doyle certainly cribbed enough from Gaboriau to give him higher marks. By Cooper out of Gaboriau, Doyle derived much of Holmes' tracking ability, and tracking constitutes a great deal of Doyle's detective stories. In the Holmes stories, Doyle pays little attention to modern criminology. Instead, almost all of the Holmes stories center on Holmes following the spoor or complaining the trail has been ruined by the impress of flat feet. We can track this motif from *A Study in Scarlet* through to the last stories. In one case, Holmes even uses plaster of Paris to preserve footprints. He imported all of this pretty directly from Gaboriau. Along these same lines, in *The Sign of the Four*, "The Missing Three Quarter" (August 1904), and "Shoscombe Old Place" (April 1927), Holmes borrows dogs to help him in his detective work. For Doyle, this was only the logical extension of the stories' multitudinous comparisons of Holmes to dogs, from hounds to fox hounds to retrievers. Doyle certainly found the detective-dog connection in Gaboriau, but it works in a somewhat different manner in the Holmes tales. The French, after all, are not a doggy nation; the British are. Gaboriau's comparisons of Lecoq to a bloodhound are, therefore, only intellectual. Doyle's comparisons bring with them the full panoply of the "view halloa," the association of British squirearchy and sport. And these things Doyle never found in Gaboriau. He did, however, find the development of the notion of the detective as the mathematically accurate crime-solving machine. In the early works, Doyle makes Holmes an instrument for detection. Holmes, Doyle says, knows nothing of literature, philosophy, or astronomy, and little of politics. He fills his cranial attic only with those things which help him solve crimes. In the early stories, Doyle applies machine images to Holmes, and many pieces begin with Holmes' complaint that Watson should describe his cases as exercises in reason rather than sensational adventures. Most of this came from Gaboriau, and Doyle, to his credit, got it out of his system pretty quickly. In the later stories, Holmes freely quotes literature from Shakespeare to Carlyle, and in his retirement he settles down not only to bee-keeping but also to the study of philosophy. By the time of the "Naval Treaty" (October, November 1893), Holmes can say "What a lovely thing a rose is!" Doyle wrote Holmes out of the world of machines and toward the world of human beings. An analogous process goes on with Holmes' use of disguise, again something which Doyle borrowed from Gaboriau. In the early stories, Holmes, like Lecoq, plays a number of costumed roles. By the time of "The Reigate Squires" (June 1893), Holmes has dispensed with the wig and grease paint and become a method actor.

With all of these elements, Doyle goes beyond Gaboriau because he adapts the ideas to his culture and his sense of the fitness of things makes an interesting narrative. He does, however, borrow a couple of specific incidents from the Frenchman. The idea of the dirty prisoner in "The Man with the Twisted Lip" (December 1891) comes directly from *Monsieur Lecoq,* and Holmes' observation about wine glasses in "Abbey Grange" depends on an incident in *The Mystery of Orcival.* These things, like the character points, stimulated Doyle's imagination and helped him make his detective and his detective stories. He completely misjudged, however, the aesthetic suitability of Gaboriau's narrative structure. As late as 1924, Doyle spoke about the "neat dove-tailing" of Gaboriau's plots. Breaking apart a detective plot to insert a sentimental narrative did not prove to be a fit way to create a detective novel. Following Gaboriau's narrative pattern went a long way toward ruining *A Study in Scarlet, The Sign of the Four,* and *The Valley of Fear,* in all of which he uses the inserted story to provide a yawning anti-climax. Doyle also used the inserted narrative in a number of short stories, like "The Gloria Scott" and "The Crooked Man" (July 1893). In the short stories, Doyle condensed the historical material to make it appropriate to the narrative form, and over a time reduced his reliance on Gaboriauesque insertions. It was fortunate, then, that Doyle discovered the short story form, for Gaboriau disabled him as a detective novelist. Tangentially related to Gaboriau, and directly connected to Doyle's success and the success of detective stories in general, is the fact that Doyle limited the subject matter of his stories. As we have seen, Gaboriau chose as one of his topics the murky and potentially frightening world of finance. Doyle, however, opted not to frighten his readers in this manner. In "The Reigate Squires," he makes Watson tell his readers they will find "no politics or finance" in the stories. Thus, although Holmes does handle a few spy cases ("The Naval Treaty," "The Bruce-Partington Plans" [December 1908], and "His Last Bow"), Doyle directs his detective stories away from disturbing or controversial public topics which might alienate readers. When he wishes to frighten his readers, he does so in the same ways English writers used from the days of Horace Walpole.

Doyle drew a good bit of his subject matter not from Gaboriau or Poe, but from Collins and the sensation novelists. Some of this shows up in his use of the Indian material in *The Sign of the Four* and "The Crooked Man." His dependence on sensation novel material, however, comes through more clearly in his use of the larger than life, gothic master criminal, as well as his frequent returns to the theme of inheritance. Holmes confronts powerfully evil men, of course, in "The Final Problem" and "The Empty House," but Professor Moriarty and Colonel Moran owe a bit more to Gaboriau than they do to the English tradition of villainy. This is not the case with "The Speckled Band" (February 1892) or "Copper Beeches."

Grimesby Roylott in the former story owes much to the villain of the sensation novel, and in fact this story of a locked-room murder harkens back to *Uncle Silas*. Even more clearly, Jethro Runcastle in "Copper Beeches" is Doyle's remake of Count Fosco from *The Woman in White*: both are fat, jovial, threatening, and very bad. The later Holmes story, "The Disappearance of Lady Frances Carfax" (December 1911), reproduces the essentials of Collins' first sensation novel, with the substitution of persons, the larger than life villain, and the law's inability to prevent the crime. Going from these particular motifs of the sensation novel, we find underneath many of the short stories Doyle introduces the sensation novel assumption that thrilling fiction can be made from the thesis that women cannot handle their own affairs, and especially cannot deal with any sort of inheritance. Thus, "The Speckled Band," "Copper Beeches," "A Case of Identity" (September 1891), and "The Solitary Cyclist" (January 1904), all build on a helpless woman receiving an inheritance which the wolves and jackals of the world will snap up unless true and chivalrous men stop them.

Up to this point, all of Doyle's sources are natural and obvious, given the history of the detective story. In the 1880s, anyone could have combined Poe, Gaboriau, and the sensation novelists to form the next step in the evolution of the detective story. Not everyone, however, could have added Joseph Bell (1837-1911) to the formula. Dr. Joseph Bell, a consulting surgeon to the Royal Infirmary and Royal Hospital for Sick Children, was one of Doyle's teachers when he attended medical school in Edinburgh. Shortly after he finished the first set of short stories about Holmes, Doyle wrote to Bell, acknowledging his debt to him:

> It is most certainly to you that I owe Sherlock Holmes...I do not think that his analytical work is in the least an exaggeration of some effects which I seen you produce in the out-patient wards.

Holmes' background in Joe Bell provides a fair amount of what is unique in him. To some extent, Doyle based Holmes' appearance on the lean-faced, hawk-nosed Bell, but this is difficult to argue since Doyle does not detail Holmes' appearance and his illustrator, Paget, established the popular notion of Holmes' looks using his brother as a model. More significant than this, Doyle drew Holmes' deduction demonstrations from Bell. Almost all of the Holmes stories begin, not with a crime, but with a curtain raiser in which Holmes demonstrates his powers of observation and analytical skill. Watson's shoes, hat, watch, and fingers all provide material for seemingly outlandish and magical assertions which Holmes proceeds to explain as simply routine results of methodical looking and thinking. This kind of "You have been in Afghanistan, I perceive," is the sort of thing Joe Bell used to do in the wards—telling patients about themselves and their ailments before they had a chance to announce where it hurt. Doyle's readers, as shown in countless parodies, clearly thought this analytical skill provided much of what was fascinating and valuable about Holmes.

Almost as important for Holmes' character as the deduction demonstrations is the fact that Doyle modelled Holmes on a physician. In his first draft of *A Study in Scarlet*, Doyle jotted down that Holmes was to be "a consulting detective." Even though Doyle threw out some of his original ideas for his protagonist, he kept the notion of Holmes as a consulting detective. This came from Bell, who was a medical consultant, as well as from Doyle's own work as a physician. Thus, in the stories and novels when Lestrade, Gregson, and assorted other Scotland Yarders run up against a case they cannot diagnose or cure, they call in Holmes, just as the perplexed general practitioner summons a consultant when he finds an ailment beyond his skill and power. Although in the later stories Doyle eases out of this concept, making Holmes simply a private detective and in the 1920s giving him a rudimentary agency, the concept of the consultant operated in the early ones. Indeed, it may have given Doyle the idea for Holmes' Baker Street rooms. Baker Street is only a stethoscope's throw away from Harley Street. The background as a physician, moreover, contributed several other things to Doyle's fashioning of his detective. On occasion, he metaphorically describes Holmes as a physician (in "Charles Augustus Milverton" [April 1904] and "Abbey Grange"), he introduces us to Holmes at St. Bartholomew's hospital, and in "The Beryl Coronet" (May 1892) he even gives the character something of a bedside manner. Holmes' constant references to historical criminal cases in the early stories smacks more of a physician reading *The Lancet* than a policeman reading *The Police Gazette*. Finally, in the last series of stories, Doyle virtually turns Holmes into a physician. Holmes diagnoses a case of leprosy in "The Blanched Soldier" (November 1926), traces peculiar behavior to monkey-gland shots in "The Creeping Man" (March 1923), and straightens out a case of poisoning and sibling rivalry in "The Sussex Vampire" (January 1924).

But Doyle derived more for Holmes from his recollections of Joe Bell than the logical diagnoses and other qualities of a physician. Bell was also a teacher and so in many ways is Holmes. We tend to forget, in these days of "that's right, but" and "that's certainly an interesting idea," that simpler times viewed humiliation and abuse as valuable ways of motivating students. Part of what Doyle put into Holmes, as a result of either using his old professor, or professors in general, is some marked pedagogical characteristics. Holmes teaches and has plenty of scholars. Doyle specifically tells us that detective Stanley Hopkins in "Black Peter" has "the respect of a pupil" for Holmes and his methods. Watson in "Abbey Grange" listens to Holmes "like an interested student who observes the demonstration of his professor," and even Lestrade in "The Norwood Builder" (November 1903) has an air of "a child asking questions of its teacher." During the course of the stories, Doyle creates for Holmes passages which can only be described as lectures—thus the cryptography material in "The Dancing Men" and the walk-through geometry lesson in "The Musgrave Ritual." In this same category come the various tests Holmes administers to Watson. Watson squeaks out a gentleman's C in the quiz about the hat in "The Blue Carbuncle," but here the importance of the test resides not in the experience itself but in that Holmes feels impelled to point out Watson's errors and to show him how to do the thing correctly. Holmes' professorial qualities show through in his little monographs, like the famous one on tobacco ash or the one about human ears mentioned in "The Cardboard Box." They also appear in his running argument with Watson about the nature of Watson's narratives. Holmes, again and again, wants the narratives to be didactic, stressing the intellectual side rather than the less dignified sensational elements incidental to crime and detection. Doyle wisely makes Watson decline to do this, but as a compensation and as intellectual veneer, he places considerable stress on the professorial qualities of Holmes. This may be, in fact, one of the secrets of the character. What we view as endearing grumpiness and delightful perversity in our teachers (usually in retrospect), becomes in unemployed geniuses like Dupin or upstart policemen like Lecoq a royal pain.

The Holmes stories also have some definite and persistent connections with the entrenched ideas about detectives and policemen as a class. As I noted at the beginning of this chapter, people, all sorts of people, willingly take their problems, trivial ones as well as big ones, to Holmes. This is a far cry from Walter's refusal to consult the police in *The Woman in White*. We find, in fact, a reversal of the detective's position shown in Gaboriau. In *L'Affaire Lerouge*, Papa Tabaret fears his friends will not shake his hand if they discover his detective activity, but in "Scandal in Bohemia" Holmes has enough self-assurance to refuse the proffered hand of the King of Bohemia. Part of this new attitude toward detectives occurs because toward the end of the century Scotland Yard and the reorganized C.I.D. established their legitimacy and competence. Part of it, too, came from the fact that Doyle was a physician. People are more helpless, honest, and willing when they visit a physician, particularly a high-powered consultant, than they are when they visit a lawyer. Here Doyle's own experience differed from that of the lawyer-writers of the last generation. Nevertheless, throughout the stories, Doyle constantly brings up the issue of the detective's discretion. Doyle's mention of royalty in two of the first three short stories serves partly to demonstrate that Holmes has been discreet for the crowned heads of Europe. He carries this theme through "The Missing Three Quarter", and in his efforts to demonstrate Holmes' sensitivity, he goes a long way toward destroying the story. The discretion theme in Doyle carries over a century's worth of fear that the police will not respect individual privacy. With the theme of discretion, of course, Doyle has to have it two ways: he is, after all, telling about the detective's locked lips at the same time he details his cases for the public. Doyle throws a sop in the direction of professional propriety by having Holmes protest against the publication of his cases, by Watson's conscious limitation to old cases in which the participants are all dead, and by telling us, in some stories, the real names have been changed. In the majority of the cases, especially those like "The Second Stain" (December 1904) and "The Noble Bachelor" (April 1892) involving important persons, Doyle appeals to the public's voyeuristic tastes. He realized, as did other late Victorian writers and publishers, the number of people who like to read gossip was far larger than the number who become the subject of gossip. This attitude reflects a major cultural shift and it, in turn, has its effect upon the tone of Doyle's detective stories. In *Caleb Williams*, detection is the stuff of tragedy. For some of Doyle's early stories, too, detection specifically touches on something akin to traditional tragedy: "The Boscombe Valley Mystery" (October 1891) and "The Five Orange Pips" (November 1891) pointedly use the term "tragic" and bring in judgment from weightier realms than mere human justice. As the Holmes stories progress, however, Doyle uses "tragedy" in its loose sense, meaning anything shockingly depressing, and he concentrates instead on writing detective stories which will appeal to and gratify his readers.

Doyle inherited another police theme from all of the detective writers before him: the boob policeman. In his early works, official policemen display all sorts of truculent ignorance and wrong-headedness. They never see the truth and frequently want to arrest the wrong person. Gregson and Lestrade are, in the traditions of the detective story, the ignoramuses installed for Holmes to dally with as he finds the real facts. Doyle, over the years, changed this. Look at what happens to Lestrade. In *A Study in Scarlet*, he is stupid and, to use Doyle's word for him, ferret-like. Friston's illustration in *Beeton's Christmas Annual* shows him as a nasty little piece of work. By the time of "The Second Stain" (1904), however, Doyle describes him as having "bulldog features", and Paget's illustrations change accordingly. Between these two stories, too, Lestrade becomes more civil and humble, and Doyle introduces other policemen, like Stanley Hopkins, whom Holmes considers almost bright. By the time of "Wisteria Lodge" (September and October 1908), we find policemen like Inspector Baynes who arrives at the correct solution at the same time the Great Detective does. To some extent, then, Doyle worked himself out of the rut of the convention of stupid policemen— probably because there were manifest examples this was wrong. He proceeded from fantasy to occasional glimpses of reality.

With another traditional detective theme, Doyle worked the other way, towards fantasy instead of away from it. The genius detective, from Poe onward, is supposed to be infallible. Contrary to popular notions of the character, Holmes fails pretty often in the early cases. He fails with Irene Adler, he fails in "The Five Orange Pips," he fails in "The Engineer's Thumb" (March 1892), in "Cooper Beeches," and in a few other stories. Holmes assures Mrs. St. Clair her husband is dead in "The Man with the Twisted Lip," he tells Grant Munro his wife is being blackmailed in "Yellow Face" (February 1893), and so on. Hardly the great detective. Doyle even has Holmes talk to Watson about his errors in the introductions to several stories. Of course, Doyle is again having it both ways, and we forget about Holmes' incompetence when we read the stories, but the evidence is there nonetheless—in the early tales. Probably because of his need to create Moriarty to dispose of Holmes in 1893, and then because of the emergence of thriller writers like John Buchan, as well as the advent of World War I, Doyle moved gradually toward stories dealing with master criminals. As a response to this, and as a response to the efficiency latent and manifest in the early stories, Doyle made Holmes much more infallible in the later tales.

In the main, Doyle displays little interest in police work. Yet he wrote the Holmes stories at a time when modern, scientific criminology was aborning. This fascinated other writers and provided details for the lesser detective writers of the 1890s and early twentieth century, but it did not greatly inspire Doyle. At best, he gives Holmes only a wash of scientific criminology. In the first series of stories, Holmes frequently alludes to parallel historical cases, but, with the exception of Palmer and Pritchard mentioned in "The Speckled Band," Doyle made most of them up. As I have said before, Holmes' practice smacks a bit more of reading medical literature than it does of police work. While Doyle eases up on these historical citations in the stories collected in *The Memoirs*, he does seed chemistry throughout the whole canon. We see Holmes fiddling with beakers and retorts in a number of stories. Holmes' chemistry, however, has only an occasional connection to criminology. Mostly he precipitates this or that without concern for its detective application. In "The Adventure of the Empty House," in fact, Holmes spends some of the missing years studying coal tar dyes, suggesting he is more interested in making a million by inventing a new color than in devising criminological tests. This lackadasical attitude toward chemistry extends to the toxicology and medicine in the Holmes stories. Doyle did not care (nor, in justice, did his readers) whether the snake in "The Speckled Band" or the poison in "The Dying Detective" (December 1913) really existed. In spite of his professional training, Doyle was willing to introduce "brain fever" whenever he wanted a character out of the way, as in "The Cardboard Box" and "The Naval Treaty." If he was casual about things he should have known about, Doyle was downright unconcerned about actual advances in scientific criminology. Holmes may mention Bertillon, but, aside from "The Norwood Builder," fingerprints do not figure in the stories. Rather than reading up on crime and criminals, Doyle developed details for his detection from his own imagination, or from perfunctory reading of popular magazines like *The Strand*, where he got the idea about the disguised horseshoes he used in "The Priory School" (February 1904).

All of this casualness with his detective stories presents a reversal of Doyle's usual practice in his historical fiction. In books like *The White Company*, he attempted to make his background information as accurate as possible. This, however, he coupled with the most puerile of story lines. But in spite of their unfitness for adult consumption, Doyle's composition of historical novels does have a real impact on the Holmes stories. One of the reasons for Doyle's affection for Gaboriau lay in the fact that the Frenchman demonstrated the stuff of the historical novel could be levered into the detective story. With the exception of *The Hound of the Baskervilles*, Doyle included in the Holmes novels stories which carry us to past events in exotic places—granting, of course, that Utah and Pennsylvania are exotic. In the short stories, too, Doyle frequently hooks on an excursion into the past after Holmes has nabbed the criminal. One of the detective story's pulls on Doyle was as a medium for telling more than one story, usually the criminal's and the detective's. If we already have two, why not add a third story, a historical one? Not only, then, did Doyle find in the detective story an excuse for including small historical romances, he also found in his own historical novels a framework for characterizing the detective. The author, like his Victorian contemporaries, was caught up in the glamorization of chivalry, chivalry modulated by contemporary attitudes toward sexuality as well as by imperialism. Much of this comes out in *The White Company*, in which Doyle depicts his own hearty and healthy view of the Middle Ages. Fundamental to this historical romance, Doyle creates the ideal of the chivalric hero who is "fearless to the strong, humble to the weak, [and who dispenses] chivalry to all women...Help to the helpless, whosoever shall ask for it." This concept forms the character basis of the Holmes stories. We can see it, specifically, in "Charles Augustus Milverton:"

> The high object of our mission, the consciousness that it was unselfish and chivalrous, the villainous character of our opponent, all added to the sporting interest of the adventure...I knew that the opening of safes was a particular hobby with him [Holmes], and I understood the joy which it gave him to be confronted with this green and gold monster, the dragon which held in its maw the reputations of many fair ladies.

Doyle certainly heaps on the metaphors of knighthood in this passage, and, indeed, interpreting the stories in light of chivalry adds another necessary level to their meaning. In the first series of stories, four women bring their problems to Holmes because they have no one else to turn to. Only one of *The Adventures of Sherlock Holmes*, "The Engineer's Thumb," involves a healthy, intelligent, and active man. That is the "chivalry toward all women" and "help to the helpless." The knight's quality of being "fearless to the strong" shows up in Holmes' anti-aristocratic bias in stories from "Scandal in Bohemia" to "Mazarin Stone" (October 1921). In the first story, we can almost say Holmes accepts Irene Adler's photograph because he cannot get her scarf or her sleeve.

The chivalry Doyle transplanted from *The White Company* to his detective stories links up directly to the element in the Holmes stories coming from the Victorian schoolboy story and its reincarnation in the popular novels of Stevenson and Haggard. *A Study in Scarlet* resembles in many ways Stevenson's *Treasure Island* (1883) and H. Rider Haggard's *King Solomon's Mines* (1886). All of these novels aim what begins as a schoolboy story at a slightly older and more mature audience. The schoolboy story originated in periodicals, like *Boys' Own Paper*, and developed in novels like Hughes' *Tom Brown's Schooldays* (1857). These outlets dispensed exciting fiction for boys, but, specifically opposed to the Penny Dreadful of the early 1800s, fiction which inculcated morality into its pubescent readers. The schoolboy story was, in effect, the tool of imperialistic values. To appeal to schoolboys, however, this class of fiction adopted character patterns familiar to boys. Thus we endlessly find the teacher and his students along with the head boy and his fags. Doyle began his career as a writer doing pieces for *Boys' Own Paper*, and we have seen his exploitation of the teacher—student side of the Holmes-Watson relationship. The teacher-student pattern, in fact, is one Doyle could not escape, and he included it in the Sir Nigel stories as well as in the Professor Challenger pieces. In the Holmes stories, too, Doyle introduces a bit of fagging with Holmes acting as the superior older boy and Watson playing the awestruck, eager fag. Further, the manly virtues of the schoolboy story join with Doyle's sense of chivalry to produce Holmes' protection of the weak, his adherence to conscience and principle versus external law, and his independence when faced with the rich and powerful. Finally, Doyle's contemporaries rather quickly picked up the Holmes stories as means of instructing boys. That Baden-Powell suggested Boy Scout group leaders have their boys read Sherlock Holmes stories not only indicates the Victorian ratification of their ways of dealing with the material world, but testifies to their moral fitness for the Empire's leaders.

With the Holmes stories, however, Doyle purposely leaned far heavier on the *dulce* of adventure than on the *utile* of imperial morality or scientific method. The detective stories and novels may start with a gloss of the intellectual, but Doyle invariably ends with adventure. In part, Doyle wrote the Holmes tales out of protest against torpid contemporary fiction. When, in "The Boscombe Valley Mystery," Watson picks up a "yellow-backed novel," he quickly becomes bored with it and drops it in favor of thinking about the business at hand. The substance of the Holmes stories is not intellectual, but emotional. Doyle, of course, knew this and went as far as incorporating Holmes' complaint "you slur over work of the utmost finesse and delicacy in order to dwell upon sensational details which may excite but cannot possibly instruct the reader." For word counters, we can see the bias of the Holmes stories in the fact that *The Strand* labelled thirty-five of the stories as "adventures." And, even in the earliest stories, words like "strange," "unusual," "fantastic," and "singular" by far outnumber terms like "reason" and "deduce." Throughout, the hunt, the chase, the capture, and the shock of action mean more than the mental questions of detection. In "The Solitary Cyclist," in fact, Doyle comes right out and says the stories depend on "the ingenuity and dramatic quality of the solution."

When he discusses Holmes' mental powers, Doyle betrays amazing casualness even in the early stories. As with stalactites and stalagmites, he confuses the meanings of the terms induction and deduction. When Holmes or Mycroft tells us about a person or material object, they do not, strictly speaking, deduce anything (i.e. reason from general to specific). If anything, they use inductive reasoning and go from specific to general. To be sure, Doyle discovered the word "deduce" does not open up the possibility of confusion which turning inductive reasoning into a verb does: Holmes can hardly say "I induce you have been ill." At any rate, by the time of "The Six Napoleons" (May 1904), he does admit the detective uses "a connected chain of inductive reasoning." Although in the early stories Doyle makes a great deal out of Holmes as a thinking machine and puts particular stress on the detective's employment of strict methodology, most of the stories show not that Holmes reasons better, but that he observes better than anyone else. In one story, in fact, he specifically says observing is his trade. Thus, the solutions to many of the fictions begin with Holmes seeing things others have missed because he is a "scientific searcher." Coupled with these facts, Doyle put new emphasis on one of the traditional metaphors for the detective's activity. When Doyle started out as a detective writer, he picked up on the standard detectival metaphor of the clue; he originally was going to entitle *A Study in Scarlet* as *A Tangled Skein* to take advantage of the thread background tied up with the word "clue." He did, in fact, keep the phrase "a tangled skein" in the finished novel. However, he switched quickly to talking about his detective forging links into a chain, rather than exclusively using metaphors of magic thread. On the one hand, the chain metaphor serves to enhance the air of reasoning about Holmes: forging links becomes akin to building syllogisms. On the other hand, it moves Doyle away from the concept of the detective simply following a preordained path to justice. As far as its total effect on character goes, however, all of Doyle's talk about calculating reason is just that, talk. Simple observation plays a part in Holmes' success in the stories, and so do intuition and imagination. Doyle eventually came to admit this in *The Case Book of Sherlock Holmes* where, in one story, Holmes says Watson "has given an exaggerated view of my scientific methods," and in another admits a "mixture of imagination and reality...is the basis of my art.

Doyle's stories succeed, in part, because he glued a scientific veneer to his detective and clamped a thin layer of reason to his sensational plots. Sherlock Holmes came from Doyle's combination and modification of pre-existing literary motifs. He succeeded because of Doyle's addition of his own flourishes and arabesques: Doyle transformed the somewhat wooden character of the detective when he made Holmes. One way Doyle followed toward making Holmes interesting was to keep him in reserve. The stories suggest Holmes is a complex and fascinating man, but they do not say much about him. Doyle effected this by using Watson as the narrator, but he also designed the action of the stories to keep the focus away from Holmes. Usually the client's story as told to Holmes and Watson takes up more space than the detective action does. In the stories, we learn nothing of Holmes' life. We do not know he has a brother until the twenty-second story, and we never hear anything about his father. The stories mention only the scantiest details of the hero's appearance, and Doyle, by omission or commission, left the physical delineation of Holmes to Paget, his illustrator. The few details we remember about Holmes are his habits, the shag tobacco, and the Persian slipper. These stick in our minds because others have harped on them, not because Doyle repeats them. On the whole, the author keeps Holmes under wraps to heighten the wonder of the surprise at the end of the story. Holmes, nevertheless, is a creature of immense attraction. Part of this comes from the character's name. If Doyle had a genius for nothing else, he had a positive genius for creating names. Grimesby Roylott in "The Speckled Band" can only be a villain, just as Hilton Cubitt in "The Dancing Men" can only be a solid English squire. Changing his detective's name from "Sherringford Holmes" in the first draft of *A Study in Scarlet* to Sherlock Holmes in the finished version was one of the smartest things Doyle ever did. We can see the power of the name in that it was the first thing parodists latched onto: burlesque creations from Sherlock Abodes to Sheerluck Omes testify to the power of the name.

Not everyone would be comfortable living with such an original and half-flamboyant name. To match the name, Doyle picked up on the genius-generated eccentricities he found in Poe's Dupin. As Watson knows, Holmes has little peculiarities, from scraping on the violin to pocking V.R. in the plaster with his revolver. He is magnificently moody and close-mouthed. Here, Doyle particularizes from hints in Poe. He also fleshes out in a practical way the genius' mind. Dupin may be intelligent, but we discover in the stories that Holmes knows everything and can do anything. The steady accretion of Holmes' knowledge and abilities depends, of course, on Doyle's writing off the top of his head. It does demonstrate genius, but it appeals only to the most naive part of our imaginations. On a slightly more

sophisticated level, Holmes attracts readers because of the dualism Doyle
consciously manufactured for his character. From Poe's romantic and
metaphysical concept of the Bi-Part Soul with which Doyle flirted in *A
Study in Scarlet,* he built into Holmes a more secular and popular split
personality. Holmes is a rational drug addict, a sloppy precision, and a
lazy athlete. He does not jog, do executive exercises, practice boxing or
singlestick, and uses his revolver only to the depredation of Mrs. Hudson's
plaster. Yet he is accomplished at all these things: he is an expert boxer,
marksman, and so on. Here he embodies almost everyone's fantasy of being
accomplished without effort, and the very fact that Holmes is an expert
without working at it and is able to snap out of lassitude into action also
contributes to our estimation of his genius. In their practical application,
these elements of Holmes' character lead to other areas of his attraction.
One of Holmes' problems as a genius is boredom. He constantly complains
about the sorry state of criminality which cannot produce a problem worthy
of his attention. Boredom, of course, is the epidemic problem of modern
life. To counter this, Doyle graciously provides things for his detective to
do, and once Holmes grabs hold of a trivial problem it quickly becomes
absorbing and, in stories like "The Red Headed League," important. Here
Doyle gives us a practical demonstration of Carlyle. Coupled with this, he
makes Holmes laugh. Especially in the early stories, Holmes laughs often
to express his joy, not only in the foibles of others but also in the exhilaration
of the hunt and chase. That Holmes can manipulate events to become jokes
in "Silver Blaze" and "The Naval Treaty" shows Doyle's beginning awareness
of new opportunities for the detective story.

Although he wrote fifty-six short stories and four novels about Sherlock
Holmes, Doyle did not invent many detective plots. Scraped down to their
essentials, Doyle's detective plots fall into a small number of categories:
the returned avenger, the unusual occupation, the circumstantial delay, the
stolen inheritance, the secret society, the duel, the hunt, and one or two
others. These he simply repeated in new guises and combined together to
write new stories. We have already seen where most of the plots came from,
and as plots they are hardly remarkable or vital or interesting. Doyle does,
nevertheless, tell stories in a workmanlike fashion, and he also happened
upon some narrative devices which look forward to the detective story of
the twentieth century. The first of these, we can find codified in the opening
sentences of "The Three Garridebs" (January 1925) when Watson says "It
may have been a comedy, or it may have been a tragedy." Although this
comes in 1925, Doyle from quite early in his career wrote many Holmes
stories as mixtures of non-serious and serious material. "The Red Headed
League," for instance, begins with the patently comic adventures of Jabez
Wilson, but then shifts tone to end with the thrilling action in the bank
vault. This is not an isolated example; many stories mix comedy with serious

action. Unlike the majority of detective writers before him Doyle came to realize, by accident or choice, the detective story can profit from a combination of non-serious, comic, and playful with the serious, tragic, and human implications of crime. By striking a balance between these two attitudes, the detective story can be both seriously moral and pleasingly entertaining. This combination is one of the things which enables the genre to be popular, and it forms the basis for one branch of twentieth-century detective fiction. The other modern narrative element of the detective story Doyle flirted with is the so-called "fair play" technique. The Holmes stories never become the kind of reader-writer game envisioned by S.S. VanDine and other twentieth-century writers. Doyle does not give readers all the facts, but, as he says in "The Crooked Man," retains "some factors in the problem which are never imparted to the reader." He, rather, builds stories so "the facts slowly evolve before your eyes and the mystery clears gradually away as each discovery furnishes a step which leads to the complete truth." That is what he says in "The Engineer's Thumb", and the stories bear out the statement. In some of the stories, however, he includes the sort of visual evidence which become a standard part of the "fair play" story. Doyle does occasionally give us architectural drawings, fragments of letters, and, of course, the code of the dancing men. He found this sort of thing in Gaboriau, and included it for the same reason—as a superficial advertisement for the realism of the stories. Although Doyle never intended to invite his readers to an intellectual wrestling match, he appreciated that curiosity played a large part in attracting the audience to the detective story. He began to learn that inviting readers to make the wrong guesses heightened the surprise at the end of the story. When he wrote "Silver Blaze," in fact, he bet his wife a shilling that she could not name the murderer. In response to this idea, Doyle made Holmes acknowledge in the later stories that the facts of the case can generate several alternate explanations: in "The Norwood Builder" Holmes says he can supply a half-dozen solutions which fit the facts of the case. Over the long haul, Doyle did not exploit this line of development. Most of the Holmes' adventures are single-option stories, principally formed to produce wonder at the detective's achievement. Indeed, the short story cannot really develop into the multiple-suspect, multiple-option detective story because it is too short. Doyle, however, thought about this a long time before it became a standard part of the detective novel.

Doyle thought about a lot of things connected with the detective story. He received the form from Poe, Gaboriau, and the sensation writers, and he passed it on to the short story writers of the 1890s and the novelists of the 1920s. It has been one hundred years, now, since Doyle wrote *A Study in Scarlet*, and over fifty since "Shoscombe Old Place," the last Holmes story. It has become increasingly difficult, however, to tell the dancer from the dance. Sherlock Holmes has become William Gillette, Eille Norwood,

John Barrymore, Clive Brook, Raymond Massey, Basil Rathbone, and a number of other twenty-feet tall faces on the cinema screen. The stories have been plagiarized, parodied, burlesqued, updated, and rewritten so many times the originals have disappeared, smothered by their progeny. For the whole culture, too often Holmes has become a deerstalker hat and a calabash pipe saying "Elementary, my dear Watson." The Holmes stories have become public domain in more ways than one. Yet Doyle did little that was entirely new. The detective story existed before him and would have continued had Watson never met young Stamford, or had Jefferson Hope never loved Lucy Ferrier. Further, in some ways it would have been the same kind of detective story Doyle wrote: some sort of fusion of Poe, Collins, and Gaboriau was inevitable. But it would not have been the same in the most significant ways. Never could the detective story have inspired the kind of popularity achieved by Holmes without Doyle. Never would the detective story have fused adventure, intellect, and sentiment without Doyle. Never would it have developed precisely the same combination of humanity and flamboyance Doyle caught in Holmes. Never would it have become more than the sum of its parts.

# Chapter 8

# Turn-of-the-Century Writers

When Doyle prematurely killed Holmes in 1894, *The Strand Magazine* announced in desperation that a new batch of Sherlock Holmes stories "will commence in an early number." Knowing this was unlikely, the editors kept their collective foot in the door Doyle had opened by promising, "meanwhile, powerful detective stories will be contributed by other eminent writers." There were, however, no authentically "eminent" detective writers around. *The Strand's* advertisement, as well as other magazines' willingness to print detective stories in the hopes of bagging a trophy like Doyle, made people into detective writers overnight. At the turn of the century, dozens of people became detective writers, and writers from Adams to Zangwill hoped to invent that better man-trap which would line up editors outside their doors. In spite of the fact that the turn of the century saw a robust crop of new detective stories, a number of things have prevented their serious assessment by historians of the genre. First of all, there are an awful lot of writers to read through. More important than this, the fiction of the period falls between Doyle on the one hand and the one-two punch of the Golden Age novel and the hard-boiled story on the other hand. Critical admiration for the predecessor and the successors has obscured what comes between them.

Also, much turn of-the-century detective fiction appeared in magazines, and even when it was collected in book form, it is difficult to find: the British Museum, for instance, lacks many American writers just as the Library of Congress does not hold the corresponding British writers of the period. Finally, turn-of-the-century stories seem much more dated and time-locked than detective stories written either earlier or later. This happens because of the derivative nature of some of the fiction, but the stories of the period often display an obsession with what contemporary readers can only view as quaintly antique technology. Nevertheless, the period did witness plenty of "powerful detective stories." In fact, turn-of-the-century stories show more widespread and conscious experimentation with the detective character and the narrative technique of the detective story than any other fiction since Poe's.

Sherlock Holmes, of course, stands behind most turn-of-the-century fiction. With Doyle in the wings, writers simply could not think about the detective story without having Holmes lurking in one synapse or another. Different writers, however, treated Holmes in different ways. From the very beginning, a whole class of people noticed Doyle provided grist for the mills of satire, parody, and burlesque. Even before Holmes' Swiss excursion, Robert Barr (1850-1912) had written "Detective Stories Gone Wrong: The Adventures of Sherlaw Kombs" (1892) and J.M. Barrie (1860-1937) had probably written "The Adventure of the Two Collaborators" (1893?). A crowd of people took to writing Holmes spoofs: A.A. Milne's first published work was "The Rape of the Sherlock" (1903), and some of the best known American writers and wits, including Twain, O. Henry, Harte, and Leacock, had a go at Doyle's creation. Much of the material in the parodies is, to be sure, superficial. Doyle's names, for instance, come in for a good bit of chaff with parody detectives named Shylock Homes, Picklock Holes, Shamrock Jolnes, Suburban Holmes, and Shirley Combs (the latter by one A. Conning Goil). In terms of substance, Watson takes a few raps, most notably in Bret Harte's description: "with the freedom of an old friend I at once threw myself in my familiar attitude at his feet, and gently caressed his boot..." Most of the satiric bastinado, however, gets applied to the detective. Almost universally, the satirists, parodists, and burlesquers thump on the intellectual pretentiousness of the great detective. Frequently, they show him throwing up a huge lump of logic which proves to be laughably wrong. John Kendrick Bangs' (1862-1922) satire, "A Pragmatic Enigma" (1908), for instance, ends with the newspaper headline:

DO DETECTIVES DETECT?
A Gazoozle Reporter, Disguised as a Harvard Professor,
Calls on Sherlock Holmes, Esq.,
And Gets Away with Two Suitcases
Full of the Great Detective's Personal Effects,
While Dr. Watson's Hero
Tells What He Does Not Know About
PRAGMATISM.

Holmes spoofs provided, indeed continue to provide, a bit of harmless recreation and sport. They do, however, point us to the motif of intellect which in various ways dominates serious turn-of-the-century detective stories. More importantly, the parodies created the playful spirit some significant writers managed to join with other more serious issues of the detective story. Although they are not thorough-going spoofs, Israel Zangwill's (1864-1926) *The Big Bow Mystery* (1892) and Mary Roberts Rinehart's (1876-1926) *The*

*Circular Staircase* (1908) anticipate the mature fusion of the comic and serious sides of the detective story which flourished during the Golden Age.

In terms of subject matter, turn-of-the-century detective writers recognized they could use the detective story as an examination of character, or as an explanation of a process, or both. Because of the surprise requirements of the detective story and because of the demands of the short story form, detective writers' examination of character limited itself largely to the presentation of the detective's character. We will get back to this in a moment. The other area open for exploration was the narrative explanation of a process. Detection remained a new enough profession so that many writers and readers found satisfaction simply in following what the detective does: the process of looking at footprints, considering medical data, putting on disguises, solving ciphers, and so on. The process of police work remains for many readers one of the continuing attractions of the form even in contemporary detective stories. At the turn of the century, moreover, describing the mechanics of detection held the added advantage of feeding back in to the inflation of the hero's intellect. Yet during the period something new started. Even though plenty of writers dealt with the traditional crime at the country house, some writers like Arthur Morrison (1863-1945) began to appreciate that the detective story could also inform readers about other kinds of processes. In other words, writers began to present, as secondary material, quick looks behind the scenes at a bicycle race, a safety deposit, or a pawn shop, and this material supplemented the satisfactions of observing the detective's practices. Because of the short story form and the focus on the great detective, however, this impulse did not fully develop until much later.

Serious detective writers, rather than following through on original impulses, stuck close to Doyle. It is very difficult, in fact, to find a detective writer of the period who does not, in one way or another, bounce off Sherlock Holmes. In some cases, writers draw their plots rather clearly from Doyle. Catherine Louisa Pirkis' (?-1910) "The Redhill Sisterhood" reflects Doyle's "The Reigate Squires" (1893) not only geographically, but also in terms of the mechanics of the crime. As late as 1910, T.W. Hanshew (1857-1914) lifted "A Scandal in Bohemia" (1891) for his "The Rainbow Pearl." Along with these and other parallels, writers found certain ways of constructing detective stories which became almost obligatory simply because he had used them. Thus, even though writers of the period did use first and third person narration, the most important writers employed Watsons: Arthur Morrison, Ernest Bramah (1868-1942) and R. Austin Freeman (1862-1943) did, as did Jacques Futrelle (1875-1912), Arthur B. Reeve (1880-1936) and Baroness Orczy (1865-1947). Writers at the turn of the century very simply perceived that fortunes or reputations could be made out of Doyle's prodigality. Each of the talents Doyle showered upon Holmes was capable of much more development and, indeed, could be made the basis of a character, a plot, or a whole subgenre of detective stories. Because Holmes acted and used disguise with consummate skill, disguising became an inevitable feature of new detective stories and formed the basis for Hanshew's *Man of Forty Faces* (1910), even though it was a minor part of Holmes' character. Likewise, Holmes' occasional perusal of the agony ads in newspapers blossoms into Samuel Hopkins Adams' (1871-1958) creation of Average Jones (1911) as an advertising advisor. Sherlock's diletantish science, in turn, inspired the development of the scientific detective story. His occasional criminal excursions begat the gentleman burglar tale, and his brushes with Professor Moriarty and Colonel Moran helped to stimulate the adventures of certain master criminals.

As far as character goes, Doyle suggested two patterns which go a long way toward dominating turn-of-the-century detective fiction. First, Doyle, following the example of Poe, insisted the detective was not quite an ordinary mortal. He demonstrated this separateness by creating for Holmes certain personal eccentricities—the cocaine, the violin, the revolver practice, etc.. Turn-of-the-century writers shared Doyle's impulse to differentiate the detective from ordinary people, but they also wanted to find an extraordinary character who was not Holmes and whose eccentricities arose from different sources. This led to the creation of women detectives, boy detectives, old detectives, blind detectives, clerical detectives, jolly detectives, grouchy detectives, and a selection of other eccentric types. In many ways, however, this was simply disguising, for turn-of-the-century detectives mostly do the same sort of things in spite of their habiliments—they think. Even though the Holmes tales hardly provide elaborate examinations of the intellectual process, the detective does protest that they should, and Doyle does go to some pains to give his stories an intellectual tint, if not an intellectual coloring. He conveys Holmes' genius in several specific ways: through surprise solutions, the enigmatic statement, the use of the awestruck sidekick, the observation test, and the deduction demonstrations which open many of the stories. Most writers of the period imitate these things. Surprises are, of course, universal. Detectives following Sherlock Holmes are as close-mouthed and enigmatic as the master. We have already seen the use of the obtuse narrator. Arthur Morrison's detective, Martin Hewitt (1894), gives his companion the same sort of observation examinations with which Holmes harries Watson. Detectives as diverse as Robert Barr's Eugene Valmont (1906) and Adams' Average Jones provide intellectual test drives for their clients in the form of Holmesian thought-reading or deduction demonstrations.

While all of this material was simply furniture to Doyle, turn-of-the-century writers began to take a more serious look at the intellectual processes implicit in the detective's role in the detective story. They began to ask why and how this person can observe or think better than other individuals. One answer to these questions was that he cannot. We can see an attack on the genius, based on the notion that it takes little in the way of exceptional intelligence to solve crimes and certainly nothing along the unbelievable lines drawn in the character of the genius detective. Detectives like the narrator of Max Pemberton's *Jewel Mysteries I Have Known* (1894) and Matthias M. Bodkin's *Paul Beck* (1898) hold with the latter's statement "I just go by the rule of thumb, and muddle and puzzle out my cases as best I can." Dick Donovan clearly points the finger when he says

> ...if I had been the impossible detective of fiction, endowed with the absurd attributes of being able to tell the story of a man's life from the way the tip of his nose was formed, or the number of hairs on his head...or one hundred and one utterly ridiculous and burlesque signs which are so easily read by the detective prig of modern creation, I might have come to a different conclusion.

Yet, in spite of these anti-sentiments, indeed coexisting with them, the majority of turn-of-the-century fiction rests on the person of the genius detective who can think better than anyone else. We do find, however, more impulse to anatomize the mental processes which lead to assembling facts into a conclusion or following the obscure clue to the hidden criminal. Common sense in itself is an explanation, albeit a flimsy one, of mental process. Some writers of the period follow through the tradition of mechanical logic founded by Gaboriau and briefly fostered by Doyle. Gaston Leroux's popular *The Mystery of the Yellow Room* (1907) contains long passages on the use of reason, and Jacques Futrelle implies the same thing by naming his detective "The Thinking Machine" (1907). Although writers can make mechanically logical detectives into interesting characters, these characters were somewhat old-fashioned. To take a closer, more informative look at the human intellect, turn-of-the-century writers evolved some subgenres of the detective story which retained the traditional attractions of the form while highlighting neglected areas of intellectual operations. We can see, therefore, in the scientific story, in Chesterton's fairy tales, and in the exploration of eccentric detectives, the evolution of a spectrum of new alternatives to the story resting solely on the rendering of logic.

The scientific detective story became, especially after the turn of the century, one of the more important manifestations of the form. It appeared in several different permutations, but chiefly scientific stories boil down to portraying the detective as a scientist or building the principal crime around some sort of scientifically technical means. These stories grew out of detective fiction's continuing definition and redefinition of the nature of human intelligence, adulation for the new manifestation of genius in the person of the inventor, and writers' and readers' fascination with the brave new world delivered by radio waves, electricity, and the practical applications of science in the new technology. In a way, the scientific tale reacted against the pseudo-scientific tidbits Doyle tossed off in the course of the Sherlock Holmes stories, and it was a new form of the detective-machine analogy Gaboriau popularized. On the other hand, it reacted optimistically and in a socially conservative manner to the same culture which induced H.G. Wells to invent modern science fiction in *The Time Machine* (1895), *The Invisible Man* (1897), and *The War of the Worlds* (1898). The first notable scientific detective stories appeared in L.T. Meade's *Stories from the Diary of a Doctor* (1894-1896) which ran, like the Holmes stories, in *The Strand*. These pieces, however, are shoddy work when compared to R. Austin Freeman's Dr. Thorndyke series (1907). In spite of Freeman, though, the scientific detective story found a more enthusiastic reception in America than it did in Britain. During the first two decades of the century, American writers adopted the scientific story as their own. We can even witness the fusion of the scientific detective story with science fiction in Hugo Gernsback's (1884-1967), the gadget king of early science fiction, foundation of the *Scientific Detective Monthly* in 1930. Gernsback, however, lagged behind the times. The scientific story had its heyday in the early teens. After the First World War, it withered away, in part because of the wide-spread opposition to it by Golden Age writers, and in part because the war itself showed just what modern technology could do.

The turn of the century witnessed real advances in scientific criminology and toxicology. Chemical tests, like the 1898 introduction of the Precipitin test which distinguishes human from animal blood stains, were invented. Fingerprinting was belatedly accepted in Britain in the Stratton case of 1905. Alfred Swaine Taylor's *The Principles and Practice of Medical Jurisprudence* (1865) and Hans Gross' *Criminal Investigation* (trans. 1907) gave academic grounding and a certain popularity to scientific criminology. Finally, several sensational trials, like that of Crippen in 1910, made the public aware of the uses of science in criminal investigations. All of these things prepared the material and the public for the subject matter the scientific detective writers used. The scientific story not only publicized the new discoveries of scientific criminology, and explained them as fascinating processes, it also served to reassure or warn people about the objectivity and infallibility of justice. Stories which concentrate solely on publicizing a real or imaginary process or gadget, however, in large measure doom themselves. Therefore, when Arthur B. Reeve tells us that Craig Kennedy (1912) or Constance Dunlap uses a telegraphone, a detectoscope, or a telautograph, it can only strike us as quaint. *The Achievements of Luther Trant* (1910) by Edwin Balmer and William MacHarg yields an even odder list of technological marvels in the pneumograph, the chromoscope, the kymograph, and the plethysmograph. These American writers centered their stories on scientific gadgets; Reeve especially tried to build up suspense by holding off his explanations of exactly what his black boxes do. All of this severely hobbles the fiction by dating it so quickly. Few can get excited over Reeve's introduction of a blood pressure cuff or Freeman's ecstasy over the invention of a miniature vacuum cleaner.

More fictionally propitious, the scientific story added new variety to the surprise element in the detective story by providing villains with an almost limitless pharmacopoeia, zoo, and physics laboratory from which to select their murder weapons. With science, almost anything becomes possible, and writers often concluded their stories not with a god but with a machine from the machine. Thus, T. W. Hanshew has Cleek contest with villains using x-rays, ultraviolet rays, and electricity on their victims. Bramah's Max Carrados finds electricity behind "The Tragedy at Brookbend Cottage" (1914), and Samuel Hopkins Adams' Average Jones discovers a murderer using a trombone's music to break a glass vial of acid suspended above explosives, as well as malefactors employing poisonous spiders and poison gas. This kind of solution, of course, provides a new sort of surprise for readers who do not question scientific pronouncements, gives the writer details he can make consistent throughout the story and sum up briefly at the close, and adds a dimension to the detective's character.

Implied by the scientific criminal who exploits the frontiers of technology is the creation of the specialist in scientific detection. This, however, does not always happen. For a detective writer aiming for popular success, the idea of building the detective hero around the potentially humdrum scientific researcher seems to be too much trouble. Thus, just as Holmes knows just about everything, so does Hanshew's Hamilton Cleek. Cleek knows about things from Apache to ultraviolet because, well, because he does, and because his creator wants to keep his options open. Less fanciful writers, however, bring the detectives character more into line with the place of technology in their stories. Thus L.T. Meade and Robert Eustace show the transformation of Eric Vandeleur in *The Sorceress of the Strand* (1903): "He was no longer Eric Vandeleur, the man with the latest club story and the merry twinkle in his blue eyes: he was Vandeleur the medical jurist, with a face like a mask, his lower jaw slightly protruding and features very fixed." This sort of Mr. Hyde and Dr. Jeckyll metamorphosis is reasonably rare. More often, we find the gadget stories show the magnification of the powers of the detective. Electronic bugs, for instance, fascinated Reeve, and he frequently used them to enable his detective to be in two places at once. The gadget story also rubs off public admiration for the inventor on the character of the detective. As a mark of genius, writers invoke the name or the accomplishments of Edison rather than trying to repeat the brooding romantic genius of Poe or even Doyle. The most influential scientific detective stories, however, rest pretty solidly on thinking, and, as such, they embody a variation of the traditional theme of the detective story. In a sense, any thinking about the material universe involves, in part or whole, scientific method, and the scientific story at its best highlights and expounds upon the nature and the uses of scientific thinking. Further, writers did this consciously and methodically. Adams, for instance, gives us this dialogue in *Average Jones*:

> "Are you conversant with the Baconian system of thought, which Old Chips used to preach to us...?" countered Average Jones.

> "Forgotten it if I ever knew it," returned Kirby.

> "So I infer from your repeated use of the word 'thief.' Bacon's principle—an admirable principle in detective work—is that we should learn things from things and not from the names of things."

This is an advance on "you know my methods, Watson." It identifies the tradition and particulars of scientific thinking. The same thing happens when Average Jones tells us Euclid was "one of the greatest detectives of all time." As concise and brilliant as Adams can be, however, he was not consistently a scientific writer; he is, further, little known to casual readers. The best known proponent of the scientific story was R. Austin Freeman.

Richard Austin Freeman usually gets most of the praise or blame which critics apportion to the scientific story. His detective hero, Dr. Thorndyke, has been described as "the greatest medico-legal detective of all time," and he has also been viewed as a tiresome flayer of insignificant facts. These views differ because of the differences in conceptions about the nature of the detective story and because Freeman chose, in Dr. Thorndyke's cases, to write one kind of detective story rather than another. Although Freeman's first experience with detective fiction was with his gentleman crook stories in *The Adventures of Romney Pringle* (1902), he did not find his metier until he created his scientific detective. Dr. Thorndyke appeared first in *The Red Thumb Mark* (1907) and continued in collections of short stories and novels until 1942. To begin with, Thorndyke depends in a number of ways upon Sherlock Holmes. Freeman narrates the stories through a Watson, Christopher Jervis, he makes Thorndyke a consulting detective just as Holmes is, and some of the early stories look backward to Doyle's material. Freeman's "31 New Inn" (1911?), for instance, began in Doyle's "The Engineer's Thumb" (1892) and "The Greek Interpreter" (1893). "The Mandarin's Pearl" (1909) and "The Echo of a Mutiny" (1912) look backward to the returned revenger in Doyle. The character of Dr. Thorndyke, too, has a certain love-hate relationship with Sherlock Holmes. On one hand, Freeman developed him as a reaction against Holmes' eccentricities and flamboyance, intending his detective to be a neutral medium through which scientific reasoning would show. Yet Freeman, like Doyle, modeled his hero on one of his own medical school heroes, Alfred Swaine Taylor, author of the famous *Medical Jurisprudence*. More importantly, try as he will to limit Thorndyke, Freeman ends up giving him some of the universal knowledge possessed by Holmes. Thus, Dr. Thorndyke knows not only about things like Ptosis and ptyalism, but also about cuneiform and Moabite script. Perhaps the most Holmesian trait developed in Dr. Thorndyke is the detective's role as a teacher, for Thorndyke not only discovers truth, he finds it in such a way as to demonstrate the principles of his intellectual method.

The Dr. Thorndyke stories are scientific stories in the fullest sense: the detective is a scientist, he uses scientific gadgets, techniques, and knowledge, and the stories often turn on scientific facts. Freeman combines all of the elements of the scientific detective story. Yet, in a real sense, the Thorndyke tales simply extend the motifs of observation, logic, and mathematics which developed from Poe to Gaboriau to early Doyle. In most of the stories, Thorndyke succeeds simply because he looks more carefully and fully than others do. The main difference in Freeman lies in the detective's use of scientific aids to augment the inherent weakness of the human senses. Thus the camera and the microscope let the detective observe things which the unaided eyes of the police miss. That is one point about science in Freeman. Another is, unlike Doyle, Freeman insisted on supplying accurate, verifiable information in the stories: when Freeman notes chemical properties or describes the criminal's means, he makes sure they are true or possible, abandoning the unknown poisons and brain fever which earlier writers had used to plot their way out of trouble. He approached his fiction, in other words, with the scientific thesis that experiments must be capable of duplication. Additionally, Freeman did realize machines produce facts, not truth. His stories, although they use gadgets, do not center on them. Indeed, Freeman directed his readers' fascination with technology toward Polton, Thorndyke's lab assistant. Wonder in the face of technology takes second place to the genius of the detective. As Freeman demonstrates by using the obtuse narrator, possession of the facts, as important as it is, cannot alone lead to the truth. To find truth, one must apply, rigorously and elegantly, scientific method. In the stories, Dr. Thorndyke presents a more insistent and realistic picture of the working of scientific logic than Sherlock Holmes does. Thorndyke actually does use deduction, approaching each case with a range of theories and then carefully examining the facts to determine which is correct. Freeman not only prosecutes his campaign for scientific method by giving Thorndyke little speeches about it, he also bases the narrative form of some of his stories on the idea that admiration for methodology could be as attractive as the traditional surprise ending of the detective story. In response to Edgar Wallace's *The Four Just Men* (1905) and the guessing contest he ran with its publication, Freeman wrote a series of "inverted" stories collected in *The Singing Bone* (1912). These inverted stories first describe the commission of the crime and then follow the detective's discovery of the truth. Here Freeman thought he provided readers an opportunity to appreciate scientific method without the customary distractions of the detective story. He was, however, wrong. His inverted stories spring from and succeed because of Freeman's combination of elements of the gentleman crook story, like his own Romney Pringle yarns, and the detective story's traditional adulation of genius. This, in fact, extends to all of Freeman's stories: when they succeed, they do not work because of the science in them but because of the fiction in them.

The scientific detective story was not, however, the only type of turn-of-the-century story or the only type of approach to the intellectual issues implicit in detective story material. Beginning with *The Innocence of Father Brown* (1911), G.K. Chesterton had a powerful impact on the detective story's portrait of human problem solving. In the Father Brown stories, which he continued to write until 1935, Chesterton also demonstrated new stylistic and thematic possibilities for the detective story. Chesterton based his priest detective on Monsignor John O'Connor whom he met in 1904 and who impressed upon him the wide range of knowledge of crime and sin priests gain in the confessional. From O'Connor, Chesterton gave his Father Brown an extensive knowledge of criminals' trade secrets as well as the understanding of the passage of sin through the guts of human life and individuals' souls. Although he plotted the Father Brown tales as detective stories, with the detective's enigmatic statements forecasting the surprise at the end, Chesterton's fictions are essentially exemplae demonstrating the nature of Roman Catholic doctrine. Several of the Father Brown stories look forward to Sayers in their contrast of mechanical, materialistic rationality as opposed to the true reason of the church, and most of them, additionally, preach the need for the power of confession. The stories, moreover, bring a new sort of writing to the genre. Simply because of their ties to logic and rationality, earlier detective fiction employs either neutral diction or the semi-comic diction common to much popular writing at the turn-of-the-century. Chesterton, however, writes the Father Brown stories in a poetic style which aids in removing them from the mundane world and helps to place them much closer to the magical world of the fairy tale.

Critics generally have a hard time with the Father Brown stories: with the detective side damning Chesterton for including too little reason in the stories and the literary side complaining he uses too much detection and reason. This, of course, cannot be. Even though the Father Brown stories do argue for Catholicism, as fiction they are detective stories and as such respond to contemporary detective literature. The most pointed example of this rests with Chesterton's introduction of Flambeau, the antagonist in three of the first four stories. Flambeau is a gentleman crook right out of the current vogue for such characters. His sense of artistry, dexterity of disguise, sense of irony, as well as Father Brown's demonstration of the moral paucity of his life in "The Flying Stars" (1911), all provide an apotheosis of this popular trend in detective fiction.

As important as this is, Father Brown develops as one of the many reactions to the character of Sherlock Holmes. Chesterton deliberately makes him quiet, unassuming, physically small, and seemingly "dull as a Norfolk dumpling." Although the didactic nature of the stories causes Chesterton to have him occasionally thunder in the vein of a Jonathan Edwards, the fairy tale atmosphere also gives his enigmatic statements the quality of a Buddhist master's wise imponderables in an oriental story.

Father Brown also possesses an amount of preternatural awareness, and this has moved detective classicists to go tsk-tsk. Chesterton, however, like his friend E.C. Bentley, freely admits that, as a detective, Father Brown both intuits and guesses. But Father Brown does not detect by brain waves or automatic writing. Chesterton bases all of the stories upon observable material or psychological facts. What Chesterton does is to depict a part of human intelligence earlier detective writers ignored. With inductive reason, no matter how many specifics the investigator collects, they will not by themselves produce a conclusion. Bacon was absolutely wrong when he thought a properly constructed experiment could by itself lead to truth. A thinking machine cannot think, but merely tabulates. A gap always exists between data and conclusion, a space of varying size over which the investigator must make the inductive leap. Chesterton shows, buoyed by the faith and higher reason of the church, Father Brown can make the inductive leap with ease. He can do this because long ago he made the more important leap of faith which guides his guesses and intuitions and enables him to solve human problems. Even if Chesterton went beyond the normal limits of the detective story with the Father Brown tales, he demonstrated new possibilities for the form and brought a new area of consciousness into the detective story's exploration of human intelligence.

Part of Chesterton's motive for creating Father Brown as an insignificant person and as a priest came from a general turn-of-the-century search for different kinds of detectives. In their exploration of the varieties of mental experience, as well as in their impulse to find unusual detective characters to contrast to Sherlock Holmes, late Victorian writers fastened on to the character of the lady detective. Although stories about women detectives date back to the 1860s, with Anonyma's *The Experiences of a Lady Detective* (1861?) and Andrew Forrester's *The Female Detective* (1864), the Sherlock Holmes boom of the 1890's set writers to creating female detectives with a vengeance. One year, 1894, saw Catherine Pirkis' *The Experiences of Loveday Brooke, Lady Detective*, M.E. Braddon's *Thou Art the Man*, featuring Coralie Urquhart, Charleton Savage's *The Beech Court Mystery* with "The Squirrel", and Mrs. George Corbett's *When the Sea Gives up its Dead, a Thrilling Detective Story*, with Annie Cory.

For the next twenty years, the female detective became a common variant for writers looking for something a bit out of the usual character pattern of the post-Doyle detective. Many important writers of the period added stories about female detectives to supplement their works about male detectives: Fergus Hume created Hagar (1899) in his fruitless attempt to follow up the success of *The Mystery of a Hansom Cab*, L.T. Meade and Robert Eustace matched their scientific searchers with Florence Cusak (1899), Matthias M. Bodkin drew Dora Myrl (1900) to match and eventually marry his Paul Beck, and Grant Allen created Miss Cayley (1899) and Hilda Wade (1900) after his success with *An African Millionaire* (1897). Writers like Anna Katharine Green and Mary Roberts Rinehart made much of their reputations from women detectives.

From the publishing point of view, the turn-of-the-century vogue for women detectives reflected an attempt to recapture the female reading public. As opposed to the characters and atmosphere of stories about male detectives, stories about women detectives slanted toward perceived women's interests. The setting and the details of stories like Rinehart's *The Circular Staircase* portray the trivia of household affairs and make incidental points like the heroine's valuation of her Spode over her Limoges china. As significant as this, we find the lady typist emerging as a popular character type. E. Phillips Oppenheim peoples his novels with lady typists, and we can note Tom Gallon's *The Girl Behind the Keys* (1903) involves a typist detective. All this reflects writers' attempts to appeal to a new class of readers upon whom the naked vigor of masculine intellect was supposedly wasted.

This approach was, however, a minority one. Women detectives became popular because, paradoxically, they were unusual. Here, women sleuths simply fit into the general search for unconventional or eccentric characters to turn into detectives. Beating the bushes for oddities flushed out grouchy detectives, criminal detectives, blind detectives, as well as a couple of child detectives. The female detective simply became the most commonly used variety of two-headed dog. We can see this in the almost omnipresent tag of "Lady" or "Female", in the book titles: *Clarice Dyke, the Female Detective* (1899); *Loveday Brooke, Lady Detective; Adventures of a Lady Detective* (1890); *Dora Myrl: the Lady Detective* (1900); *Lady Molly of Scotland Yard* (1910); and *Constance Dunlap, Woman Detective* (1916). In addition to signaling the oddity of the contents, the introduction of the term "Lady" served to mute objections of women acting in an "unladylike" role.

Until 1905, women worked at Scotland Yard only in the capacity of chars or female searchers. Writers of fiction, however, realized the value of women police agents from early on. Following up on the ubiquitous disguise motif in turn-of-the-century fiction, creators of Lady detectives discovered that simply being a woman was an almost perfect disguise: the watcher or the spy needs to be inconspicuous and few types of person were as inconspicuous as a woman in the male-dominated world of crime and detection. Loveday Brooke's agency sends her out whenever her bosses receive a request for an agent who will blend into the wallpaper. The same thing happens with George R. Sims' Dorcas Dene, and Anna Katharine Green's Violet Strange (1915) is such a precious size-nine socialite no one would dream of her being a detective.

Women detectives, too, embody a theme which became increasingly difficult to present in more hard-headed, male-oriented stories. In these stories, the theme of police discretion had almost disappeared as a subject of serious concern. Women detectives, however, frequently come into contact with fears about gossip. Conventionally seen as the guardians of social propriety, women detectives receive far more breathless confidences than do their male counterparts. As late as 1915, Green pointedly reassures her readers that Violet Strange does not air people's dirty linen. Finally, from the practical, crime-solving standpoint, the female detective story demonstrates that women observe certain classes of things more closely and scrupulously than men do. In "The Redhill Sisterhood," Loveday Brooke bases her conclusions in part on the way women care for children. Orczy's Lady Molly closes one of her cases because she knows about hats and female attitudes toward them. All of these practical points about women as detectives, however, add only incidental detail to the detective story.

Although the female detective confronts the same sort of crime problems as her male counterparts, and in spite of the fact that women do solve ciphers and reason as well as men, most women detectives were dipped rather deeply in sentiment. With the exception of Bodkin's Dora Myrl, who is a sort of British Annie Oakley, and Hugh C. Weir's Madelyn Mack (1914), who has as much get up and go as any Yankee businessman, most women detectives have distinct sentimental ballast. L.T. Meade's Miss Cusak takes on "duties at once herculean and ghastly" for romantic reasons, and some writers created slandered or imprisoned lovers whom the woman detective works to free. Grant Allen's Miss Cayley and Hilda Wade, as well as Orczy's Lady Molly, have romantic axes to grind in their adventures. Dorcas Dene, descending into the pathetic, detects to support her blind husband. This, of course, formed part of the pitch to women readers, but in practical terms it meant most women detectives were one book phenomena: success at solving crimes led to marriage, and marriage took Victorian and Edwardian women out of the detective business.

Basic to the female detective story, and joining it to the main current in turn-of-the-century detective fiction, is the thesis that women do not think the same way men do. Just as the scientific story exhibits the operation of the scientific method, so the female story demonstrates the "typical" female intellect. Sometimes we find the slander, perpetrated in the Hagar stories and by Green's Mrs. Butterworth (1897), that women are constitutionally

nosey. Widespread, and even less substantiated, is writers' exploitation of
female intuition. Here, whether in the heart or in the head, writers found
a new part of mental experience as well as a good excuse for not plotting.
As in the scientific story, women's stories have rhetorical capsules inserted
to defend or extol women's intuition. Lady Molly's assistant, for instance,
says:

> We of the Female Department are dreadfully snubbed by the men, though don't tell
> me that women have not ten times as much intuition as the blundering and sterner sex;
> my firm belief is that we shouldn't have half so many undetected crimes if some of the
> so-called mysteries were put to the test of feminine investigation.

Although stories about lady detectives mince their way toward a full
recognition of women rather than taking steps or making strides, the female
detective story does contain a bit of liberation for the detective genre. In
the main, women detectives do not roughhouse with the bad guys, and they
usually have a man on hand to make the arrest at the conclusion of the
action. Nevertheless, women sleuths do sometimes spotlight the liberating
effects of action and the excitement of being a detective. Rachael Innes,
in *The Circular Staircase*, sums up her detective experience by telling us
not about logic, but about the thrill of it all: "To be perfectly frank, I
never lived until that summer."

This sense of exhilaration with action, often subdued in the regular
detective figures of the period, comes out in other eccentric types of detective.
Harvey O'Higgins expands on Miss Innes' statement at the end of "The
Blackmailers" (1915), a story about Barney the boy detective. At the end
of the story, Barney dances a little jig which expresses "liberation from
drudgery and dull commonplace. It welcomed rhythmically a life of
adventure, in which a boy's natural propensity to lie should not only be
unchecked but encouraged—that should give him, daily, games to play,
hidings to seek, simple elders to hoodwink and masquerades to wear." This
statement not only represents one of the most perceptive analyses of the
nature of detective fiction, but also illustrates the way in which turn-of-
the-century writers used the unconventional detective character to broaden
the possibilities of the form. Although the lady detective is the most common
sort of eccentric sleuth, writers went far afield to find characters who would
appeal to readers with their novelty, serve as means of examining the nooks
and crannies of mental process, and help to vary the narrative possibilities
of the detective story. In one sense, most turn-of-the-century characters exhibit
one sort of peculiarity or another: the scientist, the priest, and the reformed
crook were not common to the detective story before 1900. Of course, the
scientist, the priest, the crook, the boy, and all of the others exist in potential
in traditional detectives like Sherlock Holmes; turn-of-the-century writers,

however, seized on the latent possibilities and thereby expanded the nature and the form of the detective story.

In terms of character, one class of writers set about creating eccentric detectives who could exhibit qualities of perception absent in the normal detective hero. From Poe onward, one of the detective's chief gifts lay in his ability to observe closely, and plenty of writers built their stories around what the detective sees as opposed to what normal people take in. At the turn-of-the-century, Richard Marsh composed a variation on this theme of observation by creating Judith Lee, a detective who reads lips, thereby exhibiting a skill which is both unusual and based solely on practice rather than on mystic muscle. Ernest Bramah did the same sort of thing, only more so. His stories about Max Carrados (1914) examine, in a witty and occasionally self-consciously outrageous way, the sensory compensation achieved by his blind detective. In both of these cases, writers use unexpected traits to say something about perception.

Rather than developing eccentric characters to explore unnoticed corners of perception, the most important manifestation of the eccentric detective appeared in its expansion of detective story as story. On the simplest level, Victor L. Whitechurch uses personal eccentricity only as decoration for his otherwise standard detective. Thorpe Hazell, the hero of Whitechurch's *Thrilling Stories of the Railway* (1912), operates as a normal detective would, but as a fillip, the author depicts him as "a strong faddist on food and physical culture...[who] carries vegetarianism to an extreme, and was continually practicing various exercises of the strangest description." Here the writer simply adds eccentricity to the usual detective, but in more important writers it has a noticeable impact on their fiction. Baroness Orczy's stories about the Old Man in the Corner (1901) show one example of this. Here a grubby, grey-beard loon transfixes a woman reporter with accounts of the true facts behind sensational crimes. Not only the Old Man's scrofulous anonymity and Queeg-like manipulation of a symbolic knotted string make him eccentric, his amorality jolts the stories from the usual moral-legal frame and toward the sort of picaresque aesthethic of the gentleman crook story. Going in a different direction, Melville Davisson Post's stories about Uncle Abner (1911) also use eccentricity to change the scope of the detective story. Even though Abner is a sort of Calvinistic Father Brown, Post's character pivots more surely on observation and secular logic than Chesterton's. The eccentricity of Post's stories comes only in part from the character; in large measure the eccentricity comes from Post's setting the stories in Pre-Civil War Virginia. This unusual setting not only colors the characters, it also brings in themes common to the historical novel, and to the frontier story for that matter, thereby making the Uncle Abner tales into something different.

Plunging into the even more eccentric, the gentleman crook story responded to some of the same impulses which brought writers to the eccentric detective. On the surface, there appears to be a contradiction: detective stories concern, well, detectives, so how does the gentleman crook fit in? Then, too, the crook story goes back to traditions slightly different from those which led to the detective story—to the Robin Hood legends, to picaresque tales, and to the Newgate story. Nevertheless, during the 1890's and early 1900's, the story about the gentleman crook fused with and responded to contemporary detective stories. Literally, some crook stories respond directly to Sherlock Holmes. Guy Boothby mentions Holmes in the beginning of "The Countess of Wiltshire's Diamonds" and Maurice Leblanc develops a character named Herlock Sholmes as an antagonist for his crook, Arsene Lupin.

On another level, the crook story touches on the detective's acknowledgment, from Dupin onward, that he is in potential a great criminal. The gentleman crook can be seen as a playful articulation of the double. Another way the crook stories respond to the detective story is that most writers make their crooks do detective work in one way or another. Dorrington, in Arthur Morrison's *The Dorrington Deed Box* (1897), acts as a detective even though he is clearly a scallawag or worse. Raffles, Arsene Lupin, Godahl, and Jimmie Dale, gentleman crooks to a man, all occasionally do detective work either to further their own crimes or to promote justice unavailable under the law. Some crook writers, in fact, use the techniques of detective story narration, mainly the surprise at the end of the story precipitated by authorial trickery, to make their stories run. Leblanc frequently structures the Arsene Lupin stories as detective pieces and Frank L. Packard frames *The Adventures of Jimmie Dale* (1917) with a detective problem.

Finally, the crook story responds to the same desire for the description of process we find in the detective stories of the same period. Just as readers wanted details of detective routine, they wanted details of criminal routine. Crook stories tell us how the burglar drills out a lock and we get a glimpse of the thief's exquisitely crafted kit of burglary tools. In both the detective story and the crook story, the effect of the information is the same: it does provide information as information but more importantly it enhances the skill, cleverness, and, ultimately, the genius of the hero. From another angle, we need to see the crook story as a response to the perceived stolidness and cliched nature of the regular detective story. Gentleman crooks have style, elan, and sprightliness missing in thinking machines or human bloodhounds. They dress immaculately, belong to the best clubs and move in the most sophisticated circles, but at the same time they can thumb their noses at all of the fakes, the ostentatious boors, and the oppressive know-it-alls. Crooks like R. Austin Freeman's Romney Pringle in *The Adventures of Romney Pringle* (1902) pull off what can only be considered jokes on people who richly deserve them, and this is something which Holmes could never do even if he tried to in stories like "Silver Blaze."

On the other side of the same issue, crook stories sometimes plunge into serious issues of social and personal morality implicit in, but ignored by, detective stories. Post's stories about his crooked lawyer, beginning with *The Strange Schemes of Randolph Mason* (1896), look at legal issues ignored in standard detective fiction, Chesterton's descriptions of Flambeau and E.W. Hornung's depiction of the relationship between Raffles and Bunny (1899) expose moral issues absent in straight detective stories.

Looking at turn-of-the-century crook stories, there are several ways to divide them up. One is by character. Out of the host of criminal trades (murderer rapist, fire bug, blackmailer, pornographer, purse snatcher, white slaver, and so on), crook stories focus on confidence men and burglars. Although neither type possesses much respectability, the bunco artist connects to the traditions of the picaro, and safe-cracking is a skilled trade. For our purposes, the con men begin with Grant Allen's Colonel Clay in *An African Millionaire* (1897), and include smooth-tongued fakes like G.R. Chester's Get-Rich-Quick-Wallingford in a book of the same title (1908), Boothby's Simon Carne from *A Prince of Swindlers* (1897), and Freeman's Romney Pringle. Burglars received most of their impetus from Raffles, and continued in Leblanc's Arsene Lupin, Frederick Irving Anderson's Godahl, and Packard's Jimmie Dale. In a sense, dividing by character does little good because most of the gentlemen burglars are confidence men as well.

The crook story, however, does generate a distinct set of plots. First comes the disguise story: all of the heroes lead double lives so disguise plays a fundamental role in their profession. Then comes the narrative concentrating on process, whether it is the procedure of selling the Brooklyn Bridge or the technique of expert burglary. After this is the escape story which dwells on the crook's ability to wriggle out of tight spots occasioned by his own foolishness, circumstance, or the police. The crook versus crook plot appears fairly often with the hero cheating or being cheated by one of his brethren. Finally, there is the sentimental story which uses, but subordinates, the character of the crook and the mechanics of larceny to love or some other estimable cause. All of these plots, additionally, can be colored by the telling, and writers could choose to narrate into their stories vicarious excitement, social satire, burlesque, moral censure, or a combination of these to reach different parts of the readers' appreciations.

Maurice Leblanc's Arsene Lupin is probably the most engaging gentleman crook of the period, and his exploits exemplify the lighter side of the crook story and its relationship to the detective story. A.J. Raffles, however, influenced more subsequent writers, and through this character Hornung exhibits some of the darker side of the tradition.

Raffles is as important for the crook story as his brother-in-law's Sherlock Holmes tales are for the detective story. Like the Holmes tales, moreover, Hornung's stories about Raffles were altered by theatrical and cinematic versions which have transmitted an inaccurate picture of the tone and purpose of the originals. In the original stories, Raffles is an amateur cricketeer who turns to thievery to get himself out of a hole, and then continues to sustain his life of ease. He continues to burgle and swindle because he discovers that "cricket...like everything else is good enough sport until you discover a better. As a source of excitement it isn't in it with other things..." When he is not gingering up his adrenalin level, Raffles lives in luxury at the Albany or goes out on the town with his adoring friend "Bunny" Manders. Hornung put very little of Robin Hood into the stories. Raffles may say "I could no more scoop a till when the shopkeeper wasn't looking than I could bag apples out of an old woman's basket," but this refusal to rob the poor results from snobbery rather than from any sort of moral, ethical, or social sense. Indeed, Raffles has none of these. He commits crimes out of a need for thrills, out of perverse puckishness, and in response to a twisted sense of art and artistry. Instead of more defensible motives, Raffles acts out of "the spirit of pure mischief in which he is prepared to risk his life and liberty." In "An Old Flame," for instance, Raffles does a bit of impromptu housebreaking, and while shinnying up the house front, he stops to bow to Bunny who watches amazed and aghast from the street. Through all of the stories, there also runs a sustained theme of decadence. When Bunny first sees Raffles' rooms, he is surprised to see the surroundings of an aesthete rather than the hearty suggested by A.J.'s cricketeering. Raffles does not simply long for excitement, he has a palate for depraved and outre human sensations. He says at one point, "I've told you before that the biggest man alive is the man who's committed a murder, and not yet been found out; at least he ought to be, but he seldom has the soul to appreciate himself." For Raffles this attitude simply reflects his espousal of "art for art's sake."

The Raffles stories have a double impact on readers. First, they appeal to the enjoyment of light-hearted nonchalance and disguised schoolboy pranks. Raffles is a carefree, insouciant undergraduate and Hornung enhances this with the undergraduate and sporting slang spiced into his speech. On the other hand, the stories evoke moral outrage. Raffles repels readers when they consider the implications of his speeches and attitudes, and the stories deliberately raise the gorge through Hornung's use of point of view.

As our estimation of Holmes increases because of Watson's decency, honesty, and humanity, so our estimation of Raffles sinks when we see him only through the eyes of Bunny. Bunny is, by any measure, naive, weak, and besotted. He is the pathetic eternal weakling who ignores even the vilest things he witnesses and joins the most despicable actions because he can only follow. He is, further, a sniveler and a kill-joy. We view Raffles solely from his perspective and this can only degrade the main character.

Additionally, the plots of the Raffles stories add to the character's unworthiness. Several stories tell of out-and-out failures of the hero, and in "The Gift of the Emperor," Raffles and Bunny get caught with their hands in the till. "The Wrong House" results only in Raffles bashing an innocent boy. In fact, in the first two collections of Raffles stories, only a minority reflects the sort of precision, style, and success which we find in less moral gentleman crook stories. The smash and grab job in "A Jubilee Present" is scarcely out of *Topkapi*, and Raffles' resolution to turn murderer in "Willful Murder" descends to Nazi mentality. In sum, Hornung made the Raffles stories so they charm, but he also made sure they bite.

If, in the story about the gentleman crook, the detective story taps into the tradition of the picaresque story, then in the story about the master criminal, detective fiction unites with the traditions and conventions of the romance. Although in the 1920's detective writers parodied and pilloried the master criminal story, it formed an important part of the mass of fiction publishers and readers viewed as detective fiction at the turn of the century. During the period, influential writers like Guy Boothby, L.T. Meade, Edgar Wallace, Sax Rohmer, and especially John Buchan, devoted themselves to the master criminal story. Sexton Blake (1893)—whose adventures, written by a stable of writers, appeared in *The Union Jack*—brought the master criminal story to countless lower class or underage readers in Britain just as the Nick Carter stories (1886) appealed to similar classes in the United States.

The master criminal story combines recognizable elements with a number of literary and social currents. It, of course, goes back to the gothic novel for the larger-than-life villain. These stories, however, refine the gothic hero through the filter of the sensation novel. Wilkie Collins' Count Fosco has plenty of sons and heirs in Boothby's Dr. Nikola (1895), Rohmer's Fu Manchu (1913), and Buchan's Blackstone (1915). Writers also took advantage of contemporary paranoias in building ever more fearsome master criminals. For one thing, the master criminal and his gang reflect turn-of-the-century anxieties about secret societies. The Camorra, the Black Hand, and international anarchists appear in standard detective writers, but they are paper trained as opposed to the malign presence of secret plots in the master criminal story. Master criminal stories, too, show the sinister obverse of the scientific story. Rather than exhibiting the genius' use of technology to build a better tomorrow, master criminals develop the mad scientist motif. These stories also make practical use of the vogue for the mystical and oriental which appeared at the turn-of-the-century. Scarcely a Napoleon of crime lacks quasi-mystical powers along with Oriental masters and a pack of alien servants, building up, of course, to Dr. Fu Manchu. Finally, the master criminal story responded in two ways to the contemporary detective story. First, the simple aesthetics of the tale of the great detective require his antagonist be either perverse circumstance which frames an inexplicable crime or the master criminal whose elaborate plans suitably test the mettle of the hero. Also, the master criminal story witnesses a reaction among popular writers against the extensive intellectual atmosphere of the contemporary detective story, along with a desire to join the elements of detection with the patterns of adventure which proved so successful in the books of Rider Haggard, Stevenson, and Anthony Hope.

These threads all combined to form the master criminal story, or, as it came to be known, the thriller. The key to these stories is the character of the villain. First of all, master criminals plan earth-shaking crimes. These people like Meade's Sorceress of the Strand (1902), want unlimited wealth, or, like Dr. Nikola, the modern equivalent of the elixir, or, like Fu Manchu or Buchan's Powerhouse (1913), world domination. Anyone, to be sure, can want these things, but the master criminal has the personality and organization to make success possible were the fictional world not governed by Providence. Drawing on Count Fosco, writers made their villains effete but magnetic, sophisticated but ruthless, suave and polite in small things but maniacal about large things. Master criminals also have large stocks of working capital, scientific genius, occult powers, and legions of yeggs and bruisers to do their dirty work.

Ranged against this avalanche of evil stand the hero and his associates. The associates exist, in the main, to be kidnapped, so the plot depends on the actions of the hero. In some important ways the heroes of these stories are detectives. Buchan's novels have cipher solving in them, the first Fu Manchu book contains a series of locked room murders, while Wallace's *The Clue of the Twisted Candle* (1916) has only one locked room murder. In fact, Guy Boothby's *A Bid for fortune or Dr. Nikola's Vendetta* (1895) contains the original of one of the devices Jacques Futrelle used in his arch-intellectual story, "The Problem of Cell 13" (1907). Nayland Smith and Dr. Petrie in the Fu Manchu yarns, as well as Sexton Blake, all look specifically back to Sherlock Holmes.

Part of the thriller hero's value comes from his ability to put two and two together, but more comes from his capacity for prompt action. Here the thriller hero differs from the detective hero. Dick Hatteras, in *A Bid for Fortune*, and Dick Hannay, in *The Thirty Nine Steps* (and several later novels), may be able to follow clues and solve problems, but they differ from conventional detectives in that they are average men who have experienced the real world of work, who have practical intelligence, and whose main strength is their commitment to decency and to the defense of it. In short, the master criminal's opponent is the end product of Victorian imperialism, and his ability to cope with the villain, who is usually a foreigner, proceeds from the principles of well-intentioned empire-building. Once we have the villain and the hero, the plotting of the master criminal story runs along traditional lines, showing confrontations which lead to a series of chases, captures, and escapes.

In some ways, the master criminal story became the most influential of the detective story products of the turn-of-the-century. It generated Sapper with his Bulldog Drummond, along with a host of other thriller writers in the twenties and thirties. It inspired Ian Fleming after World War II and became, in fact, one of the patterns for the spy novel. Regular detective writers, however, did not like thrillers. They laughed at their improbabilities and satirized their naivetee. Quick wits and even quicker fists seemed grotesquely out of place in the garden party world of the Golden Age of the detective story. The master criminal story, however, seems more relevant to the postwar world in which Hitler could almost succeed and cities can vanish in a sudden flash of light and heat.

In all parts of its development, the turn-of-the-century detective story was in international literary movement. While French writers of the period, like Leroux and Leblanc, carried through certain traditions of continental literature—the development of the picaro and the manner of Gaboriau, for instance—British and American writers wrote mostly in response to the British tradition. In large measure, too, these stories appealed to the same international English-speaking audience. The detective story market place was, however, a one way avenue: many British writers found American publishers, but few American stories appeared in Britain. A similar situation exists in criticism. Critics have generally ignored American writers or seen them as adjuncts of British detective fiction. To be sure, Americans did write plenty of inept, insipid, and derivative detective stories at the turn-of-the-century. The lugubrious nature of Pidgin and Taylor's *The Chronicles of Quincy Adams Sawyer, Detective* (1912) goes a long way toward proving this. Arthur B. Reeve's scientific stories also evince only a bumptiously naive fascination with technological toys. Nevertheless, Post, Futrelle, and Adams wrote detective stories as original, pleasing, and satisfying as their British counterparts, and American writers as a whole developed a range of themes which is absent in British detective fiction.

British detective stories at the turn of the century say very little about the nature of law enforcement. Most of them portray the bumbling policeman, but this comes from literary convention rather from any sort of social fervor. Bodkin and Barr voice a few complaints about Judges' Rules hampering effective investigation, but by and large, British stories never pretend to deal with real policemen or real police problems. American detective fiction, on the other hand, makes some powerful statements on the corruption, dishonesty, and ineptness of the police. In *The Powers that Prey* (1900), for example, Flynt and Walton present a grotesque indictment of police brutality, dishonesty, and perversion of the law. The American story of the period, in fact, shares many motives with muckraking journalism which went on at the same time. We can see this in American writers' frequent use of the corporation as villain. In Reeve, MacHarg and Balmer, Adams, and Francis Lynde, the real criminals are the railroads, the beef trust, the banks, or other assorted conglomerates, cartels, and monopolies. Along the same lines, American stories often turn to politics, and the same detectives who oppose the Robber Barons go after dirty politicians. Thus Reeve's "The Campaign Grafter" (1913) and Adams' "The One Best Bet" both deal with corrupt politicians. American detective stories display a few other incidental firsts. American writers, for instance, used Freud in their detective stories earlier and more frequently than their British fellows. The presence of real social issues, however, separates American from British detective writing. Granted, with a few rare exceptions, American writers simply insert the social statements in the conventional framework of the detective story. Their presence, however, stands in the background of the fully developed atmosphere and mood of resigned cynicism which provides part of the power for the hard-boiled story of the 1920s and 1930s.

Recognizing the role of the turn-of-the-century American detective story in the eventual development of hard-boiled fiction is an example of a process we can apply to all of the fiction of the period. As a whole, it displays fully developed, innovative, and sometimes sophisticated examples of detective story craft. The most talented writers of the period, like Chesterton, and even less talented writers like Freeman, inspired the detective writers of the next generation. Almost all of the concrete ingredients of Golden Age fiction reside somewhere in the work of turn-of-the-century writers. The writers exploited the various facets of Holmes more patiently and thoroughly than did Doyle, and they helped to heave the detective story further out of sentiment and sensation and toward the common world. Nevertheless, turn-of-the-century fiction did not take the giant steps which we find in British and American detective fiction of the 1920s, and even the real achievements went unnoticed because of the ephemeral nature of magazine publication. It was, in fact, magazine publication along with certain structural and narrative prejudices owing to Doyle and the Poe-Gaboriau tradition which effectively prevented turn-of-the-century fiction from developing further than it did.

Perhaps the outstanding fact about detective stories at the turn-of-the-century is just that—they are short stories. Few detective novels achieved any sort of real popularity and, indeed, compared with the mass of short fiction, few detective novels appeared. The long detective fiction of the period, with a very few exceptions, is windy, routine, and turgid. This does not mean, however, that writers did not try to expand the short story into the novel. They just stumbled over the difficulty of expanding over the length of a novel what is essentially a compact narrative knot, the problem and solution of a crime. The ghost of the three-volume novel complicated this problem, it being within the realm of possibility to make detective material into a vital short novel, but not a long novel given the self-imposed restrictions of subject, character, and theme. Doyle, as late as 1914, beat the dead horse of Gaboriau's novel structure in *The Valley of Fear,* but it did not work here just as it did not work in his early novels. Other writers experimented with the episode as a building block. Hume's *Hagar of the Pawn Shop* and Hanshew's *Cleek's Government Cases* (1916), both unite separate episodes with a frame story to produce a longer package of detective fiction. Some writers attempted to provide coherence to collected episodes by calling them memoirs, as in Barr's *The Triumphs of Eugene Valmont* (1906), but this did little to bring the short story to the novel. Thriller writers had a more cavalier approach. They simply inserted episodes of proper detection into the loose structure of the adventure novel.

While turn-of-the-century writers practiced these shifts, changes occurred which allowed the bona fide detective novel to begin. For one thing, assumptions about the size of the novel changed. During and after World War I, publishers were ready to accept shorter books, and readers did not invariably expect the triple decker novel invented for other kinds of readers in other times. The concept of leisure reading emerged, and the weekend book or the book for the train journey needed to be a reasonably short one. Secondly, the concept of the tightly constructed novel in high-brow literature suggested new methods and new models for the detective novelists of the 1920's. As a model, *The Moonstone* made a triumphant comeback. And finally, writers discovered the detective story knot itself contained opportunities for expansion, exclusive of multiple episodes or the inserted story. This, however, remained in the future.

The other element which restricted the development of the turn-of-the-century detective story was writers' basic conception of the mystery and readers' relationship to the mystery. Because of the speed at which they progress, short stories cannot do much with the careful development and exhibition of clues. The short detective story at the turn-of-the-century depends largely on traditional patterns of story-telling rather than following through on the idiosyncratic devices fashioned by Collins. Doyle wrestled with this and concluded the detective story unfolds a narrative rather than invites the readers' participation. Coupled with the dominance of the detective character, this means these short stories chiefly intend to advertise the detective's genius which the writer demonstrates by an apparently wonderful conclusion, but which the detective either pulls out of a hat or which is admirable only because there is no opportunity given for alternate solutions. Writers give few options. Further, writers at the turn of the century use very little narrative trickery which becomes a standard mark of the detective story in the next generation. Devices like Futrelle's murderer narrator in "The Mystery of Room 666" (1910) stand out from the usual conventional narration of the period. This device, in fact, stands out so much critics could view it as a shocking innovation when Christie used it in 1926.

At best, typical turn-of-the-century fiction, if it is a guessing game at all, resembles a rigged guessing game in which the author adds significant facts at the end to astonish the reader. Guessing games had much to do with the Golden Age novel, but turn-of-the-century writers could not properly adapt their tone or correctly gauge the perspicacity of their audience. This showed in the mailbags full of correct answers sent to Edgar Wallace when he ran a contest for the person who could correctly identify the murder weapon in *The Four Just Men*. Likewise, turn-of-the-century writers never added more than verisimilitude in the maps, drawings, and architectural plans they included in their stories.

The detective story at the turn of the century represents the term transitional in its fullest sense: the works look both backward and to the future and are significant in themselves. Turn-of-the-century tales reject some of the grosser forms of sentiment cultivated by Gaboriau and Doyle. Even though they cling to the concept of the great detective, they tone him down or do what Holmes constantly tells Watson to do, use him to illustrate mental processes. The writers of the period display a healthy deviousness in their invention of complex crimes and crime situations. This, too, escapes form Holmes and looks forward to the cuckoo complexities of the Golden Age book. They display, as well, some notable instances of wit and comedy. But most of these things were forgotten with the magazines which contained them. Fiction of the period also suffers from Doyle's semi-regular returns to detective writing: each new series of Sherlock Holmes stories robbed the newer writers of deserved attention. Writers also suffered from publishers' exploitation of thrillers. Booming thrillers as mysteries or detective stories misled and infuriated many readers. Wordsworth and Coleridge were not the first writers to think about nature or about simple folk—they were just the first Englishmen to talk about them. The same holds true of Golden Age detective writers: they, in a sense, talked about those things which mute inglorious detective writers were doing at the turn-of-the-century.

# Chapter 9

# The Golden Age

In 1928 a skywriter fogged "Murder" in the skies above Manhattan. This advertisement for *Murder,* by Evelyn Johnson and Gretta Palmer, symbolizes the three golden ages which coincided between the two world wars. The first of these, to be sure, was the golden age of the detective story. During this period, the genre attained new status, new kinds of writers modified the aims and approaches of the form, and new classes of readers adopted the detective story as their own.

But this would have amounted to little or nothing at all, were it not for the fact that the 1920's and 1930's were also the golden ages of publishing and advertising. Fortified by the technological innovations of the 1890's, like the linotype and cheap paper, publishers could, for the first time, produce really cheap books once the economies of scale created a large enough market. Andrew Carnegie's endowment of public libraries and the phenomenal growth of private lending libraries, exemplified by those at Boots the Chemists, and W.H. Smith in Britain, went part of the way toward expanding the reading public. After World War One, publishers competed with libraries for the expanding reading public by issuing cheap editions of popular books and authors, and they reached out with advertising to convince more readers to buy their books.

By the end of the 1920's, publishers in both America and Britain developed a wide range of marketing techniques and used most of them to boom the newly discovered and newly developed craze for detective novels. One innovative method of selling books was through the book club. The Book-of-the-Month Club began in 1926, and subsequent years saw the rise of the Detective Story Club and the Unicorn Mystery Book Club. Publishers appreciated with a vengeance that there was a class of people out there who would eagerly consume detective novels, and they created special lines of books to appeal to these readers. Among the offerings of U.S. publishers were Doubleday's Crime Club, Simon and Schuster's Inner Sanctum Novels, Lippincott's Main Line Mysteries, Dodd Mead's Red Badge novels, Knopf's Borzoi Murder Mysteries, and E.P. Dutton's Mystery of the Month. Most of these series had a special logo, like the Crime Club's stylized gunman, to draw purchasers directly to the goods. Publishers also evolved a whole range of gimmicks to further the addiction of readers to detective novels. In 1929, Harper's introduced a line of "Sealed Mysteries," in which the last chapters were sealed with an onion skin wrapper: if the reader returned the book with the wrapper uncut the publisher would supply a refund. The Borzoi Murder Mysteries offered an even trickier refund offer: the publisher would buy the book back if the reader returned it with a signed statement of not less than fifty words on why the mystery did not measure up.

And then there were the contests. The first of these was Edgar Wallace's spot-the-means contest for *The Four Just Men*, but this kind of thing did not really catch on until the twenties and then it took a different form. Any number of publishers invited readers to try their hands at writing detective stories, a device which offered publicity and the chance of uncovering new talent and avoided the risk of going broke the way that Wallace did with his contest. Methuen ran a detective writing contest in the late 1920's with A.A. Milne as one of the judges, and Dodd, Mead regularly advertised for writers and offered to send them the Red Badge Eight Point Test for detective stories.

The contests produced an occasional winner, like Ellery Queen's *The Roman Hat Mystery* (1929), but they also generated an awful lot of drivel. This, in fact, is generally true of the commercialism of the detective story in the 1920's and 1930's: the boring, ill-written, clumsy, and hackneyed books by far outnumber the good ones. In 1944, Raymond Chandler spoke of this when he wrote "the average detective story is probably no worse than the average novel, but you never see the average novel. It doesn't get published. The average—or only slightly above average—detective story does." Part of the blame for this situation lay with the reciprocal relations between an addicted public and mystery-pushing publishers.

Part of the blame, too, rests with the development of mystery criticism and mystery reviewing. Criticism of detective novels locked onto the idea of the puzzle and this eliminated most mature assessments of the genre. With reviews, the press went from totally ignoring detective books to developing segregated columns of mystery reviews. Newspapers and magazines, from the late twenties onward, provided capsule comments in special detective reviews whose authors made use of standards different from those applied to other kinds of books. *The Saturday Review* (U.S.), for instance, published "The Criminal Record, the *Saturday Review's* Guide to Detective Fiction" in the thirties. This item supplied, in chart form: Title and Author; Crime, Place, Sleuth; Summing Up; and Verdict. The verdicts for May 4, 1935 were "Not too good" (Mignon G. Eberhart), "Good Puzzle" (Ellery Queen), and "Hard to Beat" (Mrs. Belloc Lowndes). This sort of reviewing not only ignored the universal, human, and literary features of detective stories, it also encouraged writers to adhere to pat formulae designed to elicit the correct response in a fifty-word review.

Yet, amid all of the hurly-burly of the marketplace, and, in a way because of the commercial noise, the detective story attained its golden age. In large measure, this resulted from new writers taking up the form and working toward common goals. Between-the wars-detective story writers participated in a literary movement which was as conscious and definable as the well-known movements in regular literature. In fact, in many ways, it is difficult to fully appreciate golden age writers without seeing them as a group, simultaneously coherent and diverse, like the neo-classicists or the romantics. For one thing, instead of finding isolated authors writing for the same market as we do at the turn of the century, between-the-wars detective story writers not only knew one another, but joined together in communal enterprises. The first golden age novel, *Trent's Last Case* (1914), came about as a result of E.C. Bentley's (1875-1956) friendship with Chesterton.

During this period we also see a good bit of collaboration: Philip Macdonald (1896-1981) wrote his first few books with his father, Ronald; cousins Manfred B. Lee (1905-1971) and Frederic Dannay (1905-1982) combined to become Ellery Queen; John Palmer (1885-1944) and Hilary Saunders (1898-1951) wrote as Francis Beeding; and husband and wife G.D.H. and Margaret Cole (1889-1959; 1893-) worked together. Even writers who usually worked on their own sometimes collaborated. Dorothy L. Sayers (1893-1957) wrote *The Documents in the Case* (1930) with Robert Eustace and dramatized *Busman's Honeymoon* (1937) with Muriel St. Clare Byrne. Carr (1906-1977) put together *Fatal Descent* with John Rhode (1884-1964). Many writers, too, received enthusiastic support from families and friends, as did Margery Allingham (1904-1966) from her husband Philip Youngman Carter.

Writing detective stories between the wars became a semi-public practice of shared hypotheses, premises, jokes, and plot suggestions. Not only did authors cross one another's paths at publishers and on the radio, but in the fashion of any genuine literary movement, they met together to share ideas and conviviality. In 1928, Anthony Berkeley Cox (1893-1970) founded the Detection Club, an organizational melange of seriousness and spoof, to which every significant British author of the era belonged. As well as fostering good times and support for detective writers, the Detection Club produced the ultimate collaborations in its communal novels like *The Floating Admiral* (1931) and *Six Against Scotland Yard* (1936), books for which several authors each wrote a chapter of the finished piece. With these books, with the collaborations, and with the golden age novel in general, there was a good deal of fooling around, playing games, and having a good time. The point is that golden age writers shared and elaborated on their own games. Sharing brought a large measure of energy to the detective novel of the period, but elaborating, or at least one kind of elaborating, nudged the literary movement away from the salon and toward the academy.

Like any other self-respecting literary movement, golden age writers manifested their self-consciousness about what they were doing by developing a body of literary criticism in which they defined their goals and sought to establish their relationship to other kinds of literature. As we have seen already, the twenties saw the first attempts to trace the history of the genre with Messac's academic study and, more significantly, with Sayers' long introduction to *The Omnibus of Crime* (1929). Here we have attempts to establish that the detective story had its own unique past, as well as possibilities for future expansion.

At about the same time writers attempted to describe the history of the detective story, other writers were hard at work trying to prescribe its internal form. A number of writers and publishers devised lists of quasi-draconian rules which mandated precisely what the detective story ought, or more often, ought not to do. These rules appear in magazine articles, in authors' prefaces to their own and others' detective stories (in itself a significant development), in regulations like the Dodd Mead Eight Point Test for detective story contests, and in passages embedded in detective novels themselves. The most extensive of these sets of rules comes from S.S. VanDine (1888-1939), who, in 1928, set forth twenty rules for writing detective stories. The most reasonable rules occur when authors, like Christie (1890-1976), Sayers and others, insert passages in novels which focus attention toward one class of motives and criminals and away from another.

These rules, however, mean little in themselves. Some of the restrictions which regulators set down were patently foolish: even if VanDine says "there must be no love interest" in the detective story, most writers made a point of building up a love interest. Successful writers, in fact, flouted the rules with abandon, and the public loved it. Christie's *The Murder of Roger Ackroyd* (1926), the most widely criticized book of the era, was also its most popular mystery, in spite of the fact Christie did not "play fair." The rules, rigorously applied, made rotten fiction. They may reflect one line of detective story development in the late twenties, the puzzle story, but their only larger use is to show how thoroughly self-conscious detective writers became in the golden age.

In another, less crabbed vein, golden age writers reflected their self-consciousness in more open and extensive allusions to criminology and to detective stories themselves. Golden Age writers usually make a point of dropping the name of at least one historical criminal during the course of their novels: one cannot read many novels of the era without encountering Crippen, Palmer, Joseph Smith, Burke and Hare, and other notorious real criminals. Bringing in historical criminals established the *bona fides* of the writers (and readers) as criminologists, as did the fairly frequent descriptions of police technique.

On the other hand, golden age writers demonstrate their conscious identity by repeated allusions to other detective story writers, to detective stories in general, and to literary techniques used in detective stories. Again and again the readers come upon references to Doyle, Poe, Gaboriau, Freeman, Bentley, Christie, Sayers, and a number of other standard authors; or they encounter comments like "You're acting like a detective in a detective story"; or assertions like "I oughtn't explain 'till the last chapter, but I always think that's so unfair."

These acknowledgments do several things. They display the self-consciousness I noted above, they rivet down the playful nature of the golden age detective story, they appeal to readers knowledgeable about detective fiction, and they serve concrete ends in plotting and characterization. They do all of these things, but they also present something of a paradox. How can golden age writers with one hand give hard facts about criminology and with the other hand establish a playful sense of unreality? To find the answer to this question is to find the essence of the golden age detective story.

Even though turn-of-the-century detective fiction contained most of the story-telling elements and emphases used by golden age writers, it did not contain them all. Indeed, golden age writers perceived themselves as being revolutionary, and even if in the final analysis they were not, revolt conditions a large part of golden age detective fiction. As with their development of literary criticism, the revolution of golden age writers had to do with defining, by negatives, the kind of fiction they wrote. Their first revolt, therefore, was against popular fiction: throughout the period detective writers set out to separate detective fiction from fiction aimed at the masses. In golden age novels, consequently, one never finds a kind word directed toward Edgar Wallace, Sexton Blake, Sax Rohmer, or Sapper. Turn-of-the-century thrillers and novels patterned after them, as well as newspaper serials and pulp magazines, come in for constant parody, burlesque, and abuse—abuse for their melodramatic methods, their hackneyed characters, and their naivete about both life and art. Virtually every golden age writer attacks shoddy, lower-class mystery fiction, and in fact some of the memorable comic speeches of the golden age use thriller writers as their subjects. In John Dickson Carr's *It Walks by Night* (1930), for instance, the author aims his burlesque at Sax Rohmer and his sinister villain, Fu Manchu:

"Ooo, detectives, yes! You're not really, are you? I like to read about them. I can never go past a Chinese laundry without suspecting that the proprietor will chase me with the *wah-ha-hoonglung*, or deadly whistling worm of Lower Burma—"

"And then," I said, "there's the equally poisonous pretzel adder from the Swiss Congo. It's so called because it curls up like a pretzel and is a convenient salty color; it can be sent to your victim in a box of harmless pretzels. Sax Rohmer says there is only one way to detect the presence of this viper. You should always drink beer with your pretzels, for at the sight of beer this adder emits a faint but audible smacking of the lips, whereat you seize it with a tongs and throw it out of the window. Sax said he got the tip from an old Scotland Yard man who finds 'em in his bed every night."

"Yes! And master criminals—I love master criminals. They're called the Orange Octopus, or the Clutching Beetle..."

With attacks like this one, detective writers of the golden age clearly established the line between themselves and those who wrote schoolboy stories, newspaper serials, and thrillers. They rebelled against the triteness and shoddiness with which these forms besmirched the name of the detective story. They revolted against being lumped in with the likes of E. Phillips Oppenheim, William LeQueux, and Sidney Horler.

Golden age writers attempted to rescue the detective story from the depths of popular fiction, but they had no wish to elevate it to the status of highbrow literature. Detective writers, in fact, revolted against much of what highbrow fiction came to mean in the 1920's and 1930's. Even though golden age fiction, in its own modest way, experiments with points of view and examines human psychology, neither detective story writers nor detective readers could stomach the radical expressions of these things in *avant garde* writers like Joyce or Lawrence. Neither did they have a taste for the new Russian literature which was beginning to have its impact on the modern novel and modern theater. Faced with the fashion for Russian literature, detective writers' reactions range from the mild contempt of Georgette Heyer's (1902-1974) "It's all very well for you to say take Gogol, but nobody wants to," to the outright truculence of Carr's "the only adequate answer to one who begins rhapsodizing about the Russians is a swift uppercut to the jaw." Detective writers largely saw modern and modernist literature as incomprehensible, morbid, and prurient. With his sarcasm showing, Cox writes, "Adultery?...You can't write novels in these days without a very intimate knowledge of that particular phenomena." Even Sayers, who had the most thorough literary background of the lot, labeled modern poetry "The Whirligig School" and lambasted Joyce for destroying English syntax and Lawrence for reducing human communication to "a series of animal squeals." Detective writers announced with some emphasis that they would have no part of *avant garde* literature.

This double rebellion, or reaction, against both popular literature and literary modernism, established for detective writers certain limits of operation which they consciously chose and which a large number of readers in the 1920's and 1930's found to be congenial. Conscious avoidance of lower-class popular literature brought the golden age detective story much closer than other contemporaneous types of literature to the portrayal of normal people in quasi-normal situations. It also moved writers to pay close and strict attention to constructing plots and interior structure for their detective novels. This same motive, granted, too often moved third rate writers to place a high value on what they perceived to be the intellectual puzzle and the rehashing of the relevant facts. This over-stressing on the problem part of the detective story came from over-reacting to the thriller detective story, and during the golden age it generated a lot of mechanical, boring books.

The rejection of modernist literature, too, had its pluses and minuses. Detective writers of the period knowingly appealed to the widespread prejudice against the new wave of highbrow writers of the twenties. Yet, they were not book burners or boors, and they appealed to readers who were in many ways urbane and cultivated. Neither group, however, understood or liked the way modern writing fit into the traditions of literature. Detective stories of the golden age attempted to become the real heirs to traditional literature and the legitimate portrayers of contemporary life and taste. We can see some of this by marking the quality and type of literary allusions in the dialogue of the typical golden age novel. Characters cite Dickens by the cartload and Shakespeare by the ton. This sort of allusiveness not only threads the detective book into the great heritage of standard literature, but it also validates the book for the educated reader: it makes his or her education and reading significant and valuable rather than attempting, as modernists did, to make the readers look at things in new lights. Detective stories in the golden age, then, strove to be safe, comfortable entertainment for middle class readers.

The appeal to the middlebrow reader, however, quashed most of the serious potential latent in fiction about crime and criminals. In the golden age pattern, only in the thirties do a few writers like Cox and Graham Greene (1904—) begin to seriously prod about in the moral issues of crime. For most writers, the accumulated conventions of the detective story served as barriers against deep seriousness. While many writers briefly acknowledge the naked horror of death and the unseemliness of playing games with humans instead of pieces of wood or ivory, they nonetheless produced half-burlesque novels which were the basic form of detective fiction during the early twenties—and which remain one of the standard subgenres through today.

Stemming from its conscious attempt to ally itself with traditional literature, rejecting both the tawdry and the experimental, the golden age detective story concentrated on purity of language, so much so that attention to, and comments on, language became a fairly prominent feature of the literary movement. One article of the Detective Club oath was that its members would "honour the King's English." Detective writers, and by extension their readers, often had a sophisticated grasp of traditional language: perhaps no other branch of fiction could contain a statement like Nigel Strangeway's in Blake's (1904-1972) *There's Trouble Brewing* that "I was suckled on irregular verbs." Not only did the most prominent writers understand the ablative absolute, they made strenuous war on awkward, incorrect, or old-fashioned prose. A.A. Milne plainly set this out in his 1924 preface to *The Red House Mystery* (1922):

> The detective, however, (said the author) "was more concerned to discover how the murderer had effected an egress." It is, to me, a distressing thought that in nine-tenths of the detective stories of the world murderers are continually effecting egress when they might just as easily go out. The sleuth, the hero, the many suspected all use this strange tongue, and we may be forgiven for feeling that neither the natural excitement of killing the right man, nor the strain of suspecting the wrong one, is sufficient excuse for so steady a flow of bad language.

*Trent's Last Case, The Rasp* (1924), and many other golden age books, take time out from the action to insert broadsides on the state of the language. Thus, just as the American hard-boiled story of the same period found some of its drive in the introduction and exploitation of a new kind of language, the golden age story in Britain and America ran in part on attention to, and fascination with, words. The results in the golden age story appeared in the precision, the play, and the general self-consciousness about language in these stories. Indeed, these things provided authors with a range of techniques generally ignored by earlier detective writers. Some books, like Josephine Tey's (1896-1952) *The Man in the Queue* (1929), turn on puns; some, like Queen's *The French Powder Mystery* (1930) or Heyer's *The Unfinished Clue* (1934), have clues in their titles; and a majority of books of the period revolve around some sort of linguistic quibble in the text, like Christie's description of the false murder in *And Then There Were None* (1930) using figurative language. Golden Age writers' close attention to, and fascination with, language helped them to build not only their plots, but also their most memorable characters. Bentley's Trent, Sayers' Wimsey, Allingham's Campion, Marsh's (1899-1982) Alleyn, and many others use peppy, witty language; even Christie had a bit of linguistic fun in creating bits of fractured English for Poirot.

The amalgam of literary allusion, schoolboy slang, Americanisms, jokes, popular songs, lazy speech, hunting terms, babytalk, and other highly colored ingredients appeared frequently in the dialogue of golden age stories and became an attraction for readers in its own right. This sort of language, of course, came from the popularity of P.G. Wodehouse's comic novels, and as such, participated in a literary fad. The very act of writing this sort of dialogue, joined with the intellectual thrill of hiding the obvious facts with succinct yet devious language to provide one of the essential attractions of writing detective novels during the golden age, and the fascination of playing with words helped to introduce new sorts of people to writing detective stories.

One of the reasons that the detective story changed between the wars is that it attracted new kinds of writers. Before the 1920's, indeed after the 1920's, the most popular mystery writers were either uncultured hacks like Edgar Wallace, E. Phillips Oppenheim, and Sax Rohmer or were people with technical educations like Doyle and Freeman. Writers with the sophistication of Chesterton, in other words, were in the minority. After the Great War, new classes of writers turned to the detective story.

First, and most importantly, women took to the genre; women writers almost dominate the period. Agatha Christie was the first of them. Beginning with *The Mysterious Affair at Styles* (1920), Christie became the most popular of the golden age writers. She alone of the British golden age writers rose to the top of the best seller lists, and "a Christie for Christmas" became a regular feature of almost fifty years of publishing. Even though Christie possessed, and professed, little talent as a writer, had little to say on moral, social, philosophical, theological, or intellectual issues, and owned only a modest talent for drawing character, she excelled in creating complex crime situations of the least likely suspect school. She also demonstrated conclusively that the detective short story could become the short detective novel.

Dorothy L. Sayers did much more to establish the detective story as a semi-legitimate literary form. From *Whose Body?* (1923) onward, Sayers used the detective novel as a means of examining serious issues. In her books, therefore, we find discussions of the relationship between faith and science, the nature of sin, the roles of the sexes, and other issues crucial to the intellectual life of the times mixed with the unfolding of the detective story.

Margery Allingham wrote a mixed bag of detective story genres. She started with a book that was half spoof and half thriller, *The Crime at Black Dudley* (1929), and progressed through more mature parodies and more earnest thrillers, as well as through the detective story versions of the psychological novel and the novel of manners.

Largely known for her detective novel revolving around Richard III, *The Daughter of Time* (1951), Josephine Tey wrote little detective fiction between the wars, but her *The Man in the Queue* and *A Shilling for Candles* (1934) compare well with other cultivated and peppy detective novels of the period.

Ngaio Marsh was the last of the prominent women writers of the period. Her books, from *A Man Lay Dead* (1934) on, carry out some motifs from Sayers, especially in terms of characters, but Marsh concentrates heavily on setting, detection, and character rather than on the larger issues in Sayers.

In many ways, creating detective stories liberated women writers of the 1920's and 1930's. It may not have been as noticeable as chaining oneself to the rails at 10 Downing Street, but the detective story offered women writers and women readers an alternative to the gushy, bubble-headed love romance which was the typical popular form written by and for women at the end of the Victorian era. Although the extensive use of female detectives in turn-of-the-century fiction denied the character of the woman investigator to writers looking for fresh types to use as detective heroes, women writers of the golden age, nonetheless, accomplished much by altering the popular stereotypes of the male detective. Women's male heroes, like Wimsey, Campion, Grant, Alleyn, and even Poirot, undercut the schoolboy masculinity and neutered nature of the traditionally male detective. For one thing, most of them differ from the rugged, square-jawed he-men of turn-of-the-century fiction. For another, most of them fall in love and marry during the course of their books. Their relationships with their wives open in them a fuller, more sensitive, and more vulnerable humanity which they, in turn, bring to their detection. Women writers helped detectives to become human beings.

The other homogeneous class of writers who took up the detective story during the golden age was that of dons and intellectuals. From early in the century, the detective story appealed to people at the universities. G.D.H. Cole, the famous economist, took time out from his academic work to write *The Brooklyn Murders* (1923) in collaboration with his wife Margaret and a long succession of detective titles followed. Ronald Knox (1888-1957) became the Roman Catholic chaplain at Oxford the same year his *Viaduct Murder* (1925) appeared. Knox continued to write complex problems framed with light, amusing prose until his superiors pressured him to stop in 1937. With Michael Innes (1906- ), a professor of literature took to the detective novel. From his *Death at the President's Lodging* (1936) onward, Innes produced some of the most intricate plots and the zaniest books to appear under the title of the detective story. C. Day Lewis took to writing detective novels, in 1935, with *A Question of Proof* long before he became Poet Laureate; C.P. Snow (1905-1980) wrote *Death Under Sail* (1932) long before he became a spokesman for science and culture.

Most of these professional intellectuals started to write detective stories for the money, as have a number of later college professors and poets. They continued writing because of the money, but also because they became addicted. They contributed several things to the golden age story, not the least of which is status. When critics used to compile lists of important people who read detective stories in order to persuade the public of their legitimacy, academics ranked right behind kings, presidents, and dictators. For another thing, academic detective writers introduced the university as a setting, and it has endured as a conventional locale up to today. Finally, the academic writers solidified the high level of cultural awareness—in allusions, in dialogue, and in classical structure—which had been implicit in the detective novel since Sayers.

The last class of golden age writers is hardly a class, but a collection of miscellaneous bright young men who helped to remake the detective story of the period. The first of these was E.C. Bentley, whose *Trent's Last Case* began the whole movement and remains one of the most influential golden age books. Bentley's turn of mind shows best in his creation of the Clerihew, an intricate verse form and in his life-long friendship with G.K. Chesterton. *Trent's Last Case*, Bentley's only important detective novel, combines the comedy and cleverness inherent in the comic verse form with Chesterton's deviousness in setting up detective situations, and includes these things in a framework which became the first modern detective novel.

A.A. Milne repeats a similar pattern. He, too, invented a comic verse form, the Milnic, the spirit of which survived in some of his work as editor of *Punch*. Milne's *The Red House Mystery* established a standard of ease and playfulness which later writers either envied or, like Raymond Chandler, detested as a model of the golden age story.

Philip MacDonald drew somewhat on *Trent's Last Case* in his composition of *The Rasp*. Although his golden age books contain problems as complicated and elegant as most contemporary detective fiction, MacDonald had in him yearnings for the psychological thriller which first appeared in *Murder Gone Mad* (1931) and later in *The List of Adrian Messinger* (1959).

Anthony Berkeley Cox entered with *The Layton Court Mystery* (1925), in which he tried to build the most offensive detective possible in his Roger Sheringham. Cox demonstrated a bent for acid detective burlesque in his early books. With his three novels written under the pseudonym of Francis Iles (*Malice Aforethought*, 1931; *Before the Fact*, 1932; and *As for the Woman*, 1939), Cox turned from the golden age story and moved to probe the fissures and scrofula of the criminal mind.

The American cousins who created Ellery Queen began with S.S. VanDine's priggish hero, Philo Vance, borrowed from Clemence Dane's *Enter Sir John* (1928), and won a detective story contest with *The Roman Hat Mystery* (1929). Ellery Queen went on to rival Christie for popularity, but the energy of the creators also helped to publicize the merits of the detective story. Queen founded *Ellery Queen's Mystery Magazine* (1941) and has contributed to our knowledge of detective stories through numerous prefaces, articles, and bibliographies.

Finally, John Dickson Carr (1906-1977) hit the scene with *It Walks by Night* (1930). Carr went on to create some of the most baffling plots, the funniest characters, and the most boffo situations in detective fiction. He is also, along with Sayers, one of the most forthright and distinctive commentators on the nature of detective fiction.

Taken together, these men brought wit, energy, the urge to innovate, and the urge to publicize. They created some significant detective books, and they did much to define and promote the genre. They talked on the B.B.C., reviewed, wrote introductions, and, especially Ellery Queen, tried to explain the detective story to a much wider public than reached by the quasi-academic treatments in pioneer critical works like H. Douglas Thomson's *Masters of Mystery* (1931) and Howard Haycraft's *Murder for Pleasure* (1941).

Golden age stories, in all of their varieties and permutations, began with the essential problem of how to turn the detective short story into the detective novel. While it was locked into the short story form, the detective story faced certain limitations in its relationship to readers, in the nature of plotting, in the variety and articulation of character, and in theme. When the short story became the short novel, a whole range of technical devices became available to the writers, and the expansion into the novel also gave detective writers the opportunity to do the same things which mainstream literature accomplishes. As we have seen, turn-of-the-century writers never quite learned how to write detective novels successfully. The popularity of Gaboriau and Doyle institutionalized them as models and perpetuated the awkwardness of the inserted story structure in detective novels. Thriller writers opted for the episodic structure of the romance, and some writers, like Rinehart, attempted to sustain a detective problem for three hundred pages by maintaining gothic atmospherics and personal hysterics throughout their books. Even though these patterns continued to influence writers on the fringes of the detective story, by the 1920's, educated readers could not accept them. Inclined to expect a modest level of realism in their reading, semi-schooled by the tight structure of the modern novel, and conversant with propaganda for the "well made play," readers of detective novels demanded something more consistent, compact, and tight than what was offered by the last generation of writers.

The central problem, then, was how to expand the detective story plot, founded on economy and the sudden springing of the surprise, to the length of the novel. Golden age writers discovered a number of solutions to the problem. One answer came from the new understanding of the history of the detective story. During the golden age, writers were no longer held in total bondage by Doyle, as were turn-of-the-century authors. They could look elsewhere for models, and one of the first people they looked to was Wilkie Collins. Governed by the new aesthetics of the modern novel, detective writers began to appreciate and imitate Collins' achievements in *The Moonstone*. The first of the golden age novels, *Trent's Last Case*, bears some striking similarities to Collins' novel. Both books, for instance, break in the middle and the heroes go off on a continental jaunt, just as both books demonstrate the heroes' inability to solve the problem without outside intervention. Collins also taught golden age writers the importance of point of view. We can see his influence most clearly in the document books of the golden age, novels like Sayers' and Eustace's *The Documents in the Case* (1930) and Innes' *Lament for a Maker* (1938) which assemble the testimony of several characters. More pervasively, Collins freed detective writers from the memoirs of the obtuse assistant.

Due to the influence of Collins' manipulations of point of view in his novels, golden age writers experimented with story-telling techniques. Instead of the memoir voice, we find the wry commentary of a third person narrator taking over the job in most golden age stories. All the rules required this new narrator to play fair, but we find, as in Collins, he does not have to bend over backwards to do it. Detective writers discovered, in other words, that hiding facts by employing the elegant sleight of hand of the narrator gave a cleverer, more sophisticated effect than simply using a Watson. Collins also set the pattern for narrative consistency which golden age stories follow: if the detective mentions something in the solution, it really does appear in the body of the novel.

Several things resulted from this. First, because there was now world and time enough, writers could and did give increased attention and detailed description to the scene of the crime (the situation of the room, its contents, the dispositions of persons, etc.), and this, in turn, enlarged the explanation at the close of the book, with each fact from the beginning revisited and explained. Collins, further, demonstrated to golden age writers that one could return again and again to the consideration of a set of facts or questions without alienating readers. Turn-of-the-Century writers did none of these things. They stood mainly on the demonstration of genius, and the writer had neither the space nor the inclination to elaborate on the details of the plot. Collins showed golden age writers how to plot detective novels. He could not, alas, show them infallible ways of being vivid, dynamic, and interesting. For every writer who built an engaging detective novel on Collins' patterns of intellectual elaboration, a ream of writers produced books which were mechanical and arid.

Golden age writers, however, had other devices for making the detective story into the novel. One of the most popular of these was the "defective detective." The detective, whose main feature is his fallibility, could have appeared only in the twenties, as a part of the half-burlesque spirit which pervades the golden age. Most golden age writers carry a comic chip on their shoulders toward the tradition of the great detective. Failure to solve the crime, moreover, made a character point and suggested a method of extending the length of the narrative. All a writer had to do was write one story leading up to the detective's mistaken conclusions and then follow it with another, using the same facts, in which the detective, or someone else, succeeds in solving the case. Bentley did precisely this when he wrote *Trent's Last Case*, and Cox's Roger Sheringham novels work the same way.

From this two-step pattern, golden age writers concocted novels out of a dialectic of conclusions. Instead of offering only one false solution and one true one, writers began to introduce groups of detectives, each of whom puts his two cents' worth in. When we get a novel like Sayers' *The Five Red Herrings* (1931), or like some of Christie's and most of Carr's, the writer can spend most of the novel simply setting forth the alternate solutions before arriving at the final one.

These multiple solution books not only show one way of making a novel, they also demonstrate some spiritual essentials about the golden age story. First of all, the story in which the readers find half-a-dozen alternate explanations for the same facts, all of which seem reasonable and conclusive, cuts away at the sense of reality: readers know the last solution is the best, not because it is right or true, but because it comes last. The multiple solution story, consequently, stands not as an example of an unshakable logical edifice, but as a monument to the cleverness of the writer.

While earlier detective writers evoked astonishment from their revealed solutions, golden age writers deliberately set out to be clever. This shows not only with the multiple solution story, but also in the fact that, with golden age novels, we enter the world of the double reverse fake. It was the pinball realm of books founded on postulates like "he thinks that I think that he thinks so he'll not think but to outsmart him I'll not think either." This sort of thing occurs in the criminals and detectives of the novels, but it extends, too, to the relationship between writer and reader. Nothing is certain in golden age novels but death. Christie did things like apparently exonerating the most suspicious party, running an innocent man through a murder trial, and then proving the first man was guilty all along. And so did lots of other writers. They did this sort of thing because of their double devotion to making the detective story a novel and to exhibiting their own ingenuity.

Finally, to the process of building detective novels, golden age writers added one element conspicuously absent in turn-of-the-century short stories: they added people. Because of the nature of its form, the short story cannot introduce many people. If you mark off space for setting up the great detective, for establishing the enigmatic crime, and for explaining the surprise solution, not much room remains for characterizing, analyzing, and eliminating suspects. Turn-of-the-century stories, in fact, do not run on suspects; they semi-miraculously produce a person implied by the detective's digestion of the facts. The term "who done it," then, applied originally to golden age books, for golden age writers evolved the convention of using a group of suspects. The gathering of the millionaire, the secretary, the wife, the house guests, the malignant neighbor, and so on is a golden age idea. Suspects, of course, provide a sure-fire way of making a short story into a novel. They bulk out the fiction by adding characterization, and as writers learned from Collins, they fortify the detective story by becoming straw people among whom the author can shift suspicion, as well as being diversified centers of information to whom the detective needs to appeal. Given that even fictional people often misjudge, misperceive, and lie, the detective must also closely analyze suspects' information before making it a part of his solution.

Once golden age writers combined these elements to form the detective novel, they almost simultaneously discovered they were working toward something very like a play, and then in turn used the drama as model and inspiration for building their detective novels. Many of the golden age writers, after all, were also dramatists: A.A. Milne, Pooh notwithstanding, was principally a playwright; Tey wrote plays as Gordon Daviot, more plays than detective novels; Carr wrote dozens of radio plays for the B.B.C.; Sayers' final Wimsey novel, *Busman's Honeymoon* (1937), was a play rewritten as a novel; and, of course, more people have seen Christie's *The Mousetrap* (1952) than most other plays, and Christie had been writing plays since the early 1930's.

Detective novels are, in fact, very much like plays with their manageable groups of diverse people placed under stress by calamity, limited locale and set scenes. What actor would not love to play the detective in the summation and solution scene? Detective novels are, if nothing else, talky; they are full of dialogue. It is in speeches that detectives of the golden age detect or reflect and transact most of their business, as opposed to the lock-jawed sleuths of the last generation. The drama had something to do with this. The stylized group of suspects, in some ways, responds to the usual run of character actors: the ingenue, the vamp, the comic foreigner, Colonel Blimp, the unflappable butler, and so on. The structure of golden age novels, too, owes something to the drama. Michael Innes' novels draw extensively, and admittedly, from the patterns of stage farce.

More widespread, however, golden age detective novels observe certain rules which had governed the drama from the time of Aristotle. Golden age novels take place in one fixed, limited locale. The village, the big house, the university, the hotel, and the theater typify the cordon which writers drew around their action. The closed setting, of course, exists to eliminate the possibility that anyone in the world could have done the murder. But it also exists to provide for the audience the security of what Aristotle called the unity of place. Too much travelling, he held, disorients the spectator and destroys the illusion the dramatist is trying to create. Golden age writers knew all about this.

They also knew about Aristotle's unity of time, which prohibits the dramatist from covering more than a short chronological slice. In golden age novels, therefore, it is the exceptional case that takes more than a few days to wrap up, and as a rule, if a case takes longer than that, it becomes either a thriller or a psychological study. Keeping time limited helped golden age writers establish an illusion parallel to that which exists in the theater. All of the dramatic elements in golden age fiction, however, come as no surprise. They may have helped writers solve technical problems, but they also appear because the theater was a favorite pastime of the 1920's and 1930's. From the eternal revival of farces like *Charley's Aunt*, to Shaw, to the problem plays, puzzle plays, and eventually detective plays, people flocked to the theater. The detective novel of the period simply brought some of the same things into people's houses.

Although the theater, at its best, can transmit a real sense of tension and evoke the psychological claustrophobia so necessary to part of the detective novel, and although theater can reproduce witty repartee (even if it cannot catch the narrative voice) so vital to many golden age novels, it cannot do much with the variety of emotions experienced in the adventure plot. The hunt and the chase have no real place in the theater: they belong either to the cinema or, even better, to narrative literature. No matter how much critics, readers, and writers try to intellectualize it, the detective story inevitably contains elements of the hunt. Under all of the acting and the talk, the criminal stalks his victim and the detective hunts the criminal. On the one hand, golden age writers tried to subdue this rowdy and untoward aspect of the detective story. They wanted neither the episodic plotting nor the schoolboy heroes of Buchan and lesser thriller writers.

On the other hand, most of the prominent writers, like Christie, Philip MacDonald, Cox, Marsh, Allingham, and others, not only wrote thrillers, in addition to their detective novels, but recognized what a neutered thing a detective novel can become without flashes of thrill and panic and a strenuous hunt and chase. In addition to including moments of danger and threat (usually in the middle and the end of the plot to pick up the pace), golden age writers modified the basic elements of the thriller so they could fit the more civilized form of the detective story. The first thing they did to subversively introduce the thriller into the detective story was to play substantial attention to games. Virtually every novel of the period makes prominent mention of play and games: blindman's bluff, hide and seek, treasure and scavenger hunts, twenty questions, and sundry other party games appear in novel after novel. Bridge, chess, and in American novels, poker play large roles and, from the mid-twenties onward, golden age writers seeded into their novels analogies with the jig-saw or the newly invented crossword puzzle. Games occupy people in the novels and, as metaphors, they preoccupy writers. All of the game business has implications for characterization and for the semi-intellectual theme of the golden age novel, in addition to serving as an illustration of the ways in which middle-class people of the twenties and thirties used their leisure. But in spite of their harmless exteriors, these games appeal to the same instincts thrillers do. Few games represent anything but war or some other struggle for mastery—even puzzles and solitaire embody a struggle against an inanimate or abstract object. With the games in their detective novels, therefore, golden age writers simply substituted abstract and superficially polite contests for the more elemental combats of the thriller. When we see a chess or bridge motif run through a novel, when we find characters like Milne's Antony Gillingham who "play detective," and when we discover a game at a crucial point in a golden age novel, we really are witnessing disguised thriller motifs writers used in, and for, themselves, as well as to subdue some of the inevitable moral impact of crime. When writers close their books with suspense and danger, as does Sayers in *Unnatural Death* (1927), they use thriller craft to provide an emphatic conclusion. The action close, however, also slams the door on serious thought because it establishes good and evil in action and then disposes of the villain before readers have the opportunity to consider the plight of his suffering.

When golden age writers expanded the detective story into the detective novel, they had to modify certain traditional features of the genre, but this modification opened up new opportunities for developing plots. Just as importantly, the expansion of the detective form from short story to novel gave much more room for the development of character. Writers no longer had to establish their detective's nature in a paragraph or two with some brief action added, and they could now expand the number and nature of the other characters far beyond the non-existent or limited cast of people mandated by the short story form.

In terms of absolute numbers and technique, golden age writers went far beyond their progenitors in drawing the detective story's characters. When judged by the standards of reality, or by the standards of mainstream literature, they made only limited progress toward presenting complete human beings, and some particularly sensitive writers, like Sayers, recognized this failure. With their detective characters, golden age writers continued to be stuck in the traditions of the great detective, but, increasingly, cracks began to appear and broaden in this monument to unaging intellect.

On the whole, golden age writers began with the premise that the more sophisticated a character is, the better detective he makes. Sayers' Wimsey, VanDine's Philo Vance, Queen's Ellery Queen, Blake's Nigel Strangeways, Innes' Appleby, Marsh's Alleyn, H.C. Bailey's (1878-1961) Reggie Fortune, and a host of others, not only know what fork to use, but display exhaustive knowledge of Ming vases, post mortem lividity, Elizabethan drama, forensic ophthalmology, cocker spaniels, and a wealth of alternatingly cultured and grisly information. This sort of thing, carried to an extreme, led Ogden

Nash to compose the couplet "Philo Vance/ Needs a kick in the pance," but appearing in the detectives of more competent writers, it becomes bearable. The cultured detective arose, frankly, from the snobbishness inherent in many golden age stories—snobbishness shared by writers and readers. The detective's encyclopedic knowledge was also the logical outcome of the urge to base detective stories on trivia (a practice continued in the game of trivia in the 1970's and 1980's).

Although golden age detectives conduct, of necessity, more protracted investigations than Holmes or Thorndyke, they almost always deliver the goods at the end of the novel, and clever, intricate, ingenious goods they are. But every so often, the great detective fails. Both the desire to write the anti-detective burlesque, as well as the desire to thwart readers' expectations, stimulated a crop of detectives who make partial or complete fools of themselves. Philip Trent finds the wrong answer in *Trent's Last Case*, the novel which kicked off the golden age, and Anthony Berkeley's Roger Sheringham makes a substantial error in each of his novels. In a small group of books, including Christie's *And Then There Were None* and MacDonald's *The Rynox Murder* (1931), no one can solve the problem, but the answer arrives through the mails.

Most writers, however, avoided the fallible detective because, in part, the genius of their continuing detective heroes paid. Yet, even in more or less pure examples of the great detective, writers often showed some embarrassment, and they tried to compensate for using an old-fashioned figure by making him into a partly comic character. Christie's fastidious little Belgian was an attempt by a writer, not terribly gifted in the line, to mask the great detective as an alternately absurd and comic figure. Milne does better with Antony Gillingham, and Allingham does better yet, but no writer succeeded in combining the great detective with comedy better than did John Dickson Carr in his novels about Dr. Fell and Sir Henry Merrivale.

If the great detective sometimes errs or plays the fool for the cause or just for the fun of it, he nonetheless remains the great detective in that he controls and manages the denouement: his clever solution ties him back to Dupin and all the rest. In the twenties, Freeman Wills Crofts (1879-1957), and in the thirties Marsh, Innes, and Georges Simenon (1903—), slightly modified the mold by switching from the amateur detective to the professional policeman. Most police heroes, however, differ very little in their functions from the talented amateur, and with the exception of Simenon's Maigret, the policemen belong to the same class as the rich young toffs who take up detecting as a hobby.

But there is a difference between the great detectives of the golden age and the great detectives of the turn of the century. It lies in the differing attitudes toward mental operations. Some golden age writers do plod along the same mechanical-mathematical track laid down by turn-of-the-century fiction. Christie, when she concerns herself about Poirot's thinking, stresses method in the same way R. Austin Freeman did. Among many golden age writers, however, a revolution against mechanical logic and minute scientific investigations took place. Many writers agreed with Milne who, in 1924, wrote

> What satisfaction is it to you or me when the famous Professor examines the small particle of dust which the murderer has left behind him, and infers that he lives between a brewery and a flour mill? What thrill do we get when the blood spot on the missing man's handkerchief proves that he was recently bitten by a camel? Speaking for myself, none.

If writers like Milne (and later Marsh and Innes, who make remarks as pointed toward Freeman as this one) rejected the mental operations of the scientific story, they also questioned the whole machine-mind analogy of earlier detective fiction. *Trent's Last Case* ends with the conclusion that human reason is impotent—the same conclusion which Papa Tabaret made before Gaboriau decided to make his livelihood out of writing *romans policier*. In a more optimistic vein, Innes, in *Lament for a Maker*, compares problem solving to a complex bio-chemical reaction rather than the meshing of cogs, cams, and gears. Sayers, at the beginning of the golden age, admitted there was little that was mechanical about her detective's conclusions. At the end of *Whose Body?*, she describes Wimsey's moment of insight as:

> ...not one thing, nor another thing, nor a logical succession of things, but everything— the whole thing, perfect, complete, in all its dimensions as it were and instantaneously; as if he stood outside the world and saw it suspended in infinitely dimensional space.

Wimsey finds truth by "no logical process that the conscious mind can detect" and, consequently, Sayers seeds the description with the language of mysticism. Golden age writers, even the boldest of them, could only carry this sort of description so far. To redefine cognition in any sort of radical way, some would say accurate way, destroys the detective story which rests upon a set of assumptions about the material world and the uses, if not the nature, of rationality and perception. Some golden age writers, however, nibbled at the prevailing nineteenth-century notions of the detective as a thinking machine.

As we have seen, the cast of characters in the golden age detective novel was an innovation in itself. The listing of dramatis personae at the beginning of Ellery Queen's novels, and increasingly, in the thirties in the novels of others, points to the theatrical origins of many of these groups of characters. Aside from the major detective, however, the characters in golden age novels go little beyond stereotypes. Part of this came from the practice of using types similar to character actors in drama. Part of the general superficiality of characters in detective novels came from the necessity of hiding the criminal until the surprise solution; this meant that authors could not extensively examine the criminal's character without examining everyone's, and this, of course, is impractical. Another contributor to the slightness of characterization during the golden age is the self-imposed rules which writers, critics, and publishers promulgated. In his "Rules of the Game" appended to *Murder for Pleasure*, for instance, Howard Haycraft gave this advice to detective story writers:

> Admittedly, not all characters can be drawn with the same amount of detail as is devoted to the central sleuth in a form as compressed as the modern detective story...But they must be made clearly recognizable in outline—just as a clever caricaturist or shadowgraph artist can identify his subjects with a few strokes.

Along these same lines, Dodd Mead advised writers aiming for publication in the Red Badge series "characterization of the other persons in the novel...should be plausible and interesting without intruding on the plot." Given these artistic limitations, writers evolved simplified schemes which limited characterization by limiting allowable motives for murder. In *Peril at End House* (1932), Christie establishes there are only four possible motives for murder—gain, hatred, envy, or fear. In the abstract, these four vices can stem from a fairly large number of human circumstances. In practice, however, they reduce to rather pedestrian triggers of violence, and they certainly cannot encompass the wilderness of motives for violent crimes in literature and life. Some detective writers of the golden age realized this and tinkered with the structure of the genre in order to make points about people other than the detective. Sayers, for instance, gives only the most perfunctory camouflage to the villains in her novels in order to inspect their characters, and Cox, in *The Second Shot* (1931), made his first move toward the deeper sounding of human behavior. These two writers, indeed, most of the genuinely thoughtful detective writers of the golden age, realized that in order to thrive, the detective story had to move toward mainstream literature.

The history of the more important detective writers of the golden age is the history of writers combining other and older literary forms with the basic fabric of the detective story. Indeed, some of the worth of the detective story as a literary form resides in its adaptability, as well as its capacity for elaboration. One of the first of these other literary forms to join the detective story was the novel of manners.

In some ways, the detective story naturally leads into the novel of manners. After all, with its closed settings, as well as the selection of character types that normally inhabit those settings, the detective novel approximates the novel of manners. All that is needed is a slight shift of authorial emphasis away from the crime problem and toward portraying the manners of the particular people and place. We can observe this shift taking place in many golden age books. Any number of books of the period draw as much energy from depicting manners, morals, and personality generated by the unique setting as they do from the detective problem. Michael Innes, in fact, quoted from *Every Man in His Humour*, the grandfather of fiction about manners, when he defined the aim of his *Death at the President's Lodging*. These detective novels of manners range from the depressing, almost naturalistic portrait of the house of the dead, to the keenly satiric view of institutions and classes of people. In some cases, the satiric novel of manners deliberately descends, or ascends, into farce. Early Allingham, mid-career Innes, and almost total-career Carr display in their detective novels the desire to ladle as much slapstick, wit, and bizarre comedy into their books as they will hold.

In one of his departures from the comic detective novel, Carr also wrote a historical novel *cum* detective story in *The Murder of Sir Edmund Godfrey* (1936). With this book, Carr combined the golden age's interest in historical criminology (in Palmer and Crippen and all the rest) with the detective writer's skill and the historical novelist's capacity for recreating accurate background and people. Since the thirties, therefore, we can find detective novels about Sam Johnson, Aristotle, and Richard the Lion Heart as detectives. We can also find neo-Sherlock Holmes novels, like those of Nicholas Meyer. All of them are, in part, historical novels.

Finally, in the thirties, the detective novel merged with the psychological novel. Almost all detective stories, to be sure, have psychological potential, but short story writers ignored it for one reason and golden age writers for another. In the teens and twenties, middle class readers tarred the psychological novel with the same brush they used on Freud, and they usually saw Freud as morbid, immoral, and disgusting. To attempt a psychological detective novel for these readers was, at best, tricky. Writers began to introduce a kleptomaniac here and a megalomaniac there, but this was as far as most golden age writers dared to go. In the twenties, however, Sayers tried to center her novels around a more traditional kind of psychology, the psychology of salvation. She always felt, however, that the form of the detective story, with its detective, puzzle, and solution, restricted her serious consideration of human beings' internal lives. Detective novels moved more emphatically toward the psychological novel when Cox stood the form on its head and wrote *Malice Aforethought* in 1931. This book, along with the two other Francis Iles novels, eliminates the detective and instead gives us a case study of the kind of weak, corrupt, nasty little people who commit crimes. Even though Cox moved out of the detective story when he wrote as Francis Iles, these psychological crime novels, to some extent, liberated detective writers of the thirties to treat human beings with more depth and complexity.

At the same time some golden age novelists attempted to widen the literary appeal of the detective story, others attempted to narrow it. In the late twenties, novels appeared which followed, instead of breaking, the rules: novels which tried to banish every element but the detective and the crime puzzle. They admitted no love interest, little characterization, sparse description of the setting, and no theme beyond the solution to an intricate and complex puzzle. This movement received much of its impetus from Americans. S.S. VanDine's *The Benson Murder Case* (1926) may have started the trend toward puzzle novels, but Ellery Queen and a number of American and British writers climbed on the bandwagon. Even Sayers wrote a puzzle novel, *The Five Red Herrings*.

The puzzle novel comes from several sources. Naturally, it exploits and emphasizes the problem and surprise inherent in all detective stories. To some extent, the puzzle novel grew from the passion for games in the 1920's, and puzzle novels frequently invoke the crossword puzzle, that American invention of the decade. Inspired by these sources, the puzzle novel, for the first time, took advantage of the reader-writer contest suggested, but never fully used, in earlier detective books. Finally, the puzzle novel began and thrived because it served as a defense against detractors. Puzzle novels provided readers with the (less than valid) justification that their leisure reading was really mental exercise; they also set up a snobbish intellectual defense against the hard-boiled story.

To fortify the puzzle element in their novels, writers, sometimes encouraged by publishers, developed a list of original and rebuilt devices they used to encourage and heighten the readers' intellectual relationship with the puzzle. Increasingly, therefore, the golden age novels contain:

1.  maps or architectural drawings
2.  technical diagrams or drawings
3.  time tables
4.  lists of alibis and motives
5.  documents in cipher
6.  challenges to readers
7.  narrative gaps with warnings that something is missing
8.  sealed chapters or pages
9.  warning footnotes
10.  informative footnotes
11.  lists of questions
12.  partial documents
13.  lists of dramatis personae
14.  narrative warnings to pay attention

For all of these special devices, few readers used them. One finds few marginal jottings or queries added by readers in library or second hand copies of golden age puzzle books. The single-minded devotion to the puzzle story ran counter to most appeals made by narrative fiction over its two-thousand year history. This concentrated attention to puzzle structure was ruinous. For one thing, it produced some very bad books—to read S.S. VanDine is to understand the true meaning of stultification. Furthermore, the idea of the puzzle infected criticism of the detective story. Even an old horse like R. Austin Freeman, who disposed of puzzles in his inverted stories, became a victim of the term when he used it to define detective stories in his 1931 introduction to the Everyman edition of *The Mysteries of Udolpho*.

Instead of forming a new and continuing basis for detective fiction, the puzzle story became the basis of non-literary entertainments. In 1928, Lassiter Wren and Randle McKay produced *The Baffle Book*, a collection of "detective problems" complete with exhibits like fingerprints and tire tracks. *The Baffle Book* sets a problem, asks questions, and awards points for correct answers—the key being at the back of the book. There is no attempt at narrative fiction. Dennis Wheatley took this idea one step further with his "crime files," beginning with *File on Bolitho Blane* (1936). Actually planned by J.G. Links, these looseleaf binders contain miscellaneous documents and even bits of physical evidence (hair, matches, stained fabric) sealed in cellophane envelopes. There is no narrative other than that made by the player, but even that is controlled by the sealed answer at the end. Parker Brothers' "CLUE" becomes the ultimate child of the puzzle story.

Even if the puzzle story grew out of literature into the actual world of games, it did contribute to golden age fiction and detective stories in general. It reminded readers of Collins' practice and narrative consistency and elevated this by emphasizing "fair play." It inspired writers to increase the complexity and intricacy of their plots. And most importantly, it gave writers something to reject so they could go about the business of writing detective stories.

The last notable fact about the golden age of the detective story is that it ended. Some writers, like Knox, Sayers, and Cox, simply stopped writing detective stories. Some writers, like Philip MacDonald, turned to the thriller. Even people who continued to write detective stories changed. Innes alternated thrillers with detective novels, as did Christie. After 1939, nothing remained the same. The war changed the rules of the game, and master criminals without sane motives loosed mass destruction on humanity. This now seemed more real than the murder at the garden party.

Yet, the golden age achieved much in its twenty year duration. Its writers consciously made and remade the detective story, and they invented the detective novel. They gentled the great detective, broke him of his mechanical intellect and cultivated his humanity. Golden age writers developed a solid new class of readers for the detective story in the intelligent, educated, decent members of the middle class. And for them, they made the detective story less of an isolated form and more of a literary form. Golden age novels became more complete entertainments, and the good ones pack more wit, style, culture, elegance, and cleverness per page than almost any kind of book, and certainly any kind of popular book. But who can be witty, stylish, elegant, and clever in an instant and for all people and ages? All of these qualities rest on artificiality, and so does the golden age detective story. No one has ever been shot with an icicle and murderers' confessions never take the form of the detective story. Yet, these things happen in golden age stories and their actuality makes no difference. In making the readers feel this, golden age stories accomplished much.

By the time we reach 1939, golden age writers had explored almost every possibility of their particular kind of detective fiction. Even though many of the original writers quit or changed forms, and even though hard-boiled writers have changed attitudes toward the detective genre, the golden age story enjoys a long after-life, maintained by new writers who use its patterns and sustained by readers who still long for wit, style, culture, elegance, and cleverness.

# Chapter 10

# The Hard-Boiled Story

With the notable exception of Poe and Gaboriau, the detective story was largely a British product; it was, at least, until the 1920's. Thus, even though American writers like Post, Adams, and Futrelle wrote original, interesting, and entertaining detective stories, the international traffic in detective fiction went mainly one way—from Britain to America. During the 1920's a few American writers, S.S. VanDine, Ellery Queen, and John Dickson Carr, crashed the party, but nevertheless the golden age of the detective story remained largely a British affair. American golden age writers, with the exception of Carr, aped the character and plot patterns of British fiction and some of them, like VanDine, skewed the balance of the detective novel by bending over backwards to demonstrate that Americans could be as smart and sophisticated as their Old World relatives.

The hard-boiled detective story changed all of this. This pugnaciously American variety of detective fiction attained a status which British golden age tales never achieved. By the 1930's and 1940's, Europeans came to view the works of Dashiell Hammett (1894-1961), Raymond Chandler (1888-1959), James M. Cain (1892-1977), and Horace McCoy (1897-1977) not simply as detective stories but as significant fiction which had important things to say about life. Even in Britain, the hard-boiled story made its impact when readers turned from the golden age novel to tough guy fiction by Peter Cheyney (1896-1951), Ian Fleming (1908-1964), and Len Deighton (1929- ). Back home, the hard-boiled detective story prompted the birth of a second generation of hard-boiled writers as diverse as Mickey Spillane (1918— ) and Ross Macdonald (1915-1983). With the hard-boiled story, then, the energy and initiative of detective fiction as an on-going form shifted from Britain to America. Nevertheless, the hard-boiled story does have a number of connections, in character, in plot and even in style, with the traditional detective story. In spite of the sniping back and forth between them, hard-boiled writers have things in common with their golden age peers. Both groups reacted against Holmes and the turn-of-the-century detective story. Both maligned the thriller but appropriated its technology. Both wanted to vivify the language of the detective story. And both tried to move the detective story into the world of mainstream literature. The principal difference between golden age writers and hard-boiled writers resides in the fact that golden age writers relied almost exclusively on cultivated European literary traditions and conventions, while the American writers fortified the abundant features of the established detective story with American literary traditions and conventions and with an atmosphere that brought a bit more realism to the genre.

To trace the hard-boiled detective story back to its origins, we must step away for a moment from the middle brow literature which we have been pursuing and go back to the beginnings of American popular fiction— popular in both the descriptive and derogatory senses. Books aimed at schoolboys and other minimally literate and demanding readers appeared in real numbers only around the middle of the nineteenth century. In Britain, the schoolboy story had a large effect on the development of the adventure story written for adults, but had little impact on the detective story, which always danced around the skirts of regular literature. Something different happened in the United States. The American dime novel originated a number of motifs which eventually had much to do with the detective story. These paperbound books, which farm boys read behind the barns and city boys hid behind their schoolbooks, introduced countless young Americans to the person of the detective and thrilled them with his adventures.

The dime novel began as an exercise in slick marketing. In June of 1860, Irwin Beadle (1826-1882) found a novel entitled *Malaeska: The Indian Wife of a White Hunter.* He reprinted it and blazoned it forth as "A Dollar Book for a Dime." Within a few years, the country was overrun with dime novels. These books of 25,000 to 35,000 words sold originally at newsstands (the American News Company had a standing order with Beadle for 60,000 copies) and then through the mails. In the 1870's, postal regulations forced dime publishers to print their novels in magazine instead of book form. At the beginning, dime novels had little to do with detective stories: they were mostly either bad imitations of Scott or Cooper or poor reworkings of British fiction. As the dime novel business boomed, publishers like Beadle, Smith & Street, and Tousey employed dozens of tame writers who manufactured millions of words a year, but who also helped to develop the new kinds of fiction that widened the popularity of the dime novel. Some distinctive types of the dime novel were not quite original: Smith & Street's Frank Merriwell books came pretty directly from British schoolboy fiction. But others were. Dime novels introduced an eager public to the Western story (in tales about Deadwood Dick, the James Brothers, and so on), the technology story (like tales about Tom Swift and his amazing inventions), and the rags to riches fable (perpetrated again and again by Horatio Alger). Dime novels also introduced American schoolboys and working men to the detective.

Beginning with Kenward Philip's serial, *The Bowery Detective* (1870), the detective became a popular dime novel hero and the detective story became a regular branch of cheap fiction in America. Long before Sherlock Holmes, dime publishers filled a growing demand from American readers for more and more detective stories. Old Sleuth, the first recurring dime detective, appeared in 1872. Cap. Collier followed in 1883 and was both the hero and "author" of the first line of dime novels exclusively devoted to detective stories (*The Old Cap. Collier Library*). Old and Young King Brady made their debut in 1885. And, in the following year, Nick Carter began a career which, sadly, still continues today. Beadle's titles included dime novels about Detective Dave, Detective Dick, Detective Frank, Detective Gordon, Detective Jake, Detective Matt, Detective Paul, and Detective Zach. Frank Tousey's New York Detective Library offered its readers messenger boy detectives, bell boy detectives, journalist detectives, boot black detectives, photographer detectives, fireman detectives, mail carrier detectives, preacher detectives, and many more. Although they now seem quaint, dime novel detective stories deserved the oblivion they have achieved. They were written quickly, aimed at an immature audience, and indeed never pretended to be anything but disposable.

But they do have specific sources, and they do contribute to the shaping of the hard-boiled story. The dime novel detective story was, first of all, the Eastern. The episodic plotting, some character patterns, and the interest in local color in the dime detective story repeat the earlier practice of the dime western. Indeed, almost one-third of Tousey's books in The New York Detective Library are about the James brothers. Allan Pinkerton also contributed to the genesis and popularity of the dime detective. Pinkerton worked assiduously to spread his name and fame throughout the country. One of his means was his publications like *The Expressman and the Detectives* (1874) and *Criminal Reminiscences and Detective Sketches* (1879). Horatio Alger's boys' stories also contributed some of the moral fervor to the dime detective story. The fact that Richard K. Fox (1846-1922) took over the *National Police Gazette* in 1874 and, within a few years made it into one of the most popular magazines in the world, no doubt has something to do with the appearance of what we call dime detective stories in the periodicals of the early 1880's. But along with these native sources were several foreign sources. With the terms sleuth and ferret, Vidocq was a popular synonym for "detective" in dime novels, featured in titles like *Violet Vane, the Ventriloquist Vidocq*, and *Young Vidocq; or, Shadowing the Crooks of Gotham*. Eugene Sawyer, one of the Nick Carter writers, admitted he " 'Americanized' one of the Nick Carters from Gaboriau in three days." Among the Gaboriauesque features of dime detective novels were: the insider's information about police methods, the omnipresent use of disguise, the master criminal, the detective versus the inept or corrupt rival, and the epic nature of the detective hero.

As disposable as they were, dime novels did contribute much to the creation of the hard-boiled detective and the hard-boiled detective story. In terms of character, dime detective heroes differed substantially from the detectives in Doyle or turn-of-the-century fiction. First of all, they were not intellectuals. The professional expertise of dime detectives boiled down to disguise, tracking, and eavesdropping. Rarely do we find dime detectives faced with a complicated intellectual problem, and they do most of their work with their feet or their fists. Instead, dime writers made their detective heroes exemplars of moral qualities. Dime fiction was boys' fiction and as such held as its main responsibility to inculcate morality in its readers. Thus, the dime detective embodied those virtues deemed necessary by nineteenth-century America. Dime detectives, therefore, are exemplars of determination, tenacity, pluck, chivalry, and honesty. The writers usually contrived the action to demonstrate these qualities at work. Although they are by no means universally violent, dime detectives usually demonstrate their "manly" virtues through energetic and definitive action. Dime detectives are also almost always private detectives. This founding in private enterprise may link to Pinkerton's celebrity or to the disorganized nature of organized law enforcement, but most dime detectives work for themselves.

These qualities of the detective hero dictate the nature of dime detective plots. Dime novel plots are rooted in the episodic nature of the dime western, and they depend almost exclusively on the narrative of the hunt and the chase. This means, also, that the plots are not dependent on problems. As the detective is not an intellectual, the problems which propel most dime detective stories present not mental but physical challenges. Typically, the readers know the identity of the villain and derive enjoyment from watching and feeling the process of pursuit.

Because dime detective plots tend to be peripatetic, they also take advantage of the literary fashion of local color writing. Stories in The New York Detective Library, for instance, took readers not only to New York and the West (the two dominant settings), but also to Chicago, New Orleans, the Ozarks, Boston, Philadelphia, Baltimore, and Cincinnati. Just as they felt the need to educate American boys in their moral duties, dime writers also felt the need to familiarize them with their own country.

Finally, dime detective novels provided some things in terms of style. Although they are, in the main, written in alternately stilted and simplistic English, dime novels did introduce dialect characters, particularly dialect characters who used underworld slang. Some of the better writers also understood and practiced commercial adventure writing. Eugene Sawyer, for instance, recognized how "necessary it is to begin the plot with the first word."

Dime detective novels, then, were far different from detective stories written in Britain at the end of the nineteenth century. This is due, perhaps, to the fact that American detection began with Pinkerton, who was either an undercover agent or a spy, and who was, in spite of his Scottish birth, a Westerner. British detection, on the other hand, began amidst the British prejudice against domestic spies and went to work in a very careful and almost hyper-legal manner. No matter what their origins were, dime novels set up certain conventions which were to continue in American detective fiction. The non-intellectual, intensely moral, occasionally violent private eye who participates in a hunt and chase story reflecting local color and told in a simple language goes back to the dime novel detective. The dime novel detective, in other words, continues in the hard-boiled story, but he continues in a much altered form.

In 1896, two years before Beadle's dime novel business collapsed, Frank Munsey began to print his magazine, *The Argosy*, on cheap uncoated paper made from wood pulp. With this economical measure, the pulp magazine was born. Not only were the new pulps inexpensive to produce, their publishers also energetically sought to dominate the market for cheap fiction. They introduced cover art which was colorful, packed with action, sensational, and often finely conceived to catch the eye and the imagination of the browser at the newsstand. They also reduced their own costs by accepting advertisements which, in turn, appealed to the same fantasies about self-improvement, eroticism, and manliness exploited by the fiction on the accompanying pages. Agony ads ("sis, please write to your old pal and sister") involved readers in one way and editorial advice columns involved them in another way: *Detective Story Magazine*, for instance, had regular columns on "What Handwriting Reveals" and "Expert Legal Advice." Pulp magazines, further, had the advantage over dime novels in that each issue typically carried a complete novel, parts of serial novels, and short stories.

Although the pulps began as outlets for miscellaneous fiction, by the teens they developed into specialized magazines for particular audiences. By the 1920's, we find pulp magazines devoted exclusively to stories about the sea, the railroad, aviation, pirates, football, boxing, cowboys, romance, horror, science fiction, and espionage, as well as a number of other subjects. There were, of course, detective pulps. In 1915, Smith & Street replaced the dime novel series *Nick Carter Weekly* with the first detective pulp, *Detective Story Monthly*. From then on, pulp detective magazines exploded on to the newsstands. By the 1930's, there were magazines like *Action Detective*, *Clues*, *Greater Gangster Stories*, *Nickel Detective*, *Black Aces*, *Black Book Detective*, *Double Detective*, *Strange Detective*, *Spicy Detective*, *Triple Detective*, and *Thrilling Detective*, to name only a few.

When the pulp detective magazines began in the teens, they offered little original in the way of the detective story: they just offered a lot of it. Typically, the pulps published uninspired fare mixed with pieces by successful British thriller writers like Oppenheim and Wallace and stories by turn-of-the-century writers like Arthur B. Reeve who had made their reputations in the "slicks." Throughout the twenties and thirties, the pulps often trailed along behind the bandwagon of the golden age movement. Their novelty features (like Lawrence Treat's "Detectograms—A Puzzle Feature" in *Ace High Detective* or the narrative crossword puzzles in *Detective Fiction Weekly*) demonstrate real subservience to the point-of-view of some golden age writers. In this sense, pulp magazines, at their inception and, to some extent, throughout their thirty-year life span, served up cut-rate versions of what was going on in the more ethereal realms of the golden age movement. Chandler may have been correct in saying that the average British detective novel was unfit for print, but he should have added that the average pulp detective story was much worse than the average British detective novel.

Not all pulp detective stories deserve to be pulped, and this was due mostly to the nurturing of the new hard-boiled story by *The Black Mask* magazine. Oddly enough, *The Black Mask* was not exclusively a detective story magazine: it ran love stories, oriental adventures, and cowboy yarns alongside its detective stories. The magazine began with H.L. Mencken. To finance his highbrow ventures, Mencken invested in pulp magazines. For a time he published *Spicy Stories*, and then to bail-out *The Smart Set*, Mencken and his partner George Jean Nathan created *The Black Mask*. They floated *The Black Mask* ("our new louse" as Mencken called it) for $500 and sold it six months later for $10,000.

It was not, however, the owners who made *The Black Mask* into a potent force in the history of the detective story. Rather, it was the editors and the writers they discovered. George W. Sutton, Jr. bought the first stories by Carroll John Daly (1889-1958) and Dashiell Hammett. Philip Cody took over from Sutton and, according to Erle Stanley Gardner (1889-1970), "with Cody, the action-type of detective story took a long stride forward." Finally, Joseph T. Shaw (1874-1952) took the job as editor of *The Black Mask* from 1926 until 1936.

Under Shaw, the magazine became the most important vehicle for the new type of American fiction, the hard-boiled story. We can see the extent to which *The Black Mask* dominated the market in that several pulps added "black" to their titles (*Black Aces, Black Book Detective*) in order to ride on the coattails of *The Black Mask*. We can also see it in W.T. Ballard's (1903-1980) comments about Ken White, the editor of *Dime Detective*:

Ken White had tried to copy *Black Mask* with *Dime*, but for some reason it never came off. I had known Ken for many years and used to kid him about being jealous of Shaw, which he was.

Sutton, Cody, and Shaw discovered and encouraged almost all of the important new detective writers. They discovered Hammett and Chandler along with lesser writers like Raoul Whitfield (1898-1945), Lester Dent (1905-1959), George Harmon Coxe (1901- ), and Paul Cain (1902-1966). Editors at *The Black Mask* really edited. They advised and cajoled writers, and when this did not work, they rejected stories (including some of Hammett's) which were not up to *Black Mask* standards. The writers, in turn, often did their best work for *The Black Mask*. It is, then, to the editors of *The Black Mask* that part of the credit goes for attending and assisting the birth of the hard-boiled detective story.

The hard-boiled detective story seems, at first sight, to be a distinctly new subgenre. In Hammett, Chandler, or in the pages of Joseph T. Shaw's *The Hard-Boiled Omnibus* (1946), Ron Goulart's *The Hard-Boiled Dicks* (1965), or Herbert Ruhm's *The Hard-Boiled Detective* (1977), the hard-boiled story does not seem like the detective tales of Doyle. The detectives seem new, the criminals different, the plots fresh, and the writing original and vital. Once we look at the hard-boiled story through the perspective of the history of the detective story, not all of these things are true. Many parts of the hard-boiled story grew out of the traditional detective story or from other branches of Anglo-American literature and culture. But before we get to sorting out the roots of the hard-boiled story, we need to come to terms with what it was, for the hard-boiled story in the hands of a few writers became more than a sum of its parts.

Starting with crime and criminals, hard-boiled stories insisted crime was grotesque and criminals were sleazy, repulsive people. First of all, when murders occur in hard-boiled stories, they rarely come singly: even in short stories lots of people die violently. Furthermore, death in the hard-boiled story is never antiseptic. Writers often gravitated to putrescence and Chandler, in particular, features rotting corpses in *Farewell, My Lovely* (1940) and *The Lady in the Lake* (1943). Crimes in hard-boiled stories may most often be murders—in conscious or unconscious response to the golden age dictum that detective novels must contain murders—but hard-boiled writers introduced not merely the main crime and the criminal. The typical hard-boiled story, and especially the hard-boiled novel, introduces subsidiary crimes reflecting only degeneracy and depravity. There is drug addiction as a secondary feature of many stories, Chandler introduces pornography in *The Big Sleep*, and we even get a dose of canine gothic in J.J. des Ormeaux's "The Devil Suit" (1925) and Chandler's "The Man Who Liked Dogs" (1936), where attack dogs tear people's throats out. Indeed, in the average hard-boiled story, so many grotesque things happen it is difficult to sort the main crime out from all of the other nastiness. Correspondingly, nice people do not commit crimes, only awful people do. The hard-boiled story, therefore, is full of dope-friends, sex-fiends, gamblers, grifters, corrupt politicians, and rotten millionaires. This, like the number of crimes, became a feature of hard-boiled plotting.

In terms of character, though, hard-boiled writers maintained that only very stupid or very sick people commit major crimes. Race Williams, the first of the hard-boiled detectives, says "the simplest people in the world are crooks." Hammett, who had personal experience with criminals as a Pinkerton operative, stresses the stupidity of criminals in story after story. Chandler's last comment about Velma in *Farewell, My Lovely* is "she was stupid."

If criminals in hard-boiled stories are not stupid, then they are mentally ill. In "The Whosis Kid" (1925), Hammett highlights the deranged nature of the killer named in the title. Carmen Sternwood, in *The Big Sleep*, is another case in which the murderer's acts come from pathological insanity.

With its crimes and criminals, the hard-boiled story intends to yank readers out of their living rooms and slam them down in what Chandler in "The Simple Art of Murder" called "the mean streets." Mean here does not simply signify cruel; it also means squalid. It is with its crimes and criminals that the hard-boiled story communicated its squalid and cruel world and came closest to the goal of realism which many writers sought. Hard-boiled crimes and criminals, moreover, significantly changed the nature of the detective hero and the detective plot.

As stupidity and mental disease replaced the cunning and genius of the traditional story, the hard-boiled story had to develop a hero capable of dealing with insentient brutes and lunatics and of living and working in their world. The hard-boiled story, therefore, turned to the private eye, the detective who had to work for a living and who could not turn down even seedy little jobs, like looking for absconded husbands (Sam Spade and Philip Marlowe, in fact, both look for run away husbands in jobs not connected with the main plots of *The Maltese Falcon* (1929) and *Farewell, My Lovely*).

Even though there are exceptions, especially in early Hammett, the private eye exists between the police and the criminals, or, as Daly's Race Williams puts it, "I'm what you call a middleman—just a halfway house between the cops and the crooks." Existing between these two worlds may be convenient for the detective, but it is difficult on the human. Hard-boiled writers went on to layer other kinds of alienation on top of that literally caused by the hero's job: the hard-boiled hero becomes alienated from love, from friends, and from carefree society. None of this destroys the hero's integrity or his ideals, but it does add a veneer of cynicism. He may be a wisecracker, but in many ways the hard-boiled detective is the whore with the heart of gold. Thus Hammett's tough, fat little detective, the Continental Op, takes it upon himself to cure a woman of drug addiction in *The Dain Curse* (1929), and Chandler's Marlowe forces the metaphor of the knight saving the maiden throughout *The Big Sleep*.

As idealistic, almost as sentimental as they are, hard-boiled heroes could not endure in their worlds if they were not tough, and portraying toughness on several levels became one of the aims of the hard-boiled writer. In one of his tough moods, (and he has little else) Race Williams came up with his borrowed, but nonetheless classic, statement, "You can't make hamburgers without grinding up a little meat."

Had Daly the sense to add "You can't grind much meat without getting your fingers mangled", he would have perfectly adapted Robespierre's dictum about eggs to hard-boiled culture. The hard-boiled hero thus not only gives, but also takes, lots of knocks. Typically, he is slapped, slugged, scratched, shot, bitten, butted, punched, pistol-whipped, drowned, and drugged; and, in turn, he gives as good as he gets. Again, Daly's Race Williams sets the tone for the hard-boiled hero when he says, "I ain't a bird to fool with and am just as likely to start the fireworks as they are."

An adolescent readiness and occasional enjoyment of violence also creeps into the detective's character, witnessed in the Continental Op's somewhat uncharacteristic view of heaven as a place "where I could enjoy myself forever and ever socking guys who had been rough with me down below." His physical toughness not only brings a lot of violence into the hard-boiled story and describes the hero on the simplest physical level, it also separates him from the fictional gentleman detective, or the gentleman anything for that matter. The fact that the hard-boiled detective bites and scratches sets him off from gentlemen detectives whose only permissible target is the point of the jaw. It also enables him to survive in a world in which others fight dirty.

In addition to rendering the hero's physical toughness through his battles, hard-boiled writers often modified their villains so as to underline the hero's mental toughness. The most obvious of these are the super heavyweights who enter to beat the hero senseless, characters like the Indian in *Farewell, My Lovely*. More innovative, though, was the hard-boiled woman. The single-minded, rawhide-tough, homicidal woman comes frequently into Hammett's magazine fiction, *The Maltese Falcon*, Chandler's short stories and novels, as well as the works of other hard-boiled writers. Punching or shooting a woman comments again on the anti-gentleman side of the hard-boiled detective, but it also speaks to his mental toughness, which can squash his social inhibitions about females and get the job done. Illustrating this kind of toughness, the Continental Op, at the end of "The

Gutting of Couffignal" (1925), shoots down a woman and then tells her "You ought to have known I'd do it!. . . Didn't I steal a crutch from a cripple?"

On top of the physical and mental toughness, hard-boiled writers tried to convey toughness through the way their characters spoke. Hard-boiled detectives are wisecrackers, willing to sass anyone they meet. Their flippancy in the face of danger and in the teeth of authority goes a long way toward cementing the essential hard element of the hard-boiled hero. Staring down the muzzle of a .45 or telling an employer where to get off both illustrate, if not exactly nonchalance, then integrity and toughness in the hero.

With the mindlessly violent cretins or psychopaths as criminals and with a tough guy as the detective, we inevitably expect the action of the hard-boiled story to be sprightly. And it is. I have already quoted Erle Stanley Gardner classifying the hard-boiled story as "the action type of detective story." In his capacity as editor of *The Black Mask*, Shaw often exhorted his writers to rely on action and not talk: he wrote to Horace McCoy "my impression is that you agreed that it would have a stronger punch to a character to have his strengths brought out by his acts rather than by the writer's statement."

As action fiction, the hard-boiled story either rests upon a semi-episodic structure of capture and escape or upon the hero blasting his way through one obstacle after another until he finally reaches his objective. There is also Hammett's favorite plot of the feud, where the detective encourages criminals to destroy one another. Hard-boiled writers, even though some of them display expertise as plotters, do not do much that is new either with their adventure plots or their detective plots. We will see this later.

What is remarkable about hard-boiled plots is that their use of character and incident is enlivening and enables them to achieve some new effects. First of all, hard-boiled stories bring together so many corrupt and nasty people the writer can both play the game of the hidden criminal and prominently draw psychological points about the nature of criminals. Secondly, the hard-boiled writer can avoid giving too much away to his readers because there are so many crimes. Finally, the hard-boiled story uses all of its elements in concert in order to create confusion: the number of crimes, the number of criminals, and the pace of the action, as well as other factors, join to create one grand muddle. Ironically, however, many of the features of the hard-boiled plot go against the avowed intention of hard-boiled writers, for they serve mainly to make the detective's job more difficult, and they reduce the writer's opportunities for careful explanation. When the detective does solve the crime, therefore, he seems to be in the same genius class as the heroes of golden age writers.

The last characteristic of the hard-boiled story is its style. From the opening sentence, readers know they are reading a hard-boiled story. Hard-boiled style consists of six elements: direct, uncluttered, active description;

jokes and wisecracks; slang and street talk; purposely ungrammatical dialogue; clipped descriptions of events which have serious implications; and metaphors that vividly apprehend the everyday experience of the common man. In the tradition of the dime novel, hard-boiled writers knew their particular readers wanted direct, uncluttered description of rousing action, and they gave it to them. The narration of a hard-boiled story begins at a fast clip and keeps up the pace. The smart comeback and the wisecrack serve to enhance the hero's toughness, as do the clipped descriptions of events which have serious implications. We can see the latter in Hammett's frequent use of the unadorned "they hanged him" at the end of his stories. Ungrammatical dialogue, slang, and street talk reflect the hard-boiled writers' attempt at realism; the diction and structure of hard-boiled dialogue is the real language of grifters, hoods, and private eyes. Finally, some of the best hard-boiled writers have an ear and eye which combine to create metaphors that are at once striking, fresh, apt, and yet based on common life. When Marlowe, in *Farewell, My Lovely*, says his cigarette tasted "like a plumber's handkerchief," it means Chandler could transform a detailed observation of a mundane fact (that plumbers handle lead, oakum, and sewage and that they wipe their hands on their handkerchiefs) into a simile.

At its best, hard-boiled writing is very good because it is so easy to imitate, at its worst, it is awful. Some people connect Hammett with Hemingway, and there are similarities in their styles. Hard-boiled writers, however, never quite succeeded as stylists. Alcohol and Hollywood wrecked many of them. Even the prodigally gifted Chandler was sometimes careless and slipshod. One of the reasons so many hard-boiled authors wrote sloppily was they believed that with the detective story they were making throw away art.

The writers who evolved the particular forms of plot, character, and style which comprise the hard-boiled story came to see themselves as a coherent literary group. Not only did they have in common certain ways of executing and presenting detective stories, they also felt what they were doing was new and rebellious. Joseph T. Shaw, who saw himself as at least the midwife for the birth of the hard-boiled story, admits as much when he says:

> We meditated on the possibility of creating a new type of detective story differing from that accredited to the Chaldeans and employed more recently by Gaborieau [sic], Poe, Conan Doyle—in fact, universally by detective story writers; that is the deductive type, the crossword puzzle sort, lacking—deliberately—all other human emotional values.

Raymond Chandler, likewise, set out to define the aims of the group of writers "who wrote or tried to write realistic mystery fiction." Both Chandler and Shaw are wrong on many points, a condition aggravated by their cock-sure tone as opposed to the facetiousness of many golden age critics. Shaw's suggestion that the hard-boiled story portrays "recognizable human character in three-dimensional form" is belied by the fact there is not very much difference among most hard-boiled detective heroes. Chandler's emphasis on realism ignores the ultimate falseness of hard-boiled violence (no one can be beaten, shot, drugged, and mauled in myriad ways and continue to function at the level the typical hard-boiled hero does) as well as the basic sentimentality of the form.

Chandler and Shaw do, however, tell us some significant things about the hard-boiled story. They agree Hammett was the real inventor of the form; Shaw says he built *The Black Mask* story on Hammett's model, and Chandler clearly views him as the master. Further, they both define the hard-boiled story as a rebellion against the "crossword sort" of fiction. This, however, is an ill-stated definition. Hard-boiled stories, from the beginning to the present, revolt against the secondary characteristics of the traditional detective and the traditional villain. Nothing can make hard-boiled writers shudder like the thought of a Regie-smoking fop pursuing a master criminal or a lay criminal with a brilliant mind. They shudder at the idea of the body in the locked library stabbed with the weather vane from St. Martin's-in-the-Fields. They tried to change these things in their detective stories. But even though they may be clothed in the narrative of violent adventures of a tough guy hero amidst seedy surroundings, hard-boiled stories reduce to traditional detective stories. The hard-boiled writers did not, in fact, rebel against the most basic conventions of the detective story.

Although writers sometimes talk as if it is not, most hard-boiled detective fiction rests on the traditional stuff of the detective story. In the presentation and use of clues, in the delineation of the detective's abilities, and in the importance of the surprise ending, tough guy tales participate in the main line of the detective story's development. Since hard-boiled stories rest on unravelling crime problems, their writers realized if they did not seed the facts upon which the solution rested throughout the story, they risked arbitrary endings. Not only, then, did simple aesthetic grounds move hard-boiled writers to deal with clues, detective story readers by the 1920's and 1930's had come to expect them, and publishers too thought about detective stories mainly in terms of clues. In fact, in 1944, Dell went to the extreme of reprinting Hammett's collection of short stories, *A Man Called Spade*, as a "Map Back," a book with a golden age style room drawing on the back cover.

At any rate, hard-boiled writers are rather classical about the way in which they present, and their detectives use, clues. Erle Stanley Gardner tells us *The Black Mask* emphasized "clues of action" in its stories, thereby bringing them closer to the psychological story than to the detective story fixed on material evidence. This is at least half mistaken: many hard-boiled writers use the same kind of esoteric or trivial minutiae which appeared in stories about Throndyke, Wimsey, or Vance. In *The High Window* (1942), for instance, Marlowe uses the much maligned tobacco ash to reach his conclusions, in "Fly Paper" (1929), Hammett turns the plot on *The Count of Monte Cristo*, and in "The Devil Suit", J.J. des Ormeaux pivots things on de Maupassant.

Hard-boiled writers present their clues in the body of their stories and then later show how the detective synthesizes them into his solution. This is not *like* the practice of traditional detective writers, it *is* their practice. If hard-boiled writers do insert clues in the traditional manner, they differ in the ways in which these clues articulate with character and lead to the solution. The hard-boiled detective focuses mainly on people: most of his attention centers on the assessment of other characters. The detective-narrator's reactions to people range from cynical, flippant, and satirical portraits to objective observation to frank inability to understand others' characters. For most hard-boiled writers, retrospect is the only way in which one can accurately fathom another person's character and motives. This means, in the end, that material clues and aloof analysis of motives are the only reliable way to solve crimes, but the detective caught in the swell of action and the crush of bizarre personalities can not stop to consider material facts and discernable motives until late in the story.

Even though their gumshoes are not manufactured on custom-made lasts, and they engage in mayhem in going from problem to solution, hard-boiled detectives are nevertheless detectives. As such, they illustrate traditional themes and engage in conventional detective story relationships. From Gaboriau onward, detective stories provided readers with a peek behind the scenes to illustrate what working detectives really do. Turn-of-the-century writers knew all about this, and told their audiences about how detectives dust for fingerprints, test for poisons, and so on. Even though hard-boiled writers participated in the same anti-scientific backlash witnessed in their golden age contemporaries, they nevertheless wanted to let their readers know how detectives work. Indeed, detective routine in the hard-boiled story provides in itself the backlash to the scientific detective story. Tidbits on detective procedure occur fairly frequently in Hammett. He put his experience with the Pinkerton agency into his fiction and also into his *Smart Set* article "From the Memoirs of a Private Eye" (1923).

Hard-boiled writers, however, did add something to the age-old pattern of demonstrating procedure. After informing their readers about a few detective tricks, like how to shadow someone or how to lose a tail, hard-boiled writers tell them detective routine involves a great deal of triviality and boredom as well as mucking about in the sediment of society.

A similar invigoration of a traditional pattern occurs in the hard-boiled detective's relationship with the police. Hard-boiled detectives participate in the contest between the hero and the police, which is as old as Poe.

As in the traditional contest, when the private eye contends with the police, we always find the police lose and the hero wins. Even though there are some bright, honest, and efficient policemen in hard-boiled fiction, hard-boiled writers found a powerful way of varying the traditional contest. They made their policemen dishonest. Thus, the private eye does not compete against the moronic Prefect of past detective stories, he struggles with police who can solve crimes, but who will not because of their complicity in them.

If the hard-boiled writers introduced some new motifs into the professional part of the detective, they took over the motif of the genius whole cloth. It is worth reminding ourselves here that Hammett had published forty-two short stories before the final collection of Sherlock Holmes tales appeared in 1927. If a statement ever needed an exclamation point, the fact that Race Williams, the Continental Op, and a lot of other hard-boiled detectives were Sherlock Holmes' contemporaries does!

In a real sense, hard-boiled writers, and Hammett in particular, belong to the much larger group of detective writers who reacted to the excesses of the great detective. This shows specifically when Hammett and his fellows insist their detectives are simply men of normal competence and superior moral competence. Hammett's Op, for one, attacks the Doylean concept of the great detective when, in "The Gutting of Couffignal," he says "It's no good calling me a genius," and again in *The Dain Curse* when he stresses an anti-genius bias in his description of the thought process:

> Nobody thinks clearly, no matter what they pretend. Thinking's a dizzy business, a matter of catching as many of those foggy glimpses as you can and fitting them together the best you can.

This description puts Hammett in the company of turn-of-the-century authors like Bodkin and Dick Donovan who make a point of abjuring and discrediting the genius detective. Hammett also no more follows his own advice than do Bodkin and Donovan. Neither the hard-boiled writers nor their predecessors could do without at least a spark of genius in their heroes. Virtually every hard-boiled detective has the traditional sharp eye for detail and the rigorous thinker's capacity for synthesizing information into unforseen conclusions. Further, the value placed on surprise in the majority of hard-boiled stories insures that the detective comes off as an astute thinker. The rapidity of springing the surprise and the trimness of the explanation at the end ironically serve to inflate the hero's genius.

The principal difference in hard-boiled stories is not in the quality of the detective's thinking, which is on a par with that of most soft-boiled detectives, but rather that hard-boiled writers did not, and probably could not, dwell on the operations of the intellect in the body of their stories. Hard-boiled stories, after all, appeared in pulp magazines, a medium and climate which were either non-intellectual or anti-intellectual. Thus, even though some of the writers, particularly Chandler, wished to make their heroes literate, sensitive men, they could not do this in the American pulp magazines of the first half of the twentieth century. Marlowe, consequently, has to hide his culture behind feigned ignorance or feigned cynicism. Naturally, given the place and the time, hard-boiled writers had to obscure their detective's genius under the bushel of plot or the basket of ingenuous denials.

If the basic function of the detective and part of his character come to the hard-boiled story by way of conventions established by older writers, so too does the pattern of its narrative. Of course, the hard-boiled story is in large measure the adventure story based on a plot that strings dangerous incidents together. But the hard-boiled story weaves a detective plot into the adventure plot. Hard-boiled stories, therefore, move from a problem, to exposition of the elements in the problem, and finally, the surprise of the solution. Indeed, when we consider the surprise typical at the end of the detective story, we find the same surprise at the end of the hard-boiled story. Further surprises in hard-boiled stories are especially startling because the writers are careful not to ask the reader to try to discover the hidden criminal, and because the denouement often comes so unexpectedly.

Even though the hard-boiled story's surprise may be more emphatic than those in traditional detective stories, hard-boiled writers used many of the same explanations and devices employed by golden age writers. As often as they decried soft-boiled writers, hard-boiled writers were ready enough to use their tricks. We can find them using the subsidiary detective as the criminal (Hammett's "$106,000 Blood Money," 1927), a gimmick right out of Christie. Hammett and Chandler both base stories on criminals assuming other people's identities, and Whitfield's "Death in the Pasig" (1930) is a clumsier case of double identity than anything in golden age fiction. Hammett uses Doyle's pattern of the returned avenger. Many hard-boiled stories, too, turn on the least likely suspect. Hard-boiled writers may spring the detective story trap in some new ways, but the trap is the same.

In some basic ways, then, hard-boiled stories link up with the traditions of the detective story. Additionally, hard-boiled writers faced the same kind of structural problem that confronted detective writers of the late nineteenth century: what to do with the tight knot of the detective problem. We can see, in fact, an accelerated version of the evolution of the detective story in the structural development of the hard-boiled story. In Britain, the detective story form developed from short story, to disjointed novel, and finally, to the unified novel. Hard-boiled writers, too, began with short pieces— Hammett's first detective tale, "The Road Home" (1922), is hardly a fragment. They then moved to novels like *Red Harvest* (1929) and *The Big Sleep* which jam together several short plots to make a novel. Finally, they arrived at the fully unified novel with books like *The Maltese Falcon* and *Farewell, My Lovely*.

Even though the hard-boiled story conforms to the accustomed usages of the detective story and employs the motifs invented in other times and in other places, it is nevertheless distinct from the detective stories that came from the consciously middle-brow writers in London and New York. It bonds the traditional detective story to new elements of character, mood, theme, and style. If we are going to get a more sure grip on the hard-boiled story, we must therefore acknowledge the influences that differentiated the hard-boiled story, not only from its dime novel ancestors, but also from its golden age contemporaries.

One of the first things which made the hard-boiled story different from mainline detective stories is that it is aggressively low-brow fiction. Even if, in the hands of some writers, the hard-boiled story can achieve stylistic and thematic complexity and sophistication, the main audience for the hard-boiled story had little appreciation of irony or literary refinement. Since the main readers of the pulps were either adolescents or slow readers, writers had to communicate in reasonably rudimentary style. Usually writing aimed at this kind of audience is extremely punctilious about the burden of literature, sticking closely to correct grammar and standard diction. With the hard-boiled story, we find a number of solidly middle class writers (Herbert Ruhm tells us that "pulp writers were Columbia, Northwestern, Dartmouth, and Vanderbuilt graduates, law and medical students at Stanford and Columbia, attorneys, MA's in medieval history, and oil and advertising executives") purposely writing signally unliterary dialogue in markedly improper English.

This, in turn, became an integral part of the characterization of their heroes, who worked in the worst parts of town. Significantly, hard-boiled writers could describe the mean streets without condescension, without the air of slumming, and without sociological objectivity either. They accomplished this in part because of the way they described people at the upper end of the social see-saw. Hard-boiled writers usually contrast their heroes with the rich, and this contrast inevitably evokes hostility and contempt for the rich, the refined, the cultivated, and even the frivolously educated. The spoiled rich girl with hot pants is a fairly constant character in Hammett, and he and his colleagues frequently portray people with money and position as blusterers, weaklings, pansies, freaks, or degenerates of one sort or another. Rich people believe they have power, they throw their weight around, and they indulge in vices which would make a B-girl blush.

Some of this social contrast, no doubt, came from hard-boiled writers playing to readers, most of whom would never have the chance to be rich. Part of it, too, responds to the age old notion that realistic fiction deals in social contrasts and dwells on unpleasant things. A big part of it, however, comes from hard-boiled writers' wish to write about workers.

In this connection, particularly with Hammett, the hard-boiled story brushes against the flirtation with Marxism found in American letters of the period. But rather than being specifically Marxist, the hard-boiled story comes from less ideological sources. When hard-boiled writers went to school, Tennyson was still a great poet and Carlyle was the accepted prophet of the new age. The hard-boiled story came to be a pean to the American workman. Its hero, above all else, does his job. In spite of his lack of social polish or formal education, the hard-boiled hero is a skilled, honorable, and dedicated workman. This in some ways is only a naturalized version of the Victorian work theme, which preached the heroism of the man who works and the degeneracy of those who are idle. It also carries on this same theme from the dime novel. This theme may have gained more piquancy for readers after 1929, but it is nonsense to suggest the Great Depression had anything to do with the formation of the hard-boiled story. Hard-boiled stories, after all, started years before the bread lines formed and speculators began jumping out of windows.

If the depression made no contribution to the birth of the hard-boiled story, Prohibition did. Between 1920 and 1933, the hard-boiled story gained its maturity alongside bootleggers and rumrunners. From Prohibition, the hard-boiled story got some obvious things—the figure of the bootlegger, as well as all of the usable background material on the illegal manufacture, distribution, and dispensing of alcohol. It might also have taken the themes of organized crime, violence, corruption, and social hypocrisy from the visible effects of Prohibition, but I think this unlikely.

First of all, hard-boiled stories do not deal with the real organized crime spawned by Prohibition. There are no portraits of people like Al Capone, Dutch Schultz, or Machine Gun Kelly in the major hard-boiled writers. Kingpins of organized crime do appear in some stories, but either they have cameo roles only tenuously connected to the main crime, as in *Farewell, My Lovely*, or they come from roots unrelated to Prohibition. The violence in *Red Harvest*, for instance, stems not from Prohibition, but from an older American form of organized crime. Also, hard-boiled stories swing not on organized crime, but on the acts of a stupid or psychotic criminal. Rather than coming from life, the hard-boiled story from the late 1920's onward entered into a reciprocal relationship with the cinema in developing the gangster figure. Finally, it did not take Prohibition to give hard-boiled writers the idea of the lone hero cleaning up a corrupt society. They could find it in classical literature, and they could also find it in both muckraking journalism and cowboy fiction which thrived at the turn of the century.

We have already seen that muckraking and detective stories come together in the works of turn-of-the-century American writers who described rigged elections and the dirty business of corrupt cartels. This subject carries over into the stories of the hard-boiled writers. On the whole, hard-boiled stories present a picture of a society whose institutions are rank with corruption. Big cities bubble with dishonesty which percolates down even to the smallest hamlet. As Reuben J. Shay puts it in "Taking His Time" (1931):

All I know is what I read in the papers. And lately I have been reading a lot about the crookedness of the big town police departments.

These newspapers act like the cities are the only ones that have such grief...I know the little burgs. And how! And in these cow counties you just try to pinch one of the local crooks about election time and see how far you get.

It was the muckraking motive which moved hard-boiled writers to use the corrupted world as the setting for their stories. We can see its mark, too, in that quite a few hard-boiled heroes are not private detectives, but newspapermen. Characters like Frederick Nebel's Kennedy, George Harmon Coxe's Flash Casey, and Ed. Lybeck's Francis St. Xavier Harrigan are all newspapermen. Harrigan, the least subtle of them all, is a "Star Reporter and Deadly Gunman." The figure of the reporter-detective indicates the hard-boiled writers or their readers believed in the power of the press to uncover evil in a society where the normal engines of justice were fouled by people with wealth and power.

At the other end of the spectrum, we can also uncover a muckraking impulse in the ubiquitous figure of the tainted policeman. Hard-boiled writers, in this case, took a more narrow focus than turn-of-the-century writers: they relinquish the corporation as villain (or they did until the last half of the century) because of the limitations of their accepted motives for criminals, and they concentrate on that specific area of muck the private eye on his appointed rounds would have been most likely to encounter. This meant the police. Still, hard-boiled writers embroider their stories with subsidiary pictures of other kinds of corruption—in "The Gatewood Caper" (1923), for instance, Hammett brings in war profiteering as a secondary theme.

Whether he is a journalist or a detective, though, one important fact about the hard-boiled hero is that he almost always runs across rankness or corruption during his investigations. In a real sense, then, the hard-boiled story not only informs the readers about the tricky solution to a basically artificial crime, but it also broadens out to expose the conditions of the real world in which people pay kickbacks and own policemen and politicians. Occasionally, the hard-boiled hero can make the world safe for democracy. In *Red Harvest*, and in Roger Torrey's "The Clean Sweep" (1934), the heroes clean house rather thoroughly. Significantly, however, many hard-boiled heroes win victories that have little impact on a world in which almost everyone was putting the squeeze on someone else.

The muckrakers essentially believed in the power of the press and thought they could make a difference in the quality of American life. And, to some extent, they did. Hard-boiled writers, or the best of them, never allowed themselves or their heroes to think they could make much difference, that they could really do much to help themselves or others except, perhaps, for staying alive. Chandler in particular shows his hero's victory simply opening a swirl of ironies about individuals and society.

One class of hard-boiled stories simply shows the detective condemned to roll the stone up the hill continually, without the prospect of justice, love, or anything else. When hard-boiled stories reach this point, we can, and perhaps should, read existentialism into them. Hard-boiled works, like McCoy's *They Shoot Horses, Don't They?* (1935), have been viewed for some time as existentialist pieces. Like the existential hero, the private eye is an outsider, alienated from the law and the lawless. His world holds no hint of providence or of transcendent values. Some of what seems to be existential in the hard-boiled story may be genuine and a conscious attempt at philosophy. The fact that hard-boiled writers are given to inserting rhetorical capsules in which their characters define and justify themselves suggests that the same writers would willingly try to explain or illustrate their views of the world. Certainly Hammett's exemplum about Flitcraft in *The Maltese Falcon* seems to be conscious philosophizing, and he also seems to firmly establish a non-transcendent world view in *The Dain Curse* when the Op says

> That's why people hang on so tight to their beliefs and opinions; because, compared to the haphazard way in which they're arrived at, even the goofiest opinion seems wonderfully clear, sane, and self-evident. And if you let it get away from you, then you've got to dive back into that foggy muddle to wangle yourself out another to take its place.

Existence yields no answers or guidelines for the hard-boiled hero, who nevertheless needs to act in spite of the "foggy muddle," and who finds his own internal and external toughness is his only resource. All of this does seem like existentialism, but hard-boiled heroes, while they act like existential men, also act on hopelessly sentimental motives. Thus, we find the Op's dedication to curing the Dain girl, Spade's devotion to his worthless partner, and Marlowe's quixotic romanticism. Even here, however, hard-boiled heroes tempt us to existential explanations because they always know their motives are artificial and, as Flitcraft realizes in *The Maltese Falcon*, "men died at haphazard like that, and lived only while blind chance spared them."

As much as all of this sounds like existential philosophy and can be analyzed as a genuine philosophic assessment of life, it probably had at least some of its roots in the expression of values and attitudes indigenous to the 1920's. Some of the hard-boiled hero's attitudes can, I think, be traced to women's suffrage and the emergence of new women's roles during the 1920's, the Jazz Age. I have already observed that the hard-boiled woman character is a type which distinguishes the hard-boiled story from earlier kinds of crime fiction. She begins in this sub-genre and so, in fact, may the character of the vamp.

But these character types are not as significant as the impact of women on the hard-boiled hero. With the exception of Nick Charles, almost all hard-boiled heroes of the twenties and thirties are unmarried, just as virtually all hard-boiled heroes of the seventies and eighties, except Spenser, are divorced. Their single state, however, does not indicate these heroes are promiscuous or antipathetic to domesticity. Spade and Marlowe both have domestic routines and value quiet and culture. Further, the hard-boiled hero of the twenties and thirties is neither a homosexual nor a misogynist. He, however, wants what he can not find in his world.

Between the hero and the principal female character falls a barrier of values: the hard-boiled hero adds meaning to his life by strictly observing a code of values outside of himself (chivalry, justice, the code of the West, and so on), but the women he meets have no principles other than self-interest, whether it is sensualism like that of the Sternwood women or greed like that of Brigid O'Shaughnessy. The easy answer for these heroes would be to give up either their ideals or to give up women, but they can do neither. One suspects that if the women were conformable to the men, these stories would lose much of their existential coloring. But they don't, and the result simulates philosophic tension. This tension may, in fact, generate some of the wisecracks and flippant cynicism of the classic hard-boiled hero—wisecracks and cynicism being one refuge of the individual imprisoned between the ideal and the real.

The hard-boiled story, in this sense, may be in part a male response to the change in women's roles that began in the twenties. It certainly does show women in a new light, and often portrays them as greedy and venal forces loosed on the world. It certainly tries to show, to use Chandler's phrase, "the best man in his world." And it probably says to women, 'look at what you have made of yourselves,' 'what do you want!' 'why can't you see that we represent the best human values!' and 'why can't you be content to let us, alone, serve them!'

If the women's movement of the twenties may have influenced the hard-boiled story, hard-boiled fiction certainly absorbed some of its philosophic coloring from the Great War. A fair number of the writers served in the war. Further, pulp magazines appealed specifically to veterans as readers:

Ron Goulart suggests, in fact, that it was a pulp which began the American Legion. To be childishly obvious, war affects men deeply, and different wars make slightly different psychic scars on their participants. Each war produces its own kind of literature. Paul Fussell, in *The Great War and Modern Memory*, discusses the impact of World War I on the kind of poetry and prose that soldiers and veterans wrote, the way in which it generated specific and unique literary motifs and themes.

Although the hard-boiled story does not reflect on military combat, it does place the detective in a situation at least similar, and probably parallel, to that of the soldier in the trenches. In the hard-boiled story, one of the main facets of the detective's life is his separation from almost everyone else. The hero may have a few friends, but they are in the same line of work and they are not fast friends. None of the hard-boiled heroes gets along with his bosses—even the Continental Op's relationship with the Old Man sours in the later stories. Women have almost no place in the hero's life, and though they are demonstrably heterosexual, most hard-boiled heroes agree with Race Williams' "I never took a woman seriously. My game and women don't go well together." Also, and this happens most in Chandler, the detective possesses heightened sensitivity—a visual perception which is not only more attentive, but also more aesthetically awake than that of the average person while coupled with a capacity for recognizing the manifest ironies of life. Finally, the hero is an expert in violence, but in most cases hesitates to use it. As tough as he is, the Op contrasts himself with younger men who lust for sudden and frequent violence, and in *Red Harvest*, he recognizes he is being poisoned by Personville.

To turn this around, all we have to do is to substitute the word 'soldier' for 'detective,' because World War I drilled these traits into millions of men. In the trenches, the soldier has only his comrades, while people across the parapet shoot at him. People back home go on with their lives, which the soldier's resentment, envy, and distorted memory turn into a gay round of dissipation carried on in ignorance that somewhere in France men are dying. In the trenches, the soldier quickly recognizes the antiseptic inhumanity or general incompetence of authority. And although he is sickened by violence and death, the soldier knows the utility of violence. Finally, because of the danger, soldiers become acutely attentive to the smallest sound when sounds may mean death, and they prize beauty more intensely because of its contrast to carnage.

The hard-boiled hero, then, carried the soldier's mentality in his consciousness, and, in a way, hard-boiled literature inhabits the fringes of the literature inspired by the First World War. Unlike Blunden, Owen, and Sassoon, however, the hard-boiled writers never preached pacifism and never quite gave in to despair. This is the case because they also connected with that other product of the Great War, the post-war thriller.

Before the Great War, John Buchan established the popularity of the character and plot patterns of the adventure-detective story called the thriller. Both during and after the war, other writers built on Buchan's patterns, and the thriller became one of the most popular forms of the "mystery novel" in post-war Britain.

The most popular of the new writers who took to the thriller after the war was H.C. McNeile (1888-1937). Under the pen-name "Sapper," he began to turn out books about Bulldog Drummond and a gang of ex-soldiers who battle master criminals and protect their country from destruction. These soldiers have learned from World War I that the only way to deal with evil is with a whiff of grapeshot. Buchan, of course, is less crude than this, but he too pushes for a hearty response to evil wherever it threatens.

British thrillers made the transatlantic hop very quickly: books by Buchan, Sapper, Valentine Williams (1883-1946), Francis Beeding, Edgar Wallace, and others appeared in Britain and the United States almost simultaneously. These works—which combine adventure with detection, use a hero remarkable for his stamina, endurance, and wit, and project a traditional attitude toward evil—were quickly copied by American writers. Men like "Diplomat" (1897-1967), Van Wyck Mason (1897-1978), and others made the thriller their own.

Thrillers also had an impact on the hard-boiled story. On the surface, hard-boiled writers rejected the thriller with as much vehemence as they did the mannered detective story. Hammett's Op, for example, reads a thriller in "The Gutting of Couffignal" which

—had to do with a strong, violent fellow named Hogarth, whose modest plan was to hold the world in one hand. There were plots and counterplots, kidnappings, murders, prison breakings, forgeries and burglaries, diamonds as large as hats and floating forts as big as Couffignal. It sounded dizzy here, but in the book it was as real as a dime.

In "$106,000. Blood Money", Hammett again speaks of the thriller by calling one of its main ingredients, the master criminal, "romantic garbage."

Yet hard-boiled writers do, in a way, rely on thrillers. Ross Macdonald admits Buchan influenced him, and other hard-boiled writers owe something to the thriller. In their plots, both thrillers and hard-boiled stories rely on moving their heroes and villains through a series of confrontations, captures, and escapes. Further, thriller plots, descended from Victorian schoolboy stories, use furious action to test and prove the hero's manhood; hard-boiled stories do much the same thing.

The heroes have some similarities, too. The thriller hero is strong, tough, and capable of violence. Before the hard-boiled story began, Sapper set up the physical ideal of the heavy-weight boxer. This seems very much like the physical description of the hard-boiled hero, down to the American allusions to Primo Carnera, the heavy-weight champion, in connection with their heroes. At the very start of hard-boiled stories, Daly bound himself to British traditions by describing his Race Williams as a "gentleman adventurer." The hard-boiled writers also may have gotten some of their impulse to wisecrack from Bulldog Drummond, who speaks in a particularly breezy and flippant manner. Finally, the hard-boiled hero's militant normality at least parallels the normal quality upon which Buchan, Sapper, and others insisted.

There are, however, some real, defining differences between the two kinds of fiction. First of all, the American hero is definitely not a gentleman. Also, British gentlemen adventurers invariably adventure with their chums, while the private eye hunts alone. Finally, thrillers evoke atmosphere by serving up Old World locales (castles, dungeons, etc.), which the hard-boiled writer had to do without. With these last two points, America provided influences which overrode the influence of the thriller and helped to brand the hard-boiled story.

America gave the hard-boiled story the cowboy yarn and the new wild west of California in the 1920's and 1930's. The American detective story developed along side the cowboy story. Dime novels about cowboys preceded the dime detective story. Indeed, the movement of cowboy fiction toward the outlaw hero in the late 1870's, and the outcry against it, may have contributed to the popularity of the detective dime novel. Dime novels not only featured western detective yarns, like *Sierra Sam, the Frontier Ferret*, but we find titles which combine detective heroes with western villains, like *Old King Brady and 'Billy the Kid;' or, The Great Detective's Chase*, or *The James Boys Tricked; or, A Detective's Cunning Game*.

From its heritage in the dime novel, western material descended to the hard-boiled story. We can see a graphic example of this in Hammett's "Corkscrew" (1925) in which his private eye tames a western town and walks through a variety of typical cowboy story motifs—from the dude on the wild horse to the lawman facing down the bad guys at the saloon. In many ways, Hammett simply rewrote this in *Red Harvest*.

Although they are certainly far more sophisticated, the action orientation and the tendency toward episodic construction in hard-boiled plots comes in part from the western story's influence on the dime detective novel. Moving to more contemporary western fiction, the particular aloneness of the hard-boiled hero repeats the chosen isolation of cowboys from the Virginian to Hondo. The awkwardness toward sexuality and the drive to bring justice, not just to people but to a place where none exists, further unite the two kinds of heroes.

Additionally, the hard-boiled hero's devotion, for no apparent reason, to a job which has little to recommend it may connect to the cowboy hero's devotion to the austere life because he loves independence and has a deep affection for the land. Finally, the cowboy story contributed to the language of the hard-boiled hero. For the cowboy, and then the detective, what one says ("smile when you say that"), coupled with the style of delivery, is as important as what one does when faced with danger. Indeed, James M. Cain, in his preface to *Three of a Kind*, notes that his own style developed, became hard-boiled, only after he had moved to California and heard and internalized the speech of the "Western roughneck." Finally, the reserve of the cowboy, coupled with the western capacity for hyperbole, may have had something to contribute to the multi-layered American diction employed by the hard-boiled hero.

Just as the pattern of the isolated cowboy hero and some of his unique values replaced the character patterns of the British thriller, California substituted for Europe as the setting in the hard-boiled story. Granted, some hard-boiled stories take place in Boston, Pittsburg, New York, and other Eastern cities, but California is the setting of the hard-boiled classics. Many of Hammett's, and all of Chandler's, stories take place on the West Coast. Mark Hull is a Hollywood gumshoe and Jack McGuire works in California. There was even a pulp called *Hollywood Detective*. It was, of course, easier for hard-boiled writers to use California since many of them migrated to Hollywood. California, too, appealed to most American readers as an exotic locale and, as such, had the same pull as exotic locales in any fiction. California also became, for hard-boiled writers, the new Cities of the Plain. As John K. Butler puts it in "The Saint in Silver" (1941):

> Around every corner in Southern California you find mystics, fortune tellers...shrewd real estate schemes, fake oil companies, phoney gold mines, quack dental offices, and Swedish massage parlors where the massage is not particularly Swedish. Grifters, hustlers, promoters, swindlers...all of them making an unending source of trouble for the law.

This view of California as the place where the oldest sins are practiced in the newest ways served as an ideal background for the hard-boiled hero. It also jibed with the widespread American prejudice that the country has somehow been tilted toward the Pacific and all of the freaks have rolled into California; and this notion, significantly, provided pulp readers with the willing suspension of disbelief necessary for the hard-boiled story.

During its first twenty years, the hard-boiled story added considerably to the development of the detective story. Fusing the traditional story with diverse literary and cultural strains, it attracted new readers and exploited areas hitherto alien to the detective story. Yet, the hard-boiled story never achieved all of what its partisans claimed for it: it never quite became realistic fiction, and it only infrequently looked deeply into human character. In a sense, the hard-boiled formula became more confining than that of the classical detective story because it mandated the detective's whole character, leaving little room for the arabesques and furbelows added to their characters by "classical" writers. We can see the contrast vividly in Rex Stout's (1886-1975) novels which combine a hard-boiled detective, Archie Goodwin, and one based on a golden age pattern, Nero Wolfe.

Of the first generation of hard-boiled writers, the best eventually became embarrassed by the glib-tongued tough-guy hero. In spite of this, as far as popular fiction is concerned, the hard-boiled story was able to jump the cultural chasm created by World War II. Indeed, its hero, its plot, and its values seem more relevant to the postwar world than do the heroes, plots, and values of golden age stories. After the war, the hard-boiled story could continue to develop. In some cases, it grew out of detective fiction into the world of the spy. In some cases, it descended to trumpet the most adolescent and barbarous qualities of its culture. In some cases, it developed some of the possibilities implicit in, but never crystallized by, the original writers. And in some cases, it worked its way into the last substantial development of the detective story, the police procedural novel.

# Chapter 11

# The Police Novel

Describing the development of detective fiction becomes much more difficult once we get to the hard-boiled story. Up to the 1920's, the detective story fed mainly upon itself, with the pioneers of each new development conscious of and building on the literary features which former detective writers used. Hard-boiled writers did this too: they reacted to traditional detective literature, sometimes copying it and sometimes reviling it. But in the twenties, detective stories widened their sources. Hard-boiled stories came to be influenced not only by detective literature, but also by films about detectives and gangsters. The detective story became more than a literary form, but it is difficult to sort out how much literature influences film and film influences literature.

This whole problem becomes even more acute with the latest manifestation of the detective story, the police procedural. Police procedurals, to be sure, build upon earlier forms of the detective story. They owe much to the scientific story, the golden age plot, the thriller, and the hard-boiled story. Additionally, however, they respond to police shows on radio and television, they attempt to portray an oppressed minority group (police), and they react to a growing public perception in the 1950s and 1970s that we are witnessing the death of civilization.

To make all of this even more difficult to deal with, the term "police procedural" is an extremely loose label pasted by reviewers on a wide variety of books which have in common only police officers as their heroes. In some cases, the label distorts the character of books which are really hard-boiled stories, thrillers, and so on. In some cases, however, the term "police procedural" accurately describes writers' aims, as well as the new kind of detective fiction which differs significantly from earlier sorts of detective story. In the last thirty years, the police procedural has opened up new opportunities for the detective story writer, provided a real challenge to the underlying assumptions of the traditional detective story, and, in some cases, made contact with the realism toward which detective stories had been struggling since the 1920's.

One problem with the term "police procedural" is that all detective writers make some sort of comment about it. This is true even of pioneers like Poe. To illustrate the special capacity of his genius detective and to demonstrate the utility of genius, Poe makes special point of detailing police routine. In "The Purloined Letter," particularly, he notes the minute and

169

painstaking examination the police make of Minister D—'s rooms to demonstrate that genius is not simply the infinite capacity for taking pains.

On a different level, Dickens, Collins, and other nineteenth century writers described the policeman's social routines, the tact with which they investigate and interrogate, to convince their readers that the police did not threaten privacy, decorum, or individual liberty. With Gaboriau's *romans policier*, moreover, we find books in part devoted to presenting apologies, defenses, and descriptions of police life.

Gaboriau's attention to the aura, the criminological routines, and personal problems generated by police work mark the real beginning of the police procedural. Evoking, as he does, the atmosphere of the cells and the police court, spotlighting special techniques the police use in their work against crime, and singling out the stress police work places on normal relationships establishes practices that lie at the foundation of the procedural. But Gaboriau never got to it; he grew tired of police heroes and grew too fond of chronicling the hardships of beautiful people.

After Gaboriau, Doyle and his successors blanked out the policeman in favor of the amateur, and passed over police themes in favor of presenting sentiment and sensation in the middle classes. But from the 1920's onward, the policeman has maintained a continuous presence as the hero of detective stories. Amateur detectives enjoyed a brief spurt of popularity during World War II, and private eyes flourished for a decade after the war, but the policeman has kept up a steady presence from the twenties through the eighties. Indeed, Freeman Wills Crofts (1879-1957) made a career out of books about his meticulous Inspector French.

The problem, however, is that most earlier police detectives are only nominally policemen. By and large, police work makes no appreciable impact on their personalities, and the Coles' Superintendent Wilson, Marsh's Superintendent Alleyn, and Innes' Inspector Appleby have the same sort of character as their amateur contemporaries. They have ballet, opera, painting, books, servants, and upper class cronies to fall back on when things get too depressing. They are all bosses and act as individual agents. They always win. They are not real policemen, but were created as policemen because actual crime solving was becoming too scientific, taxing, and complicated for the private individual.

We do not get to the police procedural from the nominal British policeman in golden age novels. We get there from Georges Simenon's books about Maigret. In 1931, Simenon introduced Inspector Maigret in *M. Gallet Decede*, and developed him through bushels of subsequent books. These short novels probe the lives of petty, nasty, twisted criminals and present the wearying and depressing routine investigations conducted by Maigret and his police assistants. They show no bizarre crimes, no exalted mental triumphs, and the hero is a solid, persistent, middle class man who at the end of the day is happy just to put his feet up. The Maigret novels, films, and television programs had a real impact on the police procedural once it emerged in the last half of the century: Nicolas Freeling (1927— ) regularly alludes to Maigret, and John Creasey's (1908-1973) Gideon owes much to him. Maigret, however, did not immediately inspire a vogue for a particular brand of novel about policemen. That inspiration came from America, where various literary and social forces led writers to reevaluate the detective and the detective story.

The hard-boiled detective story developed a hero and an atmosphere that had immense attraction for the readers of the 1940's and 1950's. For postwar readers, however, the story about the hard-boiled private eye had some real weaknesses. First of all, the romantic and sentimental coloring of many hard-boiled stories was at odds with the professed realistic aims of hard-boiled writers. Both Chandler and Hammett turn an almost blind eye toward the fact that most private investigators are, in fact, unenviable characters who spend their careers working on seedy and sordid little cases. Both writers are markedly uncomfortable with the bread-and-butter of the average private investigator of their time, such as securing evidence of adultery for divorce cases. And both men take pains to point out that their heroes will not do such distasteful work. Further, in the 1940's and 1950's, organized law enforcement made the triumphs of the Pinkerton Agency historical curiosities, and this made it harder still to use the private eye as a realistic detective hero. Finally, the complexity and anonymity of urban life and urban crime ate away at the idea that one man, unaided, could track down a criminal in a city of five million souls.

Nevertheless, the hard-boiled story possessed many elements ideally suited for the detective writer inclined toward realism. The attitudes toward crime and criminals, the physical and mental toughness of the hero assaulted by horror and the philosophic implications of human absurdity, the atmosphere of the city, and hard-boiled style, dialogue, and description all seemed eminently appropriate ways of realistically describing mid-twentieth century existence. These things, however, needed to be transferred from the private eye to the policeman.

The transformation of the hard-boiled private eye into the hard-boiled policeman happened on the radio. From the 1920's onward, American broadcasting, both on radio and then television, has been obsessed with crime. J. Fred MacDonald, in *Don't Touch That Dial* (1979), notes, for instance, that by 1945 crime shows took up an average of ninety minutes of every radio broadcast day.

At first, radio detective shows reflected the golden age's fascination with the puzzle story. In 1929, WMAQ in Chicago ran a detective program entitled "Unfinished Play" which broadcast an unfinished crime story and offered a $200 prize to the listener who furnished the best solution. *The Eno Crime*

*Club*, a network program from 1931 to 1936, followed the same pattern: on Tuesday nights it aired an unfinished drama and presented the ending on Wednesday evening.

Moving away from the puzzle story, radio in the 1930's began to respond to the public's perception of an fears about a national crime wave and started to feature police officers in its crime programming. Frequently, radio shows framed their police dramas with comments by real police officers: Chief James Davis of the Los Angeles Police read introductions for *Calling All Cars*, Col. Norman Schwartzkopf narrated *Gangbusters* in 1936, and Sergeant Mary Sullivan of the New York Police added postscripts to *Policewoman* from 1946 to 1947. All of these shows demonstrate a move toward realism in radio crime drama. This move became documentary realism in the late 1940's.

In the late 1940's, radio shows like *Broadway is My Beat*, *The Man from Homicide*, and *The Line Up* introduced radio audiences to dramas that combined sordid crime, petty criminals, real surroundings, police procedure, and hard-boiled cops, the principal ingredients of the police procedural novel. The most important of these radio shows was Jack Webb's *Dragnet*, which aired first in 1949. Hillary Waugh (1920— ) notes "if there was a father of the procedural, I think it would have to be the radio program *Dragnet*." Webb's evocation of Sergeant Joe Friday's first person, terse, matter-of-fact toughness, set in a specific time and place ("It was Tuesday, November third, and I was working the day watch out of homicide"), and dotted with references to numbered police code ("We were answering a call on a 1014") while telling a story of crime and detection, played a formative role in the move toward the police procedural. Television programs followed, and programs like *Dragnet*, *Highway Patrol*, and *The Naked City* did their bit to combine the aura of official police investigation with some of the essentials of the hard-boiled story.

In addition to the influence of radio and television police dramas, the public's attitudes toward crime and policework contributed to the rise of the police procedural. Although the police procedural of the 1950's responded to conventions that were more or less literary, the surge of police novels in the mid to late 1960's resulted from events taking place in the real world. Racial prejudice, specifically police prejudice, contributed to John Ball's (1911— ) *In the Heat of the Night* (1965). The public controversy over the Supreme Court's twin decisions about suspect's rights, *Escobedo v. Illinois* (1964) and *Miranda v. Arizona* (1966), contributed significant new topics to police novels. The "police riot" at the 1968 Democratic convention in Chicago served to make the policeman a timely topic for public interest and public scrutiny. These forces, along with the periodic "law and order" campaigns of American politicians, provided a public receptive to the new variety of the detective story.

The first novel to be called a police procedural is Lawrence Treat's (1903— ) *V as in Victim* (1945). Attempting to fuse the golden age story with the hard-boiled tale, Treat created a pair of contrasting detectives. Job Freeman, like his namesake, is an enthusiastic, scientific detective who solves the crime with fancy scientific gadgets. Nothing was new about this. The second hero, Mitch Taylor, is a cop. Tutored in traditional police wisdom, overworked, cynical about his job, exhausted by the demands of police work, and rooted in the values and style of the middle class, Taylor is something new to detective fiction. Treat, however, never took full advantage of him, tied up as he was with years of routine detective writing behind him.

Hillary Waugh, however, did not have this problem. In *Last Seen Wearing* (1952), and in his series novels about Fred Fellows and Frank Sessions, Waugh wrote police procedurals intended to (and sometimes capable of) create an "aura of horror" by "the sense of authenticity of the reports." Ed McBain (1926— ) began his 87th Precinct novels in 1956 with *Cop Hater*. His combination of humor, grisly realism, sentimentality with insistence on verisimilitude in police details, and the creation of the detailed parallel world of Isola made him the most influential police procedural writer. Along with sociological issues, John Ball concentrates, like Waugh's Fred Fellows books, on the problems of small town police work. Elizabeth Linington (1921— ), writing as Dell Shannon and Lesley Egan, has produced numerous police procedurals since 1960, all of which insist on the necessity of defending fundamental morality in a decadent society. Dorothy Uhnak (1933— ) reflected some of her own experiences as a New York City police officer in *The Bait* (1968) and subsequent novels about detective Christie Opara. Featuring San Francisco detective lieutenant Frank Hastings, Collin Wilcox (1924— ) began writing police novels with *The Lonely Hunter* (1969). Finally, Joseph Wambaugh (1937— ) infused the police procedural not only with his own experiences on the Los Angeles Police force, but also raised the pitch of horrific realism and structural sophistication of the form. From *The New Centurions* (1970) to *The Choirboys* (1975), Wambaugh may have taken one kind of police procedural as far as it can go.

While all of these writers make the police procedural an American form of the detective story, it has also appeared in other countries. Maurice Procter (1906-1973) resigned from the Halifax (Yorkshire) police to write a series of novels about Inspector Martineau of the Granchester police. These novels, beginning with *Hell is a City* (1953), frequently use the police hero in traditional kinds of detective plots. Writing as J.J. Marric, John Creasey began to chronicle the heroic experiences of George Gideon of the C.I.D. in *Gideon's Day* (1955), and in spite of his expressed admiration for policemen, made significant contributions to the evolution of the multiple plot police story. Breaking away from the tendency to glorify the policeman, British-born Nicolas Freeling followed Simenon in writing psychological novels which feature a realistic hero. These began with the first Van der Valk book, *Love in Amsterdam* (1962), and continue with a French policeman, Castang, after Van der Valk's fictional death. Swedish writers Maj Sjowall (1935— ) and Per Wahloo (1926-1975) continued the tradition of Simenon with their Martin Beck novels, and broadened their research so that by the time of *Murder at the Savoy* (1971), they could cite McBain in their work. The South African James McClure (1939— ) and the Dutch Janwillein van de Wetering (1931— ) are only two of the most recent police procedural writers from countries other than the United States.

The main feature which unites all police procedural writers is, very simply, that they chose policemen and policewomen as their heroes. Individually, they differ a great deal: some write clumsy prose and some are competent stylists; some examine the complex implications of their characters and themes while others do not; some use traditional detective plots while others invent unique structures to capture the essence of police life; some write stories as unreal as most television shows; and others create shockingly accurate portraits of violence and degradation. Dell Shannon's Luis Mendoza drives a Ferrari, while Wambaugh's Bumper Morgan pilots a beat-up old Ford. McBain's Steve Carella enjoys idyllic domestic bliss while Sjowall and Wahloo's Martin Beck has become alienated from his wife and family.

Yet, looking at the heroes of the police procedural, several definite patterns emerge. First of all, procedural writers insist police are average people. In police novels, the hero can have chronic stomach trouble, as Bumper Morgan has, trouble with child care, or periodontal problems. The hero can walk off and vomit when confronted with horror or befoul himself when threatened with death. Physically, the police hero is the normal person faced with the normal deterioration of the body and its natural responses to the unnatural job of policework. Procedurals, too, demonstrate the hero's average nature by providing domestic worries. Wilcox' Hastings, for example, worries about having to have his suit cleaned if a criminal bleeds all over him. From housekeeping details to family details, like Gideon's concerns for his children or Beck's consciousness of his failing marriage, procedural writers stress that their heroes are, fundamentally, average people.

Indeed, many police officers are not just normal or average people, they are common. Treat's Mitch Taylor, with his plodding nature and his lower middle class values and tastes, sets the stage for future writers. In *Ax*, McBain devotes several pages to Cotton Hawes describing the plot of a grade C science fiction film entitled *The Locusts*. Wambaugh's characters engage in puerile jokes and adolescent prurience. The level of taste on the police force does not run to James Joyce or *novelle cuisine*. Police officers reflect the tastes, concerns, and attitudes of the lower middle class, the traditional source of police recruits. Generally, egg-heads and college boys are not welcome on the force. Indeed, one of Wambaugh's themes is the unfitness of the intellectual for policework. Police heroes tend to be proletarian heroes, and while they are not quite "dumb cops," sophisticated and complex brain work plays little part in the police novel. That the heroes solve crimes by accident, by routine, or by the fact that most criminals are abysmally stupid, places the police hero in revolt against the hard-boiled or the soft-boiled hero of detective tradition.

If the common person as hero presents some challenges to the traditional detective hero, so does the other hero pattern that evolves in the police procedural. Police work is, by its nature, a communal enterprise. More than one officer works on a case and more than one shift of workers assembles and collates information. The individual police officer depends on others to do lab work, to provide records, and to supply technical advice; he or she operates in a system of structured authority which offers advice, demands progress, and sometimes hampers effective crime solving. Thus, some police procedural novels, like some war novels, introduce the multiple or corporate hero. Corporate heroes run from the picture of partners working together, to the description of a whole squad, precinct, or division working together on one case, to a description of many officers pursuing diverse cases. The last of these types is the most difficult to write, but the plot which shows many police officers working on many cases defines the police procedural in its purest state. When we find a group of officers like those in the Gideon novels or in Egan's *Scenes of Crime* (1976) or in Wambaugh's books, we can be sure it is a police procedural. Indeed, McBain's books, taken together, tell the continuing story not of one individual policeman, but of the corporate hero, the 87th Precinct.

Whether single or corporate, however, the hero of the police procedural comes out of and, in one way or another, responds to the tradition of the hard-boiled detective. The police hero has all of the essentials of the hard-boiled detective. He is big, tough, and sexy. Literally tutored in violence, he gives and receives a lot of punishment. All of this may be modified by authors' conscious efforts to point out the police officer is not a special or exceptional human being, but most police heroes start from a hard-boiled pattern. Some of them, too, talk like hard-boiled detectives. Take this passage from McBain's first 87th Precinct novel, *Cop Hater*:

"Everybody wants to go home," Carella said, "Home is where you pack your rod."

"I never understand detectives," Kling said.

"Come in, we have a visit to make," Carella said.

"Where?"

"Up the street, Mama Luz. Just point the car; it knows the way."

Kling took off his hat and ran one hand through his blond hair. "Phew," he said, and then he put on his hat and climbed in behind the wheel. "Who are we looking for?"

"Man named Dizzy Ordiz."

"Never heard of him."

"He never heard of you either," Carella said.

This clipped, tough, wise-cracking style ties the policeman to the hard-boiled hero, and police writers use it to develop for their heroes the same psychic defenses and outlook aimed at by hard-boiled writers. Police writers, however, go on to build up a special kind of diction, cynicism, hardness, and low humor which portrays not one individual, but a group of people, police officers, who define and protect themselves with their special language.

The same transference from the individual to the group takes place in the procedural's use of other hard-boiled qualities. Alienation from family, friends, and the public at large affects not only individual officers, but the police as a class. The job causes the huddling together of people shut out from the rest of society. It causes veterans to die of heart attacks or commit suicide in loneliness and despair. The procedural concerns a class of alienated people, not just one. Further, the parallel between the soldier and the detective holds much more firmly in the police novel, which deals with a quasi-military organization, than it does in the hard-boiled novel about a lone wolf. Police heroes combine toughness and sentimentality, as do hard-boiled heroes, but the common nature of the typical police officer justifies schmaltzy behavior far more than the unexplained sentimentality of the exceptional hard-boiled hero. Finally, the police officer walks down streets far meaner than those through which the hard-boiled heroes drive. Police heroes deal with literal human garbage and filth far more degrading and dangerous than anything which confronts the hard-boiled detective. If none of them is as well written as the best hard-boiled stories, the police procedural intensifies and makes more real certain elements which are only suggested or mythical in the hard-boiled novel.

At the same time, police procedurals, or some of them anyway, proceed to debunk some of the basic assumptions of the hard-boiled story. Van de Wetering, in *Outsider in Amsterdam* (1975), acknowledges that police work sometimes simply liberates the adolescent male lust for power, which ought to be sublimated. Wambaugh gives the hard-boiled ideal close scrutiny, and *The Choirboys* is, fundamentally, an anti-hard-boiled book. In it, we find the vulnerable human psyche needs to, and has to, break out of the shell of hard-boiled demeanor imposed by the horrors of police work. At its best, then, the police procedural builds on and reevaluates the traditions of the hard-boiled hero, fitting them to the realities of police work.

Procedural writers assume police work is a unique occupation which colors all facets of an individual's character and which has never before been adequately or sympathetically described. Their principal techniques of showing what policemen really do are articulated through their plots or through descriptive digressions on how shifts are assigned, how records are kept, and so on. The human impact of police work, the particular kinds of stress with which police officers live, forms the most important procedure described by police writers. They picture police work as an unrewarding, soul-destroying alternation of boredom, coping with the ludicrous and trivial, coming to terms with the morbid and depraved, and facing rare moments of absolutely terrifying physical danger.

Every worker, of course, thinks himself worthy of his hire, and then some, and police novels begin with the assumption that we pay the police very little for collecting society's trash. This, however, hardly makes police work uniquely underpaid: firefighters, teachers, sanitation workers, and even physicians can argue they get little financial reward for doing dirty jobs. The difference with police work, and procedural novels point this out, is that by its very nature it not only denies the police officer generous pay, but it also withholds most incentive and gratifications which other jobs extend to the employee.

Over the course of the last thirty years, procedural writers have developed the unrewarding nature of the police officer's job into several conventions that not only describe police work, but portray its impact on the participants' characters. Thus, procedurals take pains to show that police officers have little in the way of external incentive or example. The theme of promotion in rank emphasizes not the competence of police forces, but their stupidity and, occasionally, corruption. The good officer spends his time making arrests and can not study for promotion exams, and the rest is Catch 22. Treat's Mitch Taylor only goes through the motions of working because he knows advancement only comes to those who have influence with the higher ups.

Why, then, work for a system that does not reward real merit? Often in the procedural, the system does not reward merit because it does not understand it. Upper echelon officers are, almost universally, anti-professional political brown nosers, boot-licking junior executives, or bird-brained efficiency experts. As in war novels, few characters above the rank of lieutenant receive much praise. Fame could make up for this, but no one remembers good and brave police officers except other police officers.

Instead, the police hero gets the reverse of fame. Procedurals invariably introduce vignettes of public contempt, fear, hostility, and indifference to the police. Police officers do not even have the satisfaction of working for justice. The dilemmas of applying abstract law to practical, immediate problems, and of ignoring shoals of lesser crimes and criminals for greater crimes and criminals erode police officers' confidence that they serve justice or that justice can be served at all. Having to choke down Supreme court rulings they perceive to be wrong and having to wink at pimps, pushers, and petty extortionists takes its toll.

This confusion and public ingratitude affects the hero of the police procedural and his or her fellow officers. It can make stupid and lumpish officers if not more stupid, then more lumpish. It can result in the violent vigilante officer who finds reward in gratifying the need for violence or in enforcing an individual's, not the Supreme Court's, notion of justice. Most often it provides material for gripes. Most police heroes respond to their unrewarding job with the same situational ethics and undefinable, indefensible romanticism characteristic of the hard-boiled detective. Somehow or other, the police novels say, exceptional people continue to work for peanuts.

On top of being unrewarding, the work of the police often grinds down to boring chores and mechanical and repetitive tasks. Here lies a real dilemma for police procedural writers. If they want to capture the actuality of police work, procedural writers must in one way or another acknowledge that it is dominated by triviality and routine. Most real crimes admit a simple solution, not the byzantine structure of fancy detective fiction: victims usually know their attackers, and criminals, on the whole, are stupid and careless people. Along the same lines, routine investigation takes up most of the police officer's time. A slice of the police officer's life, therefore, means showing a lot of trivial, routine, uninteresting activities.

No writer, of course, can set out to write a popular book centered on these things. So procedural writers have found ways around them. The digression helps here, allowing writers to note that most cases are easy and most police work is uninteresting. They can then go on to deal with the exceptional case in their plot. Sometimes writers convert trivial cases into difficult ones by demonstrating that the police have so much to do it is a wonder any crime is solved. The anonymity and complexity of urban life also complicates easy cases and allows the writer to deal with the significant theme of the city. Finally, even the simplest case brings police officers into contact with people and allows the writer to develop interest not only in the police hero, but also in minor characters.

In terms of routine, procedural writers, too, have developed various ways of lifting the potentially deadening into something else. Police routine, in procedural novels, reduces to leg work and paper work. Here again, writers tip their hats to police routine more than they really describe it. McBain, for instance, often introduces facsimile reports or forms that do not develop the plot or character but merely contribute to the aura of police work. Paper work, however, can develop into a variety of character-building points. It can indicate the bureaucratic hobbling of real police work, it can portray the cultural level of the police officer (Wambaugh speaks of "pencilographical errors" while Freeling's Van Der Valk writes masterly reports), and it can describe the hero's attitude toward authority and general rebelliousness. On top of these character points, routine can also become the basis of plot. In one type of procedural, the heroes need to discover or invent an effective routine for screening the myriad facts and people which confront them: they need to find the right seives (people born in 1943, Mid-Westerners, lawyers, etc) which will produce the criminal. With this sort of routine, we come closest to the old intellectual detective hero, but most procedural writers shy away from this label.

The boredom and triviality of most police work has its bright side, too. It can be funny and it can evoke the most human side of the police hero. The police come into frequent contact with kooks, loonies, and fanatics whom the law or God or personal obsessions have unhinged. Sociologically, these people embody petty and pathetic problems of the culture. Practically, they can be very funny. Some procedural writers, especially Wambaugh and McBain, turn these episodes from the police officer's life into comic vignettes: the man who paints himself red in *The Choirboys* or the old woman who imagines herself ravished by Dracula in McBain. Also, it is often with trivial, routine cases writers show their characters' compassion. From the cliche of the lost child in the station house with an ice-cream cone to the patient, polite and kind treatment of the distraught and dispossessed, procedural writers demonstrate the humanity of their heroes. They do this, in part, because they can not show it when the police come into contact with the elemental horrors of life.

Small instances of human folly and weakness inspire laughter and compassion, but the squalor and depravity of society needs other responses. Police officers sometimes have to act as garbage collectors of a society that tries to ignore its waste and septic products. This is one of the main points of many police procedurals. Procedurals drag into public view that the police must deal with the sickest, stupidest, most perverse, and depraved parts of modern life. Instead of the hidden criminal of fiction, the police befoul themselves by daily contact with drunks, pushers, addicts, child molesters, torturers, psychopaths, and rapists.

Procedural plots center on the most abhorrent of crimes. What sort of impact does this have on the character of the police hero? The job brings the hero into contact with the darkest parts of human nature, and it pokes away at elemental fears. Seeing arbitrary violence or violated innocence brings fears for one's own family; seeing, touching, smelling mutilated and putrefying corpses inspires the throbbing whisper which reminds the heroes of their own deaths. Thinking about these thing can incapacitate the best.

Consequently, writers develop ways for their heroes to deal with them. There is, first, the role of the hard-boiled police officer, in which the heroes simply accept the facts as facts and refuse to inquire into their personal, social, moral, or theological meaning. Akin to this stance, some writers develop the separate hero, who refuses relationships outside of the job because its horrors blight any normal relationship; these heroes find solace only in the camaraderie of other police officers who know what they know. The depravity, perverseness, and human impact of crime also serve to move some cops to philosophy: Freeling's Castang and Wambaugh's Kilvinsky both work their ways toward a social theory describing the worthlessness of civilization and the decline of the West. Finally, the occasional horror of police work inspires the compartmentalization many procedural writers fix in their characters. Thus, police heroes separate the boredom from the excitement and the pathetic from the horrific. Especially, they try to separate police work from their private lives. Babies and children fill the home lives of many police heroes: Castang's wife gives birth in *Castang's City* (1980), Mendoza's wife has twins, and cuddly Teddy Carella has cuddly kids. This is all Sergeant Cuff's roses updated, and often made more sentimental.

Some parts of police work, however, resist compartmentalization. The mental or moral fervor of criminal investigation can follow an officer home, but, more insidiously, the aftershocks of physical terror creep into the individual's whole consciousness. This is one of the effects of violence that becomes a convention in the procedural. There are others. While stressing that life-threatening situations rarely occur to the average officer, episodes of potential and real violence occur in most procedurals. These episodes, in turn, raise questions important to the writers' delineation of the police personality. The first of these is, how can a normal human being calmly face situations that palpably threaten violence or death? Who would voluntarily face down a drunken 280-pound laborer armed with a tire iron? Who would want to interrupt a drug deal or break into a room of armed urban terrorists? Who could stay cool and observe regulations about the use of force? Not many people.

Some procedural writers admit this and show the screw-ups and loosening of the bowels characteristic of normal, nervous people. They also lend perspective to police brutality before, during, and after arrests. While exceptional police officers never break heads or flip anyone with their saps, police brutality is the human, particularly the male, response to being threatened. Physical danger, too, connects to the notion of brothers in arms. The intimacy of shared terror, in the past, present, and future, causes police officers to support one another physically and emotionally. It moves them, encased in one of the most closed of closed societies, to cover up for their fellows who go on the rampage, and to go on the rampage when a brother officer is killed. Of course, the bookish or squeamish impulse moves some procedural writers to hymn police training and the fact that the police can face danger and violence simply because they have received thorough and effective training. Others explain that police officers can handle violence because of their on-the-job training of dealing with danger. Nevertheless, the physiological responses remain, the adrenalin, the increased heartbeat, etc., along with mute wonder at individuals who can calmly risk their lives while following a routine of calm and order.

Most of the character conventions developed by procedural writers show human urges interfering with police work. The hard-boiled police hero, of course, overcomes them, but in a sense the character description in procedurals moves decisively away from the psychology of detection and toward the psychology of the normal individual who does a job packed with stress. It moves away from the genius detective model and usually pictures average people solving crimes, not by powerful and original thought, but by accident, dumb luck, or dogged routine.

Procedural police officers, however, do have some character points to make out of detection. Collin Wilcox, for example, develops a minor character who is simply, inexplicably lucky. Other writers tell us police officers have a kind of sixth sense that aids them in solving crimes. This is, from the point of view of fiction, indefinable and has a ticklish legal status (*Terry v. Ohio* [1968], for example is a police favorite but a lawyer's nightmare), but somehow good police officers have the ability to read the furtive look, the nervous shuffle, the slouching gait and myriad other signs of guilt. Usually they can not say how or why they can do this: they can just do it. The other crime-fighting tool built into the procedural police officer is his knowledge of criminals and how to deal with them. Every hero has informers who detail news of the streets, and they also know most of the people involved in shady business in the precinct. As often as not, however, these police abilities offer little help in solving major crimes and simply add to the hero's knowledge of how rotten things can be.

Police procedurals define themselves by using the police officer as the hero, but they also use distinctive kinds of crime and criminals to set tone and motivate plot. With the exception of assorted picaresque stories, master criminal plots and terrorist tales, crime in the procedural builds on the trend toward realism begun by the hard-boiled story. But the procedural goes much farther than the hard-boiled story. Crime in the police procedural seems much more real. Like the hard-boiled story, the procedural uses cold, matter-of-fact narration to bring home the horrible aftermath of violent crime. We find detailed descriptions of bits of brain oozing through blood-matted hair, exit wounds as big as grapefruits, post mortem excretion, torn and bleeding sexual organs, and so on. Writers place these details not in the middle of the adventure story, to be quickly forgotten, but in realistic surroundings. Readers witness the graphic effects of violence in the gutter, in tenement rooms, or at the morgue during an autopsy. The grotesque facts, coupled with the clinical tone, and placed in real surroundings, go a long way toward making crime in the procedural seem more brutally actual.

Not only are the details more shocking in the procedural than in earlier kinds of detective stories, the crimes are also more heinous. Whether through self-censorship or societal pressure, before the procedural, certain crimes never occurred in detective stories. Procedural writers take it upon themselves to write about these unspoken, unspeakable crimes. Rape and murder is a staple of procedurals, including Ball, Creasey, and Waugh. The torture and murder of children was a taboo subject, but gives Egan's *Scenes of Crime* and, especially, Wambaugh's *The Choirboys* much of their power. Murders often have sadistic twists like the one done with a bicycle spoke in McClure's *The Steam Pig* (1971) or the crucifixion in McBain's *Let's Hear it for the Deaf Man* (1973).

The shocking nature of the details, and the crime itself, impact on both readers and hero. They define the distastefulness of the police officer's job for the reader and affect the hero's consciousness. Abhominations force heroes to be hard-boiled and compartmental. At the same time, they provide an affront to the heroes' sensibilities. Finally, they engage both the hero and the readers in the outrage and humiliation that are human responses to the suffering of innocents.

Non-police characters in procedural novels do not seem to be very nice people. As with the hard-boiled story, the comparison with the combat soldier explains much about the policeman's view of non-combatants. It is, further, more apt for police officers than private eyes, for they have few friends outside of the force and confront widespread public hostility and suspicion. As physicians see only people who are ill, police officers see people at their very worst. Most of their work is with the victimized, the destitute, or the deranged. Grieving parents and friends, balky or hostile witnesses, as well as criminals, fill the officer's day. Minor characters in the procedural, therefore, tend to be vulnerable, weak and frightened people.

For its criminals, the police procedural novel goes back to the hard-boiled story, but here again it accomplishes the intent far better than its predecessor. Because they intend to write realistic stories, procedural writers avoid using criminals with the intelligence and nerve to plan and execute a well-wrought crime. Master criminal stories, like McBain's Deaf Man books, and plots involving political terrorism may exhibit the police procedures of organization and mobilization and therefore, form a sub-group themselves, but they are at variance with the usual aims of the procedural novel.

Criminals in police procedurals fit into several clear categories. Most criminals are stupid. They commit crimes for petty reasons. The murderer in McBain's *Ax* splits another man's skull for $7.50. These criminals usually do little to cover their own tracks; after the crime, they continue doing what they have always done. The criminal's genius does not hamper detection, but the complexity and anonymity of the city makes things difficult for the police. In addition to brutish criminals, procedural writers deal with average people who commit crimes because of psychological pressure. Like the twisted woman in McBain's *Calypso* (1979), psycho-sexual diseases erupt in individuals and move them to violent crime.

Often, too, procedural writers develop characters whose mental imbalance has distinct social causes. Police procedural novels bring a sociological point of view to the detective story. We can see this in the treatment of heroes who belong to an identifiable group formed by tangible sources and practicing its own customs and mores. Ed McBain, in *Let's Hear It for the Deaf Man*, identifies the police as a minority group, bringing them under the type of analysis and degree of scrutiny which other minority groups have received in the 1960's and 1970's. Some of the same kinds of attention go to criminals in police procedurals. Procedural criminals may be stupid and influenced by the same kind of mental disease as villains in hard-boiled stories, but frequently writers trace the criminal's acts to some kind of societal cause. Sjowall and Wahloo, for instance, portray a criminal pushed to act by the perverseness of capitalism and the depredations of the welfare state in *Murder at the Savoy*. Novels about prostitutes (Waugh's *Finish Me Off* [1971] or McBain's *Calypso*) and stories which turn on narcotics (Uhnak's *The Ledger*, 1970, or Van de Wetering's *Outsider in Amsterdam*) portray the roots of evil not in the individual, but in the blind bumpings of large social trends. In this sense, the city, important in other connections, causes as many crimes as mental imbalance and cretinous behavior. Thus, the procedural takes the reader from outrage at violent, obnoxious crimes to some degree of understanding of the dispossessed, sick, victimized, pathetic personalities of criminals. By accomplishing this change in attitude, it demonstrates what the police at their best can do.

The police procedural gains many of its effects from the creation of character, but it brings character across by means of plot and atmosphere, which can differ radically from the plot and atmosphere of traditional detective stories. In terms of plot, not all procedural novels differ from traditional detective stories. I have touched on this already. Some procedurals develop as hard-boiled stories, with the hero crashing against and overcoming one obstacle after another. Others are thrillers, "how-catch-ems," or golden age stories complete with clues and surprise endings. Lawrence Treat, the founder of the form, certainly plots like a golden age writer. One of the virtues of the police procedural book, then, is that it allows writers to use a wide variety of plots. All they absolutely need is a police hero and some material describing police procedure. Thus, they mandate the heroes' characters but not their acts, and they demand description, which can be added on to many different kinds of action.

Police procedural writers, however, do have some common aims when it comes to plotting. Like some golden age writers and hard-boiled writers, they want to avoid the artificial completeness of the traditional detective story: as McBain says in *Calypso*, the police procedural does not want to be a book in which "everything [is] wrapped up neatly and tied with a pretty little bow. All the pieces in place, just like a phony fucking mystery novel." In some cases, the lure of the mystery novel is too strong, and many procedurals have the same completeness as traditional novels.

But, procedural writers also try to give the impression their plots are different form traditional mysteries. One way of doing this is to do away with the convention of the present, but unidentified criminal. To get away from the button, button game of guessing the criminal, some writers give us his identity early on. Creasey and McBain use a double focus, following the acts of both criminal and police. Other writers, like Sjowall and Wahloo in *Roseanna* (1965), identify the criminal early and concentrate on the police problem of gathering evidence against him.

At the other extreme, some procedural writers have no aesthetic bias against the *deus ex machina* and drop the criminal into the plot at the last minute as soon as a bit of new information becomes available. Although procedurals do ask the who did it question, procedural writers would rather reveal or explain identity and motive than taunt readers with a guessing game.

Just as they purposely avoid the game of choosing the murderer from a limited number of contestants, procedural writers also veer away from the surprise at the end of the plot. Or, they rig the surprise to defeat the expectations established by the traditional detective story. In the usual procedural, the guilt of the criminal is established by arduous, exhausting investigation and carries with it no exhilarating triumph, but rather a simple, weary recognition that everything in this case is over. Little joy or triumph accrues to the discovery of the pathetic criminals typical to the form. More importantly, procedural writers stress the endlessness of police work, so that a case solved can not carry with it the accomplishment of a job done. Police work never ends.

Some depart from the pattern of one crime and one solution and revolve around many crimes, some of which are never solved. Wambaugh, in particular, takes this route. Another alternative ending acknowledges, as does McClure's *The Steam Pig*, that the police only catch the small fry and the real corruptors of society escape. Waugh's *The Young Prey* exhibits perhaps the most agonizing affront to the surprise ending. In it, the rapist-murderer walks away free, in spite of his willingness to confess, because of Miranda and Escobido rules. Procedural writers do tend to move away from traditional detective story plots. The denouement, precious to Poe and Doyle as the heart of the detective story, shrinks in size and significance. Instead, procedural writers try to tell stories about, or with the air of, chaos and confusion, hard work, and everyday facts, which they perceive to be the reality of police procedure.

Any number of things make the action of a police novel different from that of a book about an amateur or private detective: the quasi-military nature of police forces, the bureaucracy, the definition of detection as a job rather than an avocation or obsession, the continuing nature of crime, the chaos of dealing with all crime instead of a single crime, and so on. All of these impact on the hero's character, but they also have specific implications for plotting which separate the procedural from other kinds of detective story. The most marked feature of the police novel appears in writers' attempts to create plots that evoke the organized confusion of police work. To really understand the job, the writers tell us, we must first understand that at any given time police departments work on a large number and variety of cases, and the solution to most cases involves the contributions of a group of people. Writers try to get this across in several ways. For procedural writers intent on using traditional, one crime, one hero plots, there are several ways of portraying the organized chaos of police work. The simplest is to use digressions. In his easier books, McBain, for instance, will stop the flow of the one hero, one problem story and give readers a snapshot of life outside the principal investigation. Thus in *Jigsaw* (1970), we get this:

"I've got that dry-cleaning store holdup, and the muggings over on Ainsley...six in the past two weeks, same m.o....I've also got a lead I want to run down on the pusher who's been working the junior high school on seventeenth. And there're two cases coming to trial this month.

Other writers accomplish the same effect in other ways. Collin Wilcox indicates the nature of police work by beginning novels with Hastings working on a case or two before settling down into the book's principal crime. In *The Young Prey*, Waugh uses policemen's anecdotes about past cases to convey the unstinting, continuous, and chaotic nature of police work.

All of these minor narrative devices get the point across, but procedural writers have also invented larger techniques to do the same thing. These change the nature of the plot-making in the police procedural, making it not only a form with a new kind of detective hero, but also one with a different kind of plot. These novels confront the reader with a number of criminal investigations carried on either simultaneously or consecutively. John Creasey pioneered this form with his Gideon books which frame a variety of investigations with Gideon's superintending one important case. In *Police Chief* (1977), John Ball uses the same idea, beginning with crimes in Los Angeles, switching to crimes in a small town in the Northwest, and following through with a hunt for a rapist. McBain's *Hail, Hail, the Gang's All Here* (1971), takes a slice of time out of the experience of the 87th Precinct and shows the variety of incidents and investigations which occur in one day.

Joseph Wambaugh has inspired other writers in his searches for novel ways of organizing a presentation of the diversity of police experience. *The New Centurions* follows a group of officers from the police academy to the Watts riots. *The Choirboys* goes to Joseph Heller's *Catch-22* (1964) and builds an organization out of repeated images, incremental repetition, and the gradual revelation of the novel's central incident. With these new kinds of plots, the police novel effectively leaves the realm of the detective story and becomes a class of fiction by itself.

Whether they follow the actions of several police officers or stick to the traditional one-hero plot, we can identify a police procedural novel by the atmosphere which the writer sets out to establish. Thus in the early fifties, when Waugh decided to try a new sort of novel, he said he "determined to write a fictional murder mystery that would *sound* as if it really happened." Making a police novel sound as if it really happened depends in large measure on building up details so its atmosphere differs from other, less real, varieties of detective fiction. The most obvious of these details, of course, are those that describe the environment in which the police work. In police novels, therefore, we find inserted paragraphs detailing how records are kept, how radio calls are answered, how witnesses are supposed to be interrogated, and how work schedules are set up. McBain starts his novels with an epigraph advertising "the police routine is based on established investigatory technique." All of these details serve to illustrate the process of police work for readers unfamiliar with it. The feel of these details, however, does something else. Treat begins *V as in Victim* by describing the down-at-the-heels look of the police station, and McBain describes the 87th Precinct station as being like "the office of a failing insurance company." Descriptions of police duty schedules evoke the hectic and exhausting hours officers work. All of the items that objectively portray the police officer's routines also give off an atmosphere that combines neglect, exhaustion, absurdity, and near squalor.

In addition to the strictly police details, other facts contribute to the atmosphere of the procedural. One of the most important of these is climate. The weather is always awful: it is always raining or snowing, bitterly cold, disgustingly damp, or unbearably hot. Frequently, the first sentence establishes the irritating nature of the weather: Sjowall and Wahloo's *Murder at the Savoy*, for instance, starts with "The day was hot and stifling, without a breath of air." This sense of discomfort pervades the police novel, replacing the gothic "it was a dark and stormy night." Although police writers do use night to establish atmosphere, they do not use it to tingle spines. Most crimes occur at night, so using night is realistic, but being dragged out of bed and investigating a crime in darkness provides added discomfort.

Atmospheric details like the weather and the time set the basic tone for the procedural. Writers, of course, sprinkle their books with shocking details—splattered internal organs, ugly facts about autopsies, and so on—but the essential pattern of atmosphere and tone in the police procedural establishes a groundwork of irritation and discomfort splashed with occasional bursts of violence.

The city plays a particularly vital role in establishing the distinctive atmosphere of the police procedural. The procedural continues and expands upon the description of the real city in the hard-boiled story. In the police novel, however, the city serves slightly different purposes and attains a much larger importance than in the earlier form. Police novels about small towns are the variants: most procedurals take place in large cities. Realistically, writers select the city because most crime is urban crime. The major social problems and many individual problems of the mid-twentieth century—juvenile delinquency, drug addiction, racial conflict—fester more obviously in cities than in small-town or rural settings where they are often urban imports. Further, at mid-century, American politicians pushing "law and order", as well as groups fighting for civil liberties, focused on the problems of cities and, particularly, of big-city police departments. Finally, because of the scale and scope of managing urban crime and urban policing, it is the city that attracts the moral and descriptive talents of the procedural writer. As a consequence of all of this, procedural novels portray the modern city going down the drain. From grimy tenements and sleazy bars to prostitutes' rooms and narcotics "shooting galleries," readers see in the police procedural a vivid portrait of the decayed city.

And yet, in the police procedural, something else enters the portrait of the decaying metropolis: it assumes a significance far beyond mere realistic setting or the occasion for complicating police work. In a fairly large class of procedurals, the city becomes the exotic place, full of danger, but also packed with fascination. Sometimes, this verges on travelogue. Martin Cruz Smith's *Gorky Park* (1981) gained some of its popularity from exploiting the exotic appeal of Soviet police procedure, but much of it came simply from Smith's descriptions of Moscow. The same travelogue interest in locale applies to Martin Beck's Stockholm, Van Der Valk's Amsterdam, and Tromp Kramer's South African cities.

In addition to this travelogue appeal, the city has other implications for the procedural. McBain, in a number of books, repeatedly describes the city as "a hairy bastard, but you get to love it." The city, in fact, ceases to be simply background and becomes a character in itself. Creasey's Gideon books, in a very real sense, show London as the most important character which the police repeatedly save from corruption or destruction. McBain's Isola, Riverhead, Clam's Point, and the rest are not, he insists, simply pseudonyms for Manhattan and environs; they are the archetypal city. They are ciphers out of a morality play in which the average man works for the salvation of the place that stands for the fruit of all human enterprise. In Wambaugh's *The Blue Knight* (1972), the love of the city and the tuition of police work transform a comic and pathetic fat man into a hero able to fight the dragon which imperils his beloved, his city. This same mythic energy stands behind the realistic trimmings of many police procedurals.

Since the 1950's, the police procedural has contributed significantly to the development of detective fiction. It has supplied the realistic challenge to traditional detective stories hard-boiled stories talked about but never achieved. It has evolved a hero who, although not quite new, was affected by a whole range of internal and external influences unique to police officers and neglected by earlier writers. It has departed from the spot-the-murderer plot and has developed settings and atmospheres which bring home both the depredations and the heroism of police work. Police procedurals, however, too often suffer from militancy and didacticism. They preach too ardently about the rigors of police work, and their sociology and psychology can be obtrusive, jejune, and predictable. They can also easily fall victim to sentimentality. Procedural writers, like other detective writers, often display weak wills, preferring to bend golden age or hard-boiled plots rather than to try to juggle multiple characters and diverse incidents. Only a few procedural writers have the confidence to adhere to the uncompromising realism that captures the police hero at his or her best and worst. Not many readers, I should add, have the stomach for a continued diet of police procedurals. But at its best, the form both plods, shocks, and portrays weak and fallible heroes faced with the very worst which life and society have to offer. The procedural story denies its readers the sophisticated stimulation of the classic detective story as well as the vicarious excitement of the hard-boiled tale. It is not the sort of book to take to the beach. At their best, procedurals can break out of the category of detective fiction and become mainstream literature. But not many of them have this potential. This comes from the manifold lures to compromise which face procedural writers. It also comes from the fact that, from the 1950's onward, the detective story has tended to homogenize itself. Fewer writers aim at pure, classic detective stories, hard-boiled pieces, or procedural novels; rather many writers produce books which at least touch on all of these traditions.

# Chapter 12

# The End

Surveys have a habit of omitting almost everything contemporary. For readers of a certain age, history stops with the events leading up to World War II, and modern literature means James Joyce and T.S. Eliot. Leaving out the last forty years is highly attractive to the critic and the historian because it means one can avoid controversy and the possibility of making erroneous predictions, projections, and analyses.

I am tempted to take the easy way out here and end by saying the golden age story and the hard-boiled story atrophied in the late thirties, and the police procedural novel is the latest and probably the last version of the detective story. From a purely formal point of view I could get away with this because it is no doubt true: no one has invented substantial alterations to either the form of the classical detective story or the hard-boiled tale since around 1940. The police procedural remains the only new way of embodying the detective story to emerge from World War II. If I stopped now, however, I would have to leave out several clusters of very popular writers, I would have to ignore the development of the form not as the detective story but as literature, and I would have to pretend the character of the detective hero had not changed. So then, here is a quick look at what happened to golden age and hard-boiled stories after World War II.

After World War II, the classical detective story stopped travelling in realms of gold. Some of the most original and energetic golden age writers, Sayers, Knox, and Cox, simply stopped writing detective stories. Other golden age writers switched over to thrillers. Carr, Queen, Allingham, Marsh, and Christie kept up the old game, but often with a difference. In Britain, the hard-boiled detective, like Peter Cheyney's Lemmy Caution, brought a variety of violence to the detective story that challenged the rococo intellectualism of the golden age novel. More thoughtful writers began to see the classical detective as a pain in the neck. Eric Ambler's Charles Latimer, the detective and detective writer in *A Coffin for Dimitrios* (1939), is not only an effete irrelevance in a world run by cartels and bossed by hired muscle, but Ambler ultimately shows us Latimer's dubious viability by murdering him in *The*

*Intercom Conspiracy* (1969). The golden age detective becomes an irrelevant and ineffective snoop for many post-war observers.

After World War II, the most vigorous and, occasionally, the most thoughtful writers turned not to the detective story, but to the spy novel, believing that there they could deal with what they and their contemporaries considered most relevant and with the most effective ways of meeting twentieth century reality. After the war, too, publishers increasingly chose to promote thrillers and spy novels. The readership of classical detective stories began a slow decline, in spite of, or perhaps because of, attempts to widen the appeal of the detective story. In the twenties and thirties, the detective story was a solidly middle-class entertainment, and some observers felt it could enter the mainstream and be accepted as literature.

But then things changed. Not only has mainstream literature come to mean high-brow literature, but ever since Edmond Wilson's "Who Cares Who Killed Roger Ackroyd?" (1945), the literary establishment has been gun shy of at least the classical detective story. It has become the province of vaguely tweedy individuals who go quietly to their public libraries and consume every "Mystery" book on the shelves. To be sure, people still write detective stories. The golden age patterns survive, and hard-boiled fiction is undergoing something of a renaissance lately. But the new writers, with a few exceptions, do not achieve the fame of the older writers. Ask even a well-read person to name a detective story writer and the reply will be Agatha Christie and not Amanda Cross, Edmund Crispin, or Robert B. Parker. The new writers are, in many cases, careful with their craft, witty or muscular in their style, vivid with their settings, and clever with their plots. In most cases, however, they lack not only the wide audience of the pre-war years, but also the innovative energy of the detective writers of the twenties. As far as the detective story goes, after World War II, we travel in realms of silver.

Even though World War II affected the development of the golden age detective story, and some of the best writers dropped the trade, there was hardly a gap in the line stretching back to E.C. Bentley. New writers stepped in to continue the tradition. Frances and Richard Lockridge (1896-1963; 1898-1983) continued the frothy detective entertainment with *The Norths Meet Murder* (1940). Christianna Brand (1907— ), starting with *Death in High Heels* (1941), kept up the flow of impossible murders under impossible conditions. Accelerating the frank acceptance that the detective's world is, in essence, unreal, Edmund Crispin (1921-1978) began a series of very funny, ironic, and erudite novels with *The Case of the Gilded Fly* (1944). Michael Gilbert (1912— ) kept the golden age going with his novels. After this transitional generation of writers, P.D. James (1920— ), Amanda Cross (1926— ), Emma Lathen, Charlotte MacLeod (1922— ), Harry Kemelman

(1908— ), H.R.F. Keating (1926— ), Peter Lovesey (1936— ), and others took up the classical detective story.

While new writers took over, golden age motifs and urges still controlled the "classical" detective story. To some extent, this is due to reviewers setting up writers of the twenties as standards against whom contemporary detective writers must be compared: thus "as good as Christie" or "the new Dorothy L. Sayers" frequently substitute for descriptive or evaluative criticism. In part, this is also the case because, frankly, contemporary detective writers do copy the golden agers. P.D. James' *Unnatural Causes* (1967), for example, seems to come right out of Sayers' *The Nine Tailors*, and we can say the same for books by other authors. Many of the new detective writers simply continue the literary movement begun in the twenties. Crispin has the same facetiousness and self-consciousness as do Innes and Carr, and P.D. James, in one of her novels, even prescribes rules for crime that are as limited and limiting as those inspired by the puzzle book. Much of this is purely derivative and, slavish or otherwise, continues trends started a generation ago.

Yet, the new writers have a real commitment to some of the substantial ideals of the golden age. The best of them believe the detective story should be a medium for pure, witty, clever, and elegant prose style. Amanda Cross, for example, takes time out to comment on the misues of "hopefully"; Michael Gilbert and Crispin can write perseflage with the best; writers like James work hard at perfecting their style. Finally, most of the new golden age writers aim at the same educated middle-class readers targeted in the twenties. Just as Sayers did, contemporary writers assume their readers know Pope, Auden, and Joyce. They take it for granted their readers want subsidiary information about how processes work (how one gets a seat on the New York Stock Exchange) and what certain institutions are like (from English departments to synagogues). They assume also that, caught in the trap of the sixties, their readers want to be dosed with relevance. These points, usually subordinated to detection in golden age fiction, balloon up in contemporary detective stories. If they do not threaten, they offer to diminish, often substantially, the role of the plot in the detective story, as well as to alter the character of the detective hero.

To look at the new hero of golden age stories first, it is clear that for many detective writers the delineation of the thinking machine has few attractions. Cognition was the obsession of the 1890's, but not the 1980's. Doyle's tidbits on Holmes' mind reflect a late nineteenth-century preoccupation. Illustrating this, H.G. Wells, when it came to inventing Martians for *The War of the Worlds* (1898), dealt mainly with brains, specifically brains with mechanical biases. Writers after World War II, if they took themselves half seriously, knew the brain was not a machine and thinking was not a mechanical procedure. Freud, bio-chemistry, and research into the process of creation all suggest mechanical analogies for thinking are, on the whole, very bad ones. As a result of this realization, new golden age detectives, like James' Adam Dalgleish, depend a good deal on subconscious helps that masticate and digest information and then throw it back in the form of sudden insights.

Consequently, we find few omniscient oddities among the new detectives. With the notable exception of Crispin's Gervase Fen, contemporary writers avoid bizarre, eccentric characters whose behavior reflects misanthropic genius. Instead, by conscious choice, writers try to tone down their detectives into smooth, intelligent, middle-class individuals. Dalgleish may write poetry, MacLeod's Peter Shandy may pull off a jape or two, but overall, new detectives are private, modest, unassuming people. In the age of the anti-hero, well-adjusted and successful people dare not attract too much attention, and so most detective protagonists do not. Although writers do search for new characters to break old Anglo-Saxon stereotypes of the detective, they also try to keep them normal. Thus, H.R.F. Keating's Indian detective, Ganesh Ghote, is as modest and unassuming as possible.

Concentrating on the hero's humanity, as opposed to his or her mental equipment, means writers can either focus on presentation of routine detective work or severely curtail the prominence of the detective plot in their stories. The new golden age writers leave the first option to the police procedural story, which accepts boredom as one of its plot and thematic points. The second option, diminishing the traditional attention to ratiocination, has become more attractive. Writing about Rabbi Small as a man, for instance, holds far more attraction for Kemelman than writing about his role as a detective. What we can see, then, in the contemporary golden age story, is the gradual wilting of the problem-based detective story. Few writers from the sixties onward can get away with things like fifty page denouements that rehash the events of the preceding one hundred and fifty pages. Few writers want to do much clue mongering, and few want to present periodical reviews of available information. Emma Lathen does not, for example, obtrude much artificial detective plot machinery into the bodies of her novels, and neither does Amanda Cross. The new writers steer clear of detective plot machinery, in part, because it is old fashioned; they avoid it because they see the novel as a flowing, organic whole and not as the kind of entertainment attempted by golden age writers of the twenties. All of this, from the technical point of view, means the surprise in many contemporary detective novels is less surprising. The writers may use old conventions, like the least likely character, but their surprises are not as amazing as those in the twenties and thirties. They are not the same because the writers' purposes are not the same.

Or perhaps that statement should be that the writers' purposes are the same, only over the last thirty years detective writers have been accomplishing those things golden age writers merely predicted for the future of their sport.

That is, detective novels have become less detective novels and more novels of manners and psychology. With a whole class of detective stories, the importance of describing milieu far outweighs the importance of the crime problem: the crime, in fact, becomes merely the justification for describing places and the people typical to them. Thus, Kemelman's interest centers on portraying the peculiarities of life in a New England Jewish community, Lathen concentrates on the world of money and banking, and Amanda Cross dwells on the quirks of various academic communities. Whereas in the old golden age story, the urge to create specific and limited settings sprang originally from the wish to draw a closed laboratory setting for a crime, contemporary writers place only secondary value on this. Instead, they depict setting because the locales are interesting and important in and for themselves, because the places generate personality types that are unusual and interesting and because most of the backgrounds chosen give rise to issues unrelated to detection but relevant to larger society. Thus, when we find Emma Lathen describing the Lake Placid Winter Olympics in *Going for the Gold* (1981), she does so to give her readers a behind-the-scenes look at an interesting event and because this event brings certain unusual character types together. We can see even a better example of manners at work in Charlotte Macleod's Balaclava University books (starting with *God Rest You Merry* 1978). Her wacky agricultural college serves not only as background, but also as the generator for character types whose primary significance lies in their entertainment value. The detection in these books, likewise, serves to bring out the particular natures of her character types.

Attention to manners not only yields comedy, but can also lead to serious social comment. And this is what we find in a group of the new golden age writers. Building background and describing manners brings some writers to the discussion of serious contemporary issues. Thus, Lathen's Wall Street serves as a lever to the consideration of racial prejudice in *Death Shall Overcome* (1966), Cross' Harvard brings up women's issues in *Death in a Tenured Position* (1981), and Cordelia Gray's work as a detective in James' *An Unsuitable Job for a Woman* (1972) likewise uses the manners of detective and police work to bring up questions about sex roles. All of this means that, for the new golden age writers, manners have become more important and useful for saying things, and purely detectival elements have become less relevant. The milieu generates characters and the characters become interesting and entertaining in and for themselves. These detective novels, then, aim at description, comedy, satire, or polemic, and the detective problem and the detective character act principally as fragile structures to provide a beginning and an ending.

Symptomatic of what has been happening to the golden age detective story over the past forty years is the attraction of anachronism. The anachronists have, in fact, emerged as a sub-group of classical detective writers. They are, simply put, contemporary writers who set their detective stories in the past. We can trace this back to Doyle's late stories which take place in the 1890's instead of the twentieth century. More consciously, Carr set things in motion by writing detective stories that are also historical novels. After the war, Lillian De La Torre (1902— ) made anachronism popular with her *Dr. Sam-Johnson, Detector* (1946). The movement continues with, among others, Margaret Doody's (1939— ) *Aristotle, Detective* (1978), Peter Lovesey's books about the Victorian policeman Sergeant Cribb, Robert van Gulik's (1910-1967) stories about ancient China, and Nicholas Meyer's (1945— ) novels about Sherlock Holmes and his real contemporaries. As we will see in a bit, this motive extends to hard-boiled stories, too. Also having an impact on this trend, the cinema and television have recently featured costume drama based on classical detective stories by the rivals of Sherlock Holmes, Christie, Sayers, Cox, and others.

All of this waltzing around between history and the detective story demonstrates a number of things about the condition of contemporary detective fiction. As it looks back to Carr, the anachronistic trend illustrates how neo-classical the newer writers are, simply copying and building on one golden age motif. Secondly, it demonstrates how much the detective story demands fabric to clothe its fixed structure. Whether writers choose comic or satiric portraits of manners or daily life in ancient Rome, China, or England, the detective story needs to go beyond crime or intellect to attract readers. Choosing a historical setting and a historical detective, the anachronistic writers can free themselves from the onerous obligation of confronting weighty contemporary issues; this reconnects them with the golden age's usual antipathy to serious or depressing literature. Finally, some anachronistic writers, like Van Gulik, use historical setting as background for reasonably formal, grueling detective plots, and this suggests that if the detective story has lost its significance for the contemporary world, it can survive in a reasonably pure state, with its full regalia of structural tricks intact, when the writer takes us backwards in time.

If the new golden age detective story fulfills the prophecy of the thirties by fusing the detective story fully and irrevocably with the novel of manners and the historical novel, it also continues the urge to use the detective novel for the examination of human psychology. Psychology, alas, is an immense field that investigates phenomena as diverse as why people remember certain items while forgetting others to why individuals engage in antisocial acts. The term "psychological novel" is so vague it defines very little: there are all sorts of psychological novels.

But as far as the detective story goes, psychology has several specific referents. First, the new writers reject the moronic assumption of golden age publishers that detective novels ought not deal with character beyond the mechanical display of how the detective hero's mind operates. Writers like Amanda Cross point out it is their detectives' interests, insights, and identifications with many things that qualify them as finders of truth. Likewise, the new writers, even those who give lip service to rules, find criminality's springs to be far more diverse and devious than those covered by the old formulas of hate, revenge, and gain. Additionally, subsidiary characters now tend to receive fuller treatment than the old rules suggested.

All of this makes for one kind of psychological novel. The next kind is, for our purposes, not a detective story at all. Reviewers like to describe novels in the tradition of John Buchan as "psychological novels of suspense." Dick Francis (1920— ), for instance, writes "psychological novels of suspense," but they are really simply thrillers that rely for craft and effects on the precedents of Boothby and Buchan. Next, we have the psychological thrust of the detective gothic or the gothic detective story. One form of this type goes back to the "had-I-but-known" fiction of Mary Roberts Rinehart, but for the second half of the century Daphne DuMaurier's (1907-1983) *Rebecca* (1938) probably serves as the chief inspiration for novels that probe the characters' traumatized psyches to wring the hearts and sweat the palms of their readers. Among the proponents of this kind of fiction, we have Charlotte Armstrong (1905-1969) and Victoria Holt (1906— ). But DuMaurier, in 1938, really only adapted the psychological motives of Francis Iles to fit a female audience. We can also find a number of contemporary writers who build on Iles' psychological examinations of the stunted personalities of people who actually commit crimes. Writers like Frederich Durrenmatt (1921— ) and Stanley Ellin (1916— ) demonstrate the suspense, horror, and pathos of individuals who actually commit crimes. This same motive extends into the pseudo-fiction or narrative reportage of Truman Capote's (1924-1987) *In Cold Blood* and Norman Mailer's *The Executioner's Song* (1979).

The difficulty of surveying the last forty years of hard-boiled detective stories lies with the fact that there is really no break in the tradition between the 1930's and 1940's. With the golden age story, the realities of the Second World War put a semicolon between the golden age and its inheritors in the post-war world. World War II brought to popular notice facets of human behavior and the human condition that affected writers and readers alike and caused the golden age story either to accede to playing the role of conventional entertainment or to edging closer to other kinds of fiction. If anything, the war ratified the uses of power and promoted the values and talents of the hard-boiled hero. It served to prove the formulae created by veterans of the last war. Further, the older hard-boiled writers were not extinguished by the war. Indeed, Chandler did not begin to write novels until 1939, and he produced some of his best work during or shortly after the war. Ross Macdonald, by most estimates one of the formative hard-boiled writers, did not invent his principal detective, Lew Archer, until 1949.

This continuum invites critics to see the hard-boiled story not simply as a kind of detective story, but also as an indigenous form of American expression that documents, if it does not explain, certain essential qualities of American culture. During the past ten years, particularly, this notion has led to numerous doctoral dissertations on Hammett, Chandler, and Macdonald. Articles about these writers have so overwhelmed detective criticism that at least one voice has called for a ban on them so people can look at other worthy writers. With the possible exception of Sayers, whose reputation has risen, educated readers, if they are likely to know any detective writers, will know those from the hard-boiled school.

A number of factors have led to this situation. Hammett's refusal to testify to Senator Joseph McCarthy boosted his stock with the American literary establishment. Chandler's critical reception in England made a splash once it was imported to the U.S.. Another factor in the popularity of the hard-boiled story was the occasionally true perception that it is an exemplum of existentialism; thus, the hard-boiled story fit in with the fifties' vogue for Sartre and Camus. Also, the hard-boiled story does measure the hero's relationships to authority and his capacity for violence, and these may be essential American themes.

Nevertheless, the hard-boiled story is a detective story and it does proceed through several marked stages of development. Further, its development depends not only upon reactions to basic or continuing facets of American reality, but also upon the proclivity it shares with other forms of detective fiction to react upon itself, making syntheses out of pre-existing elements. Over the past forty years, it doubles back to Ross Macdonald and Mickey Spillane (1918— ) to make itself over. The new relevancies the hard-boiled detective story develops alter with each decade and change to fit very different audiences. Unlike the golden age story, the hard-boiled story has fit itself to the prurient fascination of a boys' locker room and has become a form accepted and approved by academics and intellectuals.

Almost from the beginning, the hard-boiled story has developed along two different and often antithetical directions: the first appealed to the average reader of pulp magazines and the second sought to add style and restraint to the adventure story about the tough-guy hero. The pulp hard-boiled stories provided characters like Race Williams for pre-war adolescents and lower-class readers; this kind of story continued after the war as rough and tough as it ever was, and even more so. Demanding little in the way of elegance, consistency, or craftsmanship from its plot, readers of this brand of hard-boiled story asked mainly for virile episodes of violence, an extra-manly hero, and a simple, direct style decorated with an occasional bit of profanity or a wisecrack delivered in the face of danger. These stories, moreover, exist to demonstrate cliches and insist on making moral and social statements that reinforce the strongly held biases of their readers. As far as the postwar years go, Brett Halliday (1904-1977) and his hero Mike Shayne transfer the pulp story from the 1930's to the 1940's. Although the Mike Shayne novels have some clue-hunting orientation, their hero, prone to virtue and violence and often at odds with the law, opened the way for Mickey Spillane.

Starting with *I, The Jury* (1947), Spillane achieved what is perhaps the perfect articulation of the pulp hard-boiled detective story. This first novel, roughly modeled on *The Maltese Falcon*, builds on shooting, fist fights, and assorted mayhem, rendered in a supposedly frank manner. Spillane writes simple prose, spiced with occasional witticisms like "you bet your grandmother's uplift bra." Most notably, however, he creates in Mike Hammer an individual willing and fit to stay the corruption of the world, to execute justice, and to satisfy women frustrated by ineffectual and effeminate men. Much of Spillane serves as an affront to social commentators and literary critics, but several of his novels have become all-time best-sellers in the category of mystery and detection.

This success with hard-boiled novels that amplify sex and violence led other writers, like Richard Prather (1921— ), to repeat Spillane's patterns of "manliness," puritanism, and wild west Americanism. The most significant heir to Spillane, though, was Ian Fleming (1908-1964). To Spillane's embroidery on hard-boiled formulas, Fleming added brand-name dropping, motifs of character and plot drawn from the love romance, and articulation of popular Freudianism latent in Spillane, along with, of course, elements of international intrigue. Because of the immense success of the Bond books (from 1953 onward, but especially at the end of the decade), popular writers followed Fleming's lead—and followed him out of the detective story. Consequently, most pulp hard-boiled heroes of the sixties and seventies are not detectives, but spies. Nick Carter, one of the oldest names in American detection, became a super-spy in 1964: the owner of the name determined this was the only acceptable role for good, hard men. With this, the pulp hard-boiled story passes beyond the scope of this book. Even after the pulp hero becomes a spy, however, he continued to exert an influence on the writers of intellectual hard-boiled stories.

Going back to Hammett, the hard-boiled story has always possessed the potential to be something more than simply an adventure thriller featuring a tough, idealistic hero and making emphatic statements on the social utility of force and forcefulness. Chandler is the principal figure in this intellectual or artistic (neither term fits precisely) school of hard-boiled writing, and he was in some ways a post-war writer.

In terms of influence, however, Ross Macdonald's introduction of Lew Archer in *The Moving Target* (1949) had a greater impact on the shape of things to come. Macdonald quickly mastered the patterns of plot, character, dialogue, atmosphere, and tone instituted by the best hard-boiled writers, he revolted against the perceived artificialities of the traditional detective story, and he reacted against the stolid quality of much mainstream literature at mid-century. While Macdonald's novels retain the delicate balance between brutality and sensitivity so necessary for the best of hard-boiled fiction, he adds new themes to the hard-boiled detective story that give his books more relevance to him and to the 1950's and 1960's. Thus his novels, almost from the beginning, insist on psychoanalytical answers to certain enigmas of human behavior. Just as this clicked with the popular Freudianism of the fifties, so Macdonald's concern for the environment appealed to readers of the sixties and seventies.

After Ross, the other MacDonald, John D. MacDonald (1916— ), contributed most to the growth and popularity of the intellectual hard-boiled detective story. Introduced in *The Deep Blue Good-Bye* (1964), John D. MacDonald's hero, Travis McGee, has made significant alterations in the traditions of the subgenre. He combines elements from Ian Fleming (living in an ambience set up by selective allusions and acting out various motifs from the love romance) with reflections on topics ranging from what sort of woman should wear slacks to the individual's relations with the consumer society. Not content simply to state that certain things exist, John D. MacDonald made the hard-boiled story a primer for his own brand of popular philosophizing. Although this brought John D. a devoted cadre of readers, Ross Macdonald has had the greater impact on current writers. In the early 1970's, in fact, there was what can only be described as a Ross Macdonald boom: *Newsweek* put him on its cover in 1971, five doctoral dissertations (from Bowling Green, Michigan State, Texas, Boston, and Chicago) analyzed him between 1971 and 1974, and a mass of critical articles about him came out beginning in 1969. This concerted attention led to a new crop of hard-boiled detective novels by writers too young to have read Hammett or Chandler when they were first published. These new writers attempt to shape the hard-boiled story to the realities of the 1970's and 1980's, to sustain the vigor of hard-boiled style, and to bring the tough-guy hero up to date. None of these things is easy, and the new authors have recorded as many failures as did the earlier hard-boiled writers.

If there were not such a stigma attached to it, academic might be an appropriate term for recent developments in the intellectual-artistic school of hard-boiled writing. Certainly, Ross Macdonald was an academic, and among the recent writers Stuart Kaminsky (1936— ), Jonathan Valin (1948— ), James Crumley (1939— ), Richard Hoyt (1941— ), Max Allan Collins (1948— ), and Robert B. Parker (1932— ) have been college professors: Parker, in fact, wrote his dissertation on Hammett, Chandler, and Ross Macdonald.

A number of reasons move academics to the hard-boiled story. One is that the hard-boiled story is interesting and imitable. It rests on prose that is vivid and easy to copy. Perhaps the best proof of this is that Britisher Barry Fantoni can present a convincing picture of Philadelphia in the 1940's in his *Mike Dime* (1981) because he uses the Hammett-Chandler prose style. Then, too, some of the college professors listed above teach writing and Hammett and Chandler have come to replace, for students and professors alike, some of the writers traditionally used as prose models. Many recent hard-boiled stories are, frankly, adulations. Anachronistic hard-boiled writers—Kaminsky's, and Andrew Bergman's (1945— ) books and a number of other individual novels, like Joe Gores' (1931— ) *Hammett*, take place earlier in the century— in part, look to the past out of wistfullness about lost culture or character, and in part, they turn to the past in homage to the creators of the hard-boiled story. Bill Pronzini's (1943— ) Nameless Detective may live in the present, but he mutters asides to the shades of Spade and Marlowe. Anachronism, further, appeals to those of the academic bent because building setting, atmosphere, and dialogue involves research. Kaminsky, for instance, has simply transferred his research on Hollywood's Golden Age into his Toby Peters novels. Both Max Allan Collins and James Sherburne append to their novels discursive lists of their historical sources. In a more specific kind of homage, much recent hard-boiled fiction looks to Ross Macdonald. Macdonald demonstrated to the fifties and sixties that the hard-boiled story could become a vehicle for serious themes, and his successors have, in many cases, adopted Macdonald's version of high seriousness, and, in some cases, have built their fiction on Macdonald's themes of psychoanalysis and environmental concern.

From the American Studies point of view (and both Hoyt and Parker are Ph.D's in American Studies) the hard-boiled story has served and, therefore, can continue to serve, as a container for traditional American literary themes and as an exhibitor of American culture. It is not surprising, in this connection, that when new hard-boiled writers summon up archetypes, they bring in not only Macdonald, Chandler, and Hammett, but also Huck Finn and Natty Bumppo.

The academic approach means, generally, that the workmanship of recent hard-boiled fiction can be relatively high. It should also mean the form is dead and hard-boiled fiction has become a field for parodists, anachronists, and imitators. Some critics, like Donald Westlake, believe this. Hard-boiled fiction, after all, exploits a tone and character type invented in the 1920's: can these be endlessly repeated? Perhaps not endlessly, but academic hard-boiled writers have discovered facets of tone and character glossed-over, ignored, or unimagined by the inventors of the form. And by exploring these, the new writers have sought to make the hard-boiled story relevant to the seventies and eighties.

Most of the new hard-boiled writers matured in the 1960's and their fictions reflect the cultural changes encountered by these writers as they move into middle age. Compared with the old hard-boiled heroes, many of the new detectives seem to be either puritans or gourmets or both.

Lawrence Block's (1938— ) *A Stab in the Dark* presents an analysis of alcoholism that would gladden the heart of the WCTU, and Robert B. Parker has been featured in the food section of *The Washington Post*. Gone are the days of strength and endurance without exercise, for many of the new heroes jog. These characters are, in essence, built to be, and to appeal to, Yuppies; young, upwardly-mobile professionals.

Some new writers, like the hard-boiled writers of the twenties and thirties, steadfastly refuse to identify their heroes with causes beyond those demanded by the hero's situation and identity. This, in fact, is one of the attractions of anachronism to writers like Bergman and Kaminsky, in that setting a novel in the thirties or forties avoids involvement in the inevitable causes of the seventies and beyond.

Many new writers, however, have adapted the hard-boiled hero to the new culture. The genre has witnessed the evolution of the non-violent, soft-boiled detective in books like Stephen Greenleaf's (1942— ) *State's Evidence* (1982) and Marcia Muller's (1944— ) books. The detectives, too, have changed to fit the broadening culture of the second half of the century. Not all of them are WASPs. Ernest Tidyman's (1928— ) John Shaft is tougher and smarter than all of his white peers. Kaminsky's Toby Peters, Roger Simon's (1943— ) Moses Wine, and Bergman's Jack LeVine are all Jewish. In his Dave Brandstetter books, Joseph Hansen (1923— ) develops a homosexual hard-boiled hero, and in *Lamaar Ransom Private Eye* David Galloway introduces a lesbian hard-boiled detective. Finally, Sue Grafton (1940— ) and Sara Paretsky have succeeded in creating credible hard-boiled private eyes who happen to be women.

Along with these changes, many of the new heroes have adopted the causes of the era. Roger Simon makes his hard-boiled hero a Marxist who refuses to surrender his Berkeley radicalism. The most popular cause for the new hard-boiled hero is feminism. Parker presents the best example of hard-boiled feminism in his *Looking for Rachel Wallace* (1980), but almost all of the new writers pay lip-service, at least, to women's equality. While the idealism and romanticism of the old hard-boiled heroes was repressed or consciously quixotic, in the new heroes, it becomes manifest in their active and vocal concern for the oppressed. Many of the new heroes are, in fact, social workers with guns, and while the writers have built them on the same lines as Spade and Marlowe, they are, in fact, different kinds of characters.

There also have been several attempts to build a hard-boiled hero who is not the old hero made respectable and given a social conscience. Richard Hoyt portrays his John Denson as a picaresque hard-boiled detective, James Crumley draws alcoholic, drug-ridden, redneck detectives who may be the most original contribution to the genre by this generation of writers, and

Loren Estleman (1952— ) consciously takes an anti-Yuppie and anti-Preppie stance.

The works of Crumley and Hoyt, along with some others like Donald Zochert's (1938— ) *Another Weeping Woman* (1980), present another way in which the new writers expand on the potential of the original hard-boiled story. The original hard-boiled story maintained a cautious relationship with the western: it, in part, drew upon the western story, but became too consciously urban to want to openly and honestly acknowledge the relationship. Crumley, Hoyt, and Zochert use the West—Montana, Oregon, and Colorado—as the setting for their novels, and they draw upon it not only for local color, but they evoke explicit parallels between the hard-boiled hero and the cowboy.

The cowboy hero aside, much recent hard-boiled fiction draws upon the attractions of local color. The new hard-boiled heroes may still work in New York and California, but many large American cities have their own hard-boiled heroes. Boston has Parker's Spenser, Cincinnati has Valin's Stoner, Indianapolis has Michael Z. Lewin's (1942— ) Albert Samson, New Orleans has George Ogan's (1912— ) Johnny Bordelon, Detroit has Loren Estleman's Amos Walker, and so on. In some cases, the development of local color leads the new writers to be not only social workers, but social critics. Thus, they present the modern American city not merely as a collection of mean streets or a contrast between the obscenely rich and the working poor, but as an example of obtuse urban planning, crass commercialism, benign or malignant neglect, and simple bad taste.

In these things, the new hard-boiled writers build on the patterns established half a century ago. And they have changed the hard-boiled hero. Although the new heroes are often just as intelligent, resilient, witty, dogged, tough, and idealistic as were the heroes of the twenties and thirties, it is much more difficult for them. The inviolable identity of the old hero has become less possible when it is invaded, as it must be, by the new and often bewildering demands of consciousness. Some of the new hard-boiled fiction, in fact, reflects male disorientation and confusion in the face of the various manifestations of feminism in the culture. Some recent writers, nevertheless, have created approximations of a figure who will endure in detective fiction. However, just as alcoholism and Hollywood prevented the first generation of hard-boiled writers from elevating their creations out of the ranks of popular fiction into regular literature, so commercial success and self-indulgence threaten to do the same to their successors.

Indeed, commercial success and self-indulgence have followed the detective story from the days of Gaboriau onward. In many cases, the history of the detective story is the history of cleverness rather than that of sustained insight, perception, discipline, and all of those other things that separate art from artifice. Yet, the detective story has endured for over one hundred and forty years. It has made several transatlantic journeys, and it has changed and adapted. It has been stubbornly anachronistic, but it has also portrayed contemporary problems and issues. It has been, by turns, pedantic, humorous, charming, exciting, and brutal. And it has been, and continues to be, enormously popular. This has been the case because detective story writers have consciously chosen entertainment as their first priority, just as their readers have chosen it as their first priority. Entertainment, of course, does not preclude sustained insight, perception, discipline, and all the rest. It makes the writer's task harder, but entertainment does not preclude art. Over the past one hundred and forty odd years, there, in fact, have been a number of detective stories that rise to the level of art, and to encourage people to look for them has been one of the purposes of this book.

# Further Reading

### Chapter 1

In addition to the general histories cited in the Bibliography, see Dorothy L. Sayers' introduction to *Great Short Stories of Detection, Mystery and Horror* (London:Gollancz, 1928); and E.M. Wrong's introduction to *Crime and Detection* (New York: Oxford University Press, 1926). For a golden age perspective on *The Mysteries of Udolpho*, see R. Austin Freeman's introduction in the Everyman edition of the book (1931).

### Chapter 2

Again, consult the general histories and, particularly, Ian Ousby's *Bloodhounds of Heaven*. See also George Woodcock's "Things as they Might Be: Things as They Are: Notes on the Novels of William Godwin," *Dalhousie Review*, 54 (1974-5), 685-697; and Gary Kelly's *The English Jacobin Novel, 1780-1805* (Oxford: Clarendon Press, 1976).

### Chapter 3

Some of my own notions about Poe appear in "Play and Games: an Approach to Poe's Detective Tales,"*Poe Studies*, 10 (1977), 39-41, and "Poe and Long's *Hoyle*," *Studies in Short Fiction*, 16 (1979), 344-348. Robert A. Lowndes lists Poe's firsts and Liahna K. Babener discusses Poe's use of the double in pieces in *The Mystery and Detection Annual* (Beverly Hills: Donald Adams, 1972). For views of Poe and Mary Rogers, see John E. Walsh's *Poe the Detective; the Curious Circumstances Behind The Mystery of Marie Roget* (New Brunswick: Rutgers, 1968) and Raymond Paul's *Who Murdered Mary Rogers* (Englewood Cliffs: Prentice Hall, 1971). Thomas O. Mabbott's *Collected Works of Edgar Allan Poe* (Cambridge: Harvard, 1969) is the standard edition.

### Chapter 4

Nadya Aisenberg's *London Crimes* (Boston: Rowan Tree, 1982) contains Dickens' detective journalism. In addition to Ousby, consult the bibliographies cited in my Bibliography with the warning that most of the works on Dickens deal with *Edwin Drood*.

### Chapter 5

See Ousby. T.S. Eliot's essay first appeared in the *TLS* but is also in the Oxford edition of *The Moonstone* (1928). Sayers also wrote an introduction to *The Moonstone* (London: Dent, 1948). H.P. Suckworth's introduction to *The Woman in White* (London: Oxford, 1975) contains valuable information, as does Norman Page's *Wilkie Collins: The Critical Heritage* (London: Routledge & Kegan Paul, 1974). See also Norman Donaldson's introduction to *Lady Audley's Secret* (New York: Dover, 1975).

### Chapter 6

Consult all of the French histories of detective literature cited in the Bibliography. See also Samuel Edward's *The Vidocq Dossier* (Boston: Houghton Mifflin, 1979).

### Chapter 7

I hesitate to mention anything about reading further about Doyle since so much of the literature is facetious. John Dickson Carr's biography *The Life of Sir Arthur Conan Doyle* (New York: Harper and Brothers, 1949) was the classic. Owen Dudley Edwards' *The Quest for Sherlock Holmes: a Biographical Study of Arthur Conan Doyle* (New York: Barnes and Noble, 1983) is the most recent biography.

### Chapter 8

On Female detectives, consult Michele B. Slung's *Crime on Her Mind* (New York: Pantheon, 1975). Hugh Greene's introductions to *The Rivals of Sherlock Holmes* (London: Bodley Head, 1970-76), 4 vols, provide some information. Norman Donaldson's *In Search of Dr. Thorndyke* (Bowling Green: Popular Press, 1971) deserves to be read. On thrillers, see William Butler's *The Durable Desperadoes* (London: Macmillan, 1973), and Colin Watson's *Snobbery with Violence* (New York: St. Martins, 1971).

### Chapter 9

One could do worse than to read my *Watteau's Shepherds*. A number of monographs on Sayers and Christie exist: consult the bibliographies cited below. S.S. VanDine's rules first appeared in "I Used to be a Highbrow but Look at Me Now," *American Magazine*, 106 (September 1928): 14 ff., but is reprinted in Howard Haycraft's collection *The Art of the Mystery Story* (New York: Simon and Schuster, 1946).

### Chapter 10

There is little reliable criticism on the dime novel. Most writers depend on Edmond Pearson's *Dime Novel; or, Following an Old Trail in Popular Literature* (Boston: Little, Brown, 1929). J. Randolph Cox's "The Detective Hero In the American Dime Novel," in *Dime Novel Round-Up*, 50 (1981), 2-13, has some useful information, as does E.F. Bleiler's edition of *Eight Dime Novels* (New York: Dover, 1974). Gary Hoppenstand's edition, *The Dime Novel Detective* (Bowling Green: Popular Press, 1982) contains texts and lists of dime novel titles. Hard-boiled writers, on the other hand, have received much attention. In addition to the editions of Ruhm, Goulart, and Shaw cited in the text, see Ron Goulart's *Cheap Thrills* (New Rochelle: Arlington House, 1965), John Stuark's "Horace McCoy, Captain Shaw" and the 'Black Mask,' in *Mystery and Detection Annual* (Beverly Hills: Donald Adams, 1972) and other items cited in the bibliographical works.

### Chapter 12

The principal work on the police procedural is George Dove's *The Police Procedural Novel* (Bowling Green: Popular Press, 1982). Hillary Waugh's comments on the police novel are found in his essay "The Police Procedural," in *The Mystery Story*, ed. John Ball (San Diego: University Extension, University of California, 1976).

### Chapter 13

Two works on recent hard-boiled fiction are William Ruehlmann's *Saint with a Gun* (New York: New York University Press, 1974), and David Geherin's *Sons of Sam Spade* (New York: Ungar, 1980).

# Bibliography

Compiling a bibliography of critical works about the detective story presents a staggering number of editorial dilemmas. Should one include those books which Jon Breen calls "coffee table books?" Should one list volumes chiefly aimed at detective story fans? Should one catalogue obviously rummy books like those based on the assumption that Sherlock Holmes was real? Should one collect all titles about major writers like Poe and Dickens? Should one do spy criticism as well as detective story material? The list could go on. In the following bibliography, I am going to avoid all of these problems: it includes only reference works and general monographs about detective stories. Readers interested in individual authors or in periodical literature on detective fiction should consult the specialized bibliographies listed below.

# Reference Works

Adey, Robert C.S. *Locked Rooms and Other Impossible Crimes*. London: Ferret Fantasy, 1979.

Barnes, Melvyn. *Best Detective Fiction: A Guide from Godwin to the Present*. Hamden, Conn.: Linnet, 1975.

Barzun, Jacques, and Wendell H. Taylor. *A Catalogue of Crime*. New York: Harper & Row, 1971.

Breen, Jon L. *The Girl in the Pictoral Wrapper; An Index to Reviews of Paperback Original Novels in the New York Times' "Criminals at Large" Column, 1953-1970, and The Saint Mystery Magazine's "Saint's Ratings" Column, 1957-1959*. Dominguez Hills: California State College, Dominguez Hills, 1973.

Breen, Jon L. *What About Murder? A Guide to Books About Mystery and Detective Fiction*. Metuchen, N.J.: Scarecrow, 1981.

Cook, Michael L. *Murder By Mail: Inside the Mystery Book Clubs—With Complete Checklist*. Evansville, Ind.: Cook, 1979.

Glover, Dorothy, and Graham Greene. *Victorian Detective Fiction: A Catalogue of the Collection*. London: Bodley Head, 1966.

Gribbin, Lenore S. *Who's Whodunit*. Chapel Hill: University of North Carolina, 1968.

Hagen, Ordean A. *Who Done It? A Guide to Detective, Mystery, and Suspense fiction*. New York: Bowker, 1969.

Herman, Linda, and Beth Stiel. *Corpus Delicti of Mystery Fiction: A Guide to the Body of the Case*. Metuchen, N.J.: Scarecrow, 1974.

Hubin, Allen J. *The Bibliography of Crime Fiction, 1749-1975*. San Diego: University Extension, University of California, in cooperation with Publisher's Inc., 1979.

Johnson, Timothy, and Julia Johnson. *Crime Fiction Criticism: An Annotated Bibliography*. New York: Garland, 1981.

Mundell, E.H., Jr., and G. Jay Rausch. *The Detective Short Story: A Bibliography and Index*. Manhattan: Kansas State University Library, 1974.

Nieminski, John. *EQMM 350: An Author/Title Index to Ellery Queen's Mystery Magazine, Fall 1941 through January 1973*. White Bear Lake, Minn.: The Armchair Detective, 1974.

Nieminski, John. *The Saint Magazine Index: Authors and Titles, Spring 1953—October 1967*. Evansville, Ind.: Cook & McDowell, 1980.

Penzler, Otto, *et al. Detectionary*. Woodstock, N.Y.: Overlook Press, 1977.

Queen, Ellery. *The Detective Short Story: A Bibliography*. Boston: Little, Brown, 1942.Queen, Ellery. *Queen's Quorum: A History of the Detective - Crime Short Story as Revealed by the 106 Most Important Books Published in this Field Since 1845*. New York: Biblo and Tannen, 1969.

Reilly, John M. *Twentieth-Century Crime and Mystery Writers*. London: Macmillan, 1980.

Skene-Melvin, David, and Ann Skene Melvin. *Crime, Detective, Mystery, and Thriller Fiction and Film.* Westport, Conn.: Greenwood, 1980.

Steinbrunner, Chris, and Otto Penzler. *Encyclopedia of Mystery and Detection.* New York: McGraw-Hill, 1976.

Stevenson, W.B. *Detective Fiction: A Reader's Guide.* London: Cambridge University Press, 1949.

Stilwell, Steven A. *The Armchair Detective Index.* New York: Mysterious Press, 1979.

# History And Criticism

Adams, Donald K. ed. *The Mystery and Detection Annual, 1972*. Beverly Hills, Cal.: Donald Adams, 1972.

Adams, Donald K. ed. *The Mystery and Detection Annual, 1973*. Beverly Hills, Cal.: Donald Adams, 1974.

Aisenberg, Nadya. *A Common Spring: Crime Novel and Classic*. Bowling Green, Ohio. Bowling Green University Popular Press, 1980.

Arnold, Armin, and Josef Schmidt. *Kriminal Roman Fuhrer*. Stuttgart: Philipp Reclam, 1979.

Ball, John, ed. *The Mystery Story: An Appreciation*. San Diego: University Extension, University of California, 1976.

Bargainnier, Earl, ed. *Ten Women of Mystery*. Bowling Green, Ohio: Bowling Green University Popular Press, 1981.

Barzun, Jacques, and Wendell H. Taylor. *A Book of Prefaces to 50 Classics of Crime Fiction, 1900-1950*. New York: Garland, 1976.

Becker, Jens P. *Der Detektivroman*. Darmstadt, 1973.

Benvenuti, Stefano, and Gianni Rizzoni. *The Whodunit: An Informal History of Detective Fiction*. Trans. Anthony Eyre. New York: Collier Macmillan, 1980.

Boileau-Narcejac. *Le Roman Policier*. Paris: Petite Bibliotheque Payot, 1964.

Boucher, Anthony. *Multiplying Villanies: Selected Mystery Criticism, 1942-1968*. eds. Robert E. Briney and Francis M. Nevins, Jr.. Boston: A Bouchercon, 1973.

Brean, Herbert, ed. *The Mystery Writer's Handbook*. New York: Harper, 1956.

Butler, William Vivian. *The Durable Desperadoes*. London: Macmillan, 1973.

Caillois, Roger. *Le Roman Policier*. Buenos Aires: S.U.R., 1941.

Cawelti, John G. *Adventure, Mystery and Romance*. Chicago: University of Chicago, 1976.

Champigny, Robert. *What Will Have Happened: A Philosophical and Technical Essay on Mystery Stories*. Bloomington: Indiana University Press, 1977.

Charney, Hana. *The Detective Novel of Manners: Hedonism Morality and the Life of Reason*. Madison, N.J.: Fairleigh Dickinson University Press, 1981.

Depken, Friedrick. *Sherlock Holmes, Raffles, and Their Prototypes*. Chicago: Fanlight, 1949.

Dove, George. *The Police Procedural Novel*. Bowling Green, Ohio: Bowling Green University Popular Press, 1982.

Dupuy, Josee. *Le Roman Policier*. Paris: Librairie Larousse, 1974.

Eames, Hugh. *Sleuths, Inc.: Studies in Problem Solvers: Doyle, Simenon, Hammett, Ambler, Chandler*. Philadelphia: J.B. Lippincott, 1978.

Freeman, Lucy. *The Murder Mustique: Crime Writers on their Art*. New York: Ungar, 1982.

Geherin, David J., *Sons of Sam Spade: The Private Eye Novel in the 70's*. New York: Ungar, 1980.

Gilbert, Elliot L. *The World of Mystery Fiction; A Guide.* Del Mar: University Extension, University of California, 1978.

Gilbert, Michael F. ed. *Crime in Good Company: Essays on Criminals and Crime-writing.* London: Constable, 1959.

Goulart, Ron. *Cheap Thrills: An Informal History of the Pulp Magazines.* New Rochelle, New York: Arlington House, 1972.

Grossvogel, David I. *Mystery and Its Fictions: From Oedipus to Agatha Christie.* Baltimore: Johns Hopkins University Press, 1979.

Gruber, Frank. *The Pulp Jungle.* Los Angeles: Sherbourne, 1967.

Harper, Ralph. *The World of the Thriller.* Cleveland: Press of Case Western Reserve University, 1969.

Haycraft, Howard, ed. *The Art of the Mystery Story: A Collection of Critical Essays.* New York: Simon & Schuster, 1946.

Haycraft, Howard. *Murder for Pleasure: The Life and Times of the Detective Story.* New York: Appleton-Century, 1941.

Hersey, Harold B. *Pulpwood Editor: The Fabulous World of the Thriller Magazines Revealed by a Veteran Editor and Publisher.* New York: Stokes, 1937.

Hughes, Winifred. *The Maniac in the Cellar: Sensation Novels of the 1860's.* Princeton: Princeton University Press, 1981.

Jones, Robert Kenneth. *The Shudder Pulps: A History of the Weird Menace Magazines of the 1930's.* West Linn, Ore: Fax Collector's Editions, 1975.

Keating, H.R.F. *Murder Must Appetize.* London: Lemon Tree Press, 1975.

Keating, H.R.F., ed. *Whodunit.* New York: Van Nostrand, 1982.

Lacassin, Francis. *Mythologie du Roman Policier.* Paris: Union Generale d'Editions, 1974.

Lacombe, Alain. *Le Roman Noir Americain.* Paris: Union Generale d'Editions, 1975.

La Cour, Tage, and Harold Mogensen. *The Murder Book: An Illustrated History of the Detective Story.* New York: Herder & Herder, 1971.

Lambert, Gavin. *The Dangerous Edge,* New York: Grossman, 1976.

Landrum, Larry N., Pat Browne, and Ray B. Browne, eds. *Dimensions of Detective Fiction.* Bowling Green, Ohio: Bowling Green University Popular Press, 1976.

Madden, Cecil, ed *Meet the Detective.* Harrisburg, Pa.: Telegraph, 1935.

Madden, David, ed. *Tough Guy Writers of the Thirties.* Carbondale: Southern Illinois University Press, 1968.

Marsh, Edgar. *Die Kriminalerzahlung: Theorie, Geschichte, Analyses.* Munich: Winkler, 1972.

Mason, Bobbie Ann. *The Girl Sleuth A Feminist Guide.* Old Westbury, Conn.: Feminist Press, 1975.

Messac, Regis. *Le "Detective Novel" et l'Influence de la Pensee Scientifique.* Paris: H. Champion, 1929.

Murch, A.E. *The Development of the Detective Novel.* New York: Philosophical Library, 1958.

Narcejac, Thomas. *Esthetique du Roman Policier.* Paris: Le Portulan, 1947.

Narcejac, Thomas. *Une Machine a lire: le Roman Policier.* Paris: Denoel/Gonthier, 1975.

Nevins, Francis M., Jr., ed. *The Mystery Writer's Art.* Bowling Green, Ohio: Bowling Green University Popular Press, 1970.

Ousby, Ian. *Bloodhounds of Heaven: The Detective in English Fiction from Godwin to Doyle.* Cambridge, Mass.: Harvard University Press, 1976.

Palmer, Jerry. *Thrillers: Genesis and Structure of a Popular Genre.* New York: St. Martin's, 1979.

Panek, LeRoy Lad. *Watteau's Shepherds: The Detective Novel in England, 1914-1940.* Bowling Green, Ohio: Bowling Green University Popular Press, 1979.

Pate, Janet. *The Book of Sleuths.* Chicago: Contemporary Books, 1977.

Pearson, Edmund. *Dime Novels: Or Following an Old Trail in Popular Literature.* Boston: Little, Brown, 1929.

Penzler, Otto, ed. *The Great Detectives.* Boston: Little, Brown, 1978.

Penzler, Otto. *Private lives of Private Eyes, Spies, Crimefighters, and Other Good Guys.* New York: Grosset & Dunlap, 1977.

Porter, Dennis. *The Pursuit of Crime.* New Haven: Yale University Press, 1981.

Queen, Ellery. *In the Queens' Parlor and Other Leaves from the Editors' Notebook.* New York: Simon & Schuster, 1957.

Rodell, Marie F. *Mystery Fiction. Theory and Technique.* New York: Duell, Sloan and Pearee, 1943.

Routley, Erik. *The Puritan Pleasures of the Detective Story: A Personal Monograph.* London: Gollancz, 1972.

Ruehlmann, William. *Saint with a Gun: The Unlawful American Private Eye.* New York: New York University Press, 1974.

Sandoe, James. *The Hard-Boiled Dick.* Chicago: Lovell, 1952.

Schulz-Buschhaus, Ulrich. *Formen und Idelogien des Kriminel-Romans: Ein gattiengsgeschichtlicher Essays.* Frankfurt: Athenaion, 1975.

Scott, Sutherland. *Blood in their Ink: The March of the Modern Mystery Novel.* London: Stanley Paul, 1953.

Skenazy, Paul. *The New Wild West:* The Urban Novels of Dashiell Hammett and Raymond Chandler, Boise: Boise State University Press, 1982.

Stewart, R.F. *And Always a Detective: Chapters on the History of Detective Fiction.* North Pomfret, Vt: David & Charles, 1980.

Symons, Julian. *Mortal Consequences: A History—From the Detective Story to the Crime Novel.* New York: Harper & Row, 1972.

Thomas, Gilbert. *How to Enjoy Detective Fiction.* London: Rockliff, 1947.

Thompson, H. Douglas. *Masters of Mystery A Study of the Detective Story.* London: Collins, 1931.

Usborne, Richard. *Clubland Heroes.* London: Constable, 1953.

Watson, Colin. *Snobbery with Violence: Crime Stories and their Audience.* New York: St. Martin's, 1971.

Wells, Carolyn, *The Technique of the Mystery Story.* Springfield, Mass.: Home Correspondence School, 1913.

Winks, Robin W., ed. *Detective Fiction: A Collection of Critical Essays.* Englewood Cliffs, N.J.: Prentice Hall, 1980.

Winks, Robin W. *Modus Operandi: An Excursion Into Detective Fiction.* New York: Godine, 1981.

Winn, Dilys, ed. *Murder Ink: The Mystery Reader's Companion.* New York: Workman, 1979.

Winn, Dilys, ed. *Murderess Ink: The Better Half of the Mystery.* New York: Workman, 1979.

# Index